XINJIANG: VAST AND VARIED

微观新疆

（汉英版）

左 锋　主编

SINCE 1897
The Commercial Press

2015年·北京

摄影：赵勤

丛书策划　周洪波　聂晓阳
本书策划　袁　舫　昆　石
主　　编　左　锋
副 主 编　周军成　王　晖
编　　写　（按音序排列）
　　　　　北　野　毕　亮　毕婷婷　陈　超　陈　霞
　　　　　韩连赟　韩子勇　黄　毅　姜继先　蒋小寒
　　　　　刘慧敏　刘　力　刘亮程　刘湘晨　刘学堂
　　　　　全玉莉　尚崇龙　沈　苇　王　晖　王　族
　　　　　郁　笛　袁　舫　周军成　周　涛
审　　订　宋　全

英文翻译　梅　皓
英文审订　钱厚生
英文编辑　张显奎

责任编辑　刘玥妍
装帧设计　东方美迪
项目合作　一心悦读文化科技有限公司

Chief Producer　Zhou Hongbo　Nie Xiaoyang
Producer　Yuan Fang　Kun Shi
Chief Compiler　Zuo Feng
Deputy Compiler　Zhou Juncheng　Wang Hui
Compilers　Bei Ye　Bi Liang　Bi Tingting　Chen Chao　Chen Xia
Han Lianyun　Han Ziyong　Huang Yi　Jiang Jixian　Jiang Xiaohan
Liu Huimin　Liu Li　Liu Liangcheng　Liu Xiangchen　Liu Xuetang
Quan Yuli　Shang Chonglong　Shen Wei　Wang Hui　Wang Zu
Yu Di　Yuan Fang　Zhou Juncheng　Zhou Tao
Reviewer　Song Quan

English Translator　Mei Hao
English Reviewer　Qian Housheng
English Editor　Zhang Xiankui

Executive Editor　Liu Yueyan
Art Design　EmDesign
Project Coordinator　Yixinyuedu Co. Ltd.

微距体验大美

2012 年底，朋友王晖找到我，想请我牵头，编写一本介绍新疆的书。同时，他带来了商务印书馆此前出版的《微观西藏》一书。拜读后，我感觉耳目一新，其写作形式新颖，文字生动、简洁，图文并茂，中英文对照，能带给读者直观而别样的阅读感受，是当今微时代一种很好的传播方式。于是欣然地接受了这项任务。经过一年多的努力，在各位作者的热情参与和大力支持下，《微观新疆》就要付梓了。这是大家辛勤劳动的成果，衷心希望能得到读者的认可。

《微观新疆》是商务印书馆策划的"微观中国"系列丛书中的一本。本书尝试将广角度、多维度、大视野置于细节之中，从细微处观察新疆，以微距体验新疆，以"微博体"书写新疆，通过大量生动的图片、鲜活的小细节和微故事，向读者呈现新疆人的生活实态、发展状况、生存方式以及积淀在其民众性格当中的精神质地，为读者奉献真实、独特而细腻的"新疆印象"。

新疆究竟是个什么样的地方？不同的人可能会有不同的答案，正如"有一百个读者，就有一百个哈姆雷特"。新疆维吾尔自治区党委宣传部曾在北京召开"新疆形象塑造与对外传播"专题座谈会，邀请国内不同领域的 40 余名知名专家学者就新疆的形象塑造"把脉""支着儿"。正式座谈前，主持人请大家用几个关键词概括对新疆的印象，结果众说纷纭，但出现频率最高的几个词是"遥远""地大""美丽""恐怖""落后""神秘"。这或许是很多人对新疆的大体认识。

新疆是个十分神奇而又有些令人纠结的地方。《在那遥远的地方》《吐鲁番的葡萄熟了》《达阪城的姑娘》《最美还是我们新疆》等耳熟能详、脍炙人口的歌曲，使人们对它充满向往，但近年来这里发生的一系列暴恐事件，又让许多人对它充满恐惧和不安。因为援疆，我有幸在新疆生活了 3 年，亲身感受这里的风土人情；与新疆各界人士、各族人民近距离接触和深入交流，使我对新疆和新疆人有更客观、真切的认识。如果要让我介绍新疆，我觉得用"美""大""多""好"这四个字来概括较为恰当。

一是"美"。新疆自然景观神奇独特，是中国真正可以称得上大美或最美的地方。曾经多次跟媒体界的朋友聊起新疆的"美"，当问及能否用一个简单的词来表述时，大家搜肠刮肚一番，结果除了"大美"就是"最美"。新疆的美的确是一种醉人的美，无论你是初次踏上这片土地还是来过多次，每一次都会有新的感受，每一次都会有新的惊喜。高山湖泊天山天池、人间仙境喀纳斯、绿色长廊吐鲁番葡萄沟、空中草原那拉提、地质奇观可可托海、亚欧中心万花园裕民以及"此景只应天上有，人间能有几回现"的九曲十八弯等著名景区数不胜数，让人流连忘返；在横亘5000多公里的古"丝绸之路"南、北、中三条干线上，分布着交河故城、楼兰遗址、克孜尔千佛洞等数以百计的人文奇观，蜚声中外，令人感慨。新疆的美景数不胜数，各具特色，无论你用多么华丽的辞藻来概括和形容新疆的美都不过分。新疆的美不仅是自然的美，还体现在人文、饮食等方方面面。用新疆著名诗人、作家黄毅先生的话来说，从来没有哪个地方能像新疆这样，同时让你的视觉、听觉、味觉、嗅觉和触觉得到满足，你会看到无法用语言描绘的色彩，你会听到仿若天籁的乐音，你会品尝到让人垂涎的美食，你会闻到令人窒息的芬芳，你会触摸到远古和现代。这是调动所有感官的一次盛宴，是一种全方位的精神大餐。

二是"大"。新疆位于亚欧大陆中部，地域面积166.67万平方公里，占全国陆地总面积的六分之一，相当于3个法国的面积、7个英国的面积。陆地边境线5700多公里。周边与蒙古、俄罗斯、哈萨克斯坦、吉尔吉斯斯坦、塔吉克斯坦、阿富汗、巴基斯坦、印度等8个国家接壤，是中国地域面积最大、陆地边境线最长、交界邻国最多的省区。疆内各地州市首府到自治区首府乌鲁木齐的平均距离400多公里，这在国内其他任何省市区是绝无仅有的。辖区内有世界最大的内陆盆地塔里木盆地，有中国最长的内陆河塔里木河，有中国最大、世界第二的沙漠塔克拉玛干沙漠。

三是"多"。新疆的"多"体现在诸多方面，它是一个多民族、多宗教、多文化聚集的地区。全区总人口2260余万，少数民族人口占60%以上，共有55个民族成分，13个世居民族。因其特殊的地理位置，新疆历史上是"丝绸之路"的通衢之地，是各民族迁徙融合的走廊，是多宗教、多文化的交汇之地。佛教、伊斯兰教、基督教、天主教、道教等多种宗教在这里和谐并存，古代四大文明在这里汇流，各种文化在这里碰撞和融合，形成独特而丰富的多元文化。正如国学大师季羡林先生所说："世界上历史悠久、地域广阔、自成体系、影响深远的文化体系只有四个：中国、印度、希腊、伊斯兰，再没有第五个，而这四种文化交汇的地方，只有中国的敦煌和新疆。"新疆的"多"还体现在生物资源种类繁多、矿产资源极其丰富上，新疆野生植物达4000多种，野生动物近700余种。这里的煤炭、石油、天然气预测资源量分别占全国陆上资源量的40%、30%、34%，居全国之首。

四是"好"。公元前60年西汉政权在乌垒（今巴音郭楞蒙古自治州轮台县）设立西域都护府，自此新疆正式纳入中国版图，两千多年来，生活在这片广袤土地上的各族人民休戚与共、共御外侮，共同开发和保卫着祖国的边疆，用勤劳和智慧创造了各族人民的美好生活，也创造了灿烂的历史和文明。数千年的历史变迁，无数个的朝代更迭、江山起落，流淌在各族人民血液中的热情、淳朴、善良经久不衰，无论您走进毡房、蒙古包、农家小院还是城市居民楼，热情好客的新疆人会给您宾至如归的温暖。今日的新疆，经济社会快速发展，特色产业迅速兴起，文化事业日趋繁荣，各族人民生活水平稳步提高，全区进入了大开发、大发展、大繁荣的黄金期，经过各族人民的团结奋斗，未来的新疆必定会更加繁荣、富裕、和谐、稳定、文明。

美哉新疆！美好新疆！朋友，闲暇之余您不妨翻翻《微观新疆》，可能的话，请您到新疆走走看看，大美新疆将张开双臂欢迎您，这里的山水，这里的人民，这里的美食，这里的歌舞，一定会给您留下美好而别样的体验。

左锋

2015 年 1 月

A Close-up View of Great Beauty

Towards the end of 2012, my friend Wang Hui sought me out to ask me to compile a book introducing Xinjiang to the readers. At the same time, he brought a copy of *Tibet: Fast and Furious*, published by the Commercial Press. It was a refreshing read for me – a great book with nice pictures and high-quality, straightforward text in both Chinese and English, arranged in a format that takes readers straight into the action – fitting in with all the "micro" culture that we have nowadays – microblogs, microfilms, and the like. For this reason I was of course interested in producing a new book in the same vein. After a year of hard work with the participation and support of various authors, *Xinjiang: Vast and Varied* has finally come out. I hope this book, the product of the hard work of a number of people, meets with a positive reception from readers.

Xinjiang: Vast and Varied is part of the "1-Minute China" series. These books seek to widen the angle of view and expand the field of vision, revealing new details and dimensions. Looking at Xinjiang close-up, these microblogs get the readers very close to the topical matter, bringing the details further to life with a large amount of vibrant pictures, giving the reader a view into the conditions, the life styles and the state of development in Xinjiang, and providing the readers with a real, unique and detailed impression of Xinjiang.

What kind of place is Xinjiang? Different people will have different answers, just as "a hundred readers will have a hundred versions of Shakespeare's Hamlet". A seminar on "Shaping and Spreading the Image of Xinjiang" was held in Beijing, and more than 40 distinguished experts and scholars were invited to give their ideas and suggestions on how to shape the image of Xinjiang. Just before the seminar started, they were asked to use a few key words to describe Xinjiang, the most commonly appearing ones include: "far", "large", "beautiful", "awesome", "backwards", "mysterious" and the like.

Xinjiang is a very mysterious and at times confusing place. The place is famous through many popular songs extolling its virtues as a far-off beautiful place, but in recent years a number of violent incidents have provoked feelings of worry and unease about the region. I have been lucky enough to live in Xinjiang for 3 years, supporting the local development, and getting close to the place and the people that inhabit it. Interacting with all kinds of people and ethnic groups has given me a new view on the place and its people – a true understanding. If I had to pick a few words to describe the place now, "beautiful", "vast", "bountiful" and "good" would be the ones.

First, "beautiful" – Xinjiang has unique natural scenery, and can be called one of the most beautiful places in China. In past conversations with my friends in the media, we have discussed Xinjiang's beauty, and have found that to describe the place the two best phrases seem to be "great beauty" and "most beautiful". It is a kind of intoxicating beauty – whether it's your first time there or one of many trips, you will always have a new feeling and meet with new surprises. The high-altitude lakes in the Tianshan Mountains, the beautiful scenes of Kanas, the green corridors of grapevines in Turpan, the Narat grasslands, the serene Kokotay Sea, the famed scenic pastoral areas, covered in the typical floral cover of the Central Asian plains leave visitors with unforgettable memories. The southern, middle and northern routes of the Silk Road, along with the Jiaohe City Ruins, the Loulan Ruins, the Kizil Buddha Grottoes and countless other sceneries renowned both in China and abroad, make for amazing sceneries to behold. Xinjiang is full of countless beautiful sights all with their own characteristics – no matter how you go in describing them in flowery prose, you will still not have gone too far. The beauty of Xinjiang is not only in natural aspects, but also in the people, food, customs, and other areas. The famous poet Huang Yi said: "I've never been to another place like Xinjiang – it lights all five senses on fire, dazzling you with indescribable colours, enchanting music, beautiful cuisine, almost stifling aromas, and the tactical sensations of past and present. This is a banquet for the senses, a feast for one's spirit."

Second, "vast" – Xinjiang is situated in the centre of the Eurasian continent with an area of 1.66 million square kilometres – one sixth of the total area of China, three times larger than France and seven times larger than the United Kingdom. Its land border with other countries runs for 5,7000 kilometres, touching Mongolia, Russia, Kazakhstan, Kyrgyzstan, Tajikistan, Afghanistan, Pakistan and India. It is China's largest province or region in terms of area, border length and number of foreign countries bordered. The average distance between the seats of the various cities and sections of Xinjiang and the capital city of Urumqi exceeds 400 kilometres – something unheard of in China's inner provinces. The region contains the world's largest inland basin, the Tarim Basin, as well as China's longest inland river, the Tarim River, in addition to the Taklimakan Desert – the world's second largest.

Third, "bountiful" – It refers to many aspects of Xinjiang: from race to religion to culture. This is an area in which many interact. With a total population of 22.6 million people, comprising more than 60% of ethnic minorities in 55 groups, with 13 groups of native peoples. Historically, specific geographic features made Xinjiang the main trunk of the Silk Road, a corridor through which numerous peoples traveled and mixed, especially in the areas of religion and culture. Buddhism, Islam, Christianity, Taoism and other religions have co-existed here; the four great classical civilisations and various other cultures have collided and mixed here, creating a rich multi-dimensional culture. Prof. Ji Xianlin, a master of Chinese culture studies, said, "In the long history of our world with its broad expanses and complex system, those cultures with the farthest reach number only four, without a candidate for fifth: China, India, Greece and classical Islamic Civilisation. The areas in which they came together are of course only Xinjiang and Dunhuang." The bounty of Xinjiang also appears in its plentiful biological and mineral resources – more than 4,000 plant species, 700 species of wild animals are found in Xinjiang. Coal, petroleum and natural gas exist in predicted amounts totalling 40%, 30%, and 34% of national reserves, first in the nation.

And fourth is "good". In the year 60 B.C., the Western Han Government established at Wulei (the present-day Luntai County of Bayangol Mongol Autonomous Prefecture) the Protectorate of the Western Region, and from this point onward, Xinjiang was drawn into Chinese maps. For more than two thousand years, the people of the region have worked together supporting each other, repelling foreign aggressions and developing and protecting the border of our country, building a beautiful life for all groups through hard work and intelligence, creating a splendid history and culture together. Through the fluctuations of history, the rise and fall of dynasties, rivers and mountains themselves, the passion for honesty and good flowing through the veins of these people is reflected in their hospitality when they receive you, whether in a yurt, small traditional courtyard, or urban building. Modern-day Xinjiang is a place of rapid economic development, innovation in new industries, and brilliant cultural produce, where the standard of living is constantly rising in what is shaping up to be a golden area that will be brighter, more harmonious, and better cultured through the efforts of everyone who works hard on this land.

How beautiful Xinjiang is! And what a nice place it is! If, after you read this book, you have the chance to visit Xinjiang yourself, I welcome you to do so, experiencing the sites for yourself as the region welcomes you with both arms open – you'll find the scenery, people, food, songs, and dance all unforgettable additions to your experience – a beautiful and different experience.

Zuo Feng
January, 2015

目 录
Contents

地理·行旅	1	Geography and Travel
历史·传承	51	History and Traditions
宗教·民俗	75	Religion and Folklore
城市·乡村	107	City and Village
兵团·边境	149	Construction and Defence
传奇·逸事	161	Legends and Anecdotes
奇珍·异宝	177	Miracles and Treasures
艺术·体育	191	Art and Sports
语言·杂话	215	Languages and Stories
美食·美服	233	Food and Dress
索引	258	Index

地理·行旅
Geography and Travel

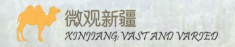
**难以概括的
新疆**

Xinjiang:
A Place
So Hard to
Describe

你的风，你的雪峰，你的草原，你的白杨树，你的天空……这些说法多么精练、多么传神！但是这些有关对风、雪峰、草原、白杨以及天空的概括，仍然不是对整个新疆的概括。概括新疆是一件困难的事。

The wind, snow-capped peaks, grasslands, white poplars, and the sky – these descriptions of Xinjiang are so captivating! However, wind, snow-capped peaks, grasslands, white poplars, and sky aren't all that Xinjiang has. It's hard to describe the region in a few words.

旅行的困惑

The
Confusion of
Travel

在内地，一个小时可能穿越几个城市，而在新疆，一个小时只是旅行的开始。

In China's more populous inland areas, an hour can take you through a few cities, whereas in Xinjiang, it's only the start of a trip.

摄影：张克红

摄影: 张宏

大与野的新疆
Big and Wild Xinjiang

在新疆,即使一片不大的森林,一个不大的湖泊,那种自然的生长,野性的呼啸,当得起一个"大"字,一个"野"字。大是格局,野是本质,是生命的自然勃发。

In Xinjiang, even an ordinary forest or lake deserves the appellations "grand" and "wild". The former reflects its geographic layout, and the latter its character – the natural vibrancy of life.

丝路要冲
On the Silk Road

新疆地处东西方交通要冲,在一千多年前,新疆就是中国与中亚和欧洲交流的唯一通道。虽然历史在后来的时间里选择了海上丝路,东南沿海成为中国与欧洲交往的必经之地,但中国向西的通道并未湮没在风沙中。路,一直在那里。

East-west travel in Xinjiang runs at breakneck speed – more than a millennium ago, Xinjiang was the only transit corridor between China, Central Asia, and Europe. Although the "maritime silk road" became the route of choice later, and the southerly sea route became the main transit channel between China and Europe, the former route from China to the West was not swallowed up by the desert. It has always been there.

3

新疆的包容美
The Beauty of Xinjiang

她把冰峰的绝顶崇高，火洲盆地的彻底塌陷，草原的妩媚秀丽，戈壁的粗砺坦荡，沙漠的荒芜神秘，绿洲的自然亲切，河流的充沛和干涸，果园的丰饶和废垒的凄清，湖泊的澄碧和山岩的铁硬……种种对立、矛盾、极端，全都包容在自己身下，形成一种独特而健康的美。这美，只在新疆。

The highest ice-capped peaks, the sweltering Qarakhoja basin, the beautiful grasslands, the coarse and broad Gobi Desert, the vast arid expanses, the pleasant and natural oases, the full and dry times of the riverbeds, the lush orchards, the green and bright lakes and iron-hard mountains – these contrasts, contradictions and extremes are all part of the body of Xinjiang, a unique and healthy beauty. This kind of beauty is only found in Xinjiang.

摄影：张宏

新疆之"新"
"New" in Xinjiang

新，就是她的本质，她的活力；新，也是她的渴望，她的未来；让她日新月异吧！她有权利，也有能力成为一个最富饶、最优美的地方！她纵然是我们无法概括的，但她自己早已找到了概括自己的话，那就是"新疆"。

New is the character and power, as well as the hope and future of Xinjiang. Let us see it change rapidly for the better! Xinjiang has the right and the power to become an abundant, beautiful place. Even though we may not be able to describe it fully, Xinjiang early on found a good name for itself, which means "new frontier" in Chinese.

乌鲁木齐克拉玛依东路立交桥　摄影：陈辉

丝绸之路
The Silk Road

丝绸之路绵延 7000 余公里。两千多年间，这条路上走过无数的驼队、马队，走过法显、鸠摩罗什、玄奘，走过征战的罗马士兵、波斯士兵、中国士兵。由此，瓷器、茶叶、造纸术、祆教、景教、佛教、伊斯兰教得以传播浸润到欧亚两个大陆，四大文明由此交汇绵延至更为广大的地域。

The Silk Road extends for more than 7,000 kilometres. In more than 2,000 years of history, countless horse and camel teams have walked it. It has been walked by Faxian, Kumarajiva, Xuanzang and others. It has been marched upon by Roman, Persian and Chinese armies. Through it, porcelain, tea, papermaking, Zoroastrianism, Nestotarianism, Buddhism, and Islam crossed between Europe and Asia, and the four great ancient civilisations expanded their reaches.

塔里木盆地
The Tarim Basin

塔里木盆地是装满沙子的大容器。这个大容器有 53 万平方公里，是世界上最大的内陆盆地，里面有 9 条河流，从盆地周边的天山、昆仑山、喀喇昆仑山、帕米尔高原向盆地中心汇聚流淌，大部分最终汇入并构成中国最长的内陆河——塔里木河。

The Tarim Basin is a large container filled with sand. Encompassing 530,000 square kilometres, it is the world's largest inland basin, with nine rivers. Runoff water from the Tianshan, Kunlun and Karakoram mountains as well as the Pamir Plateau collects within, and these flows combine to form China's longest inland river – the Tarim River.

新疆大视野
A Vast Space

苍苍茫茫地平线，苍苍茫茫天地间，360 度的宽幅画面……新疆是室外的、露天的、敞开的，是视野的大解放。空旷的环境，人们寻找着焦点，一棵树，一个人，一座山，一块绿洲，一片在地上移动的云影。新疆在路上，在地尽头，在天边外。

A vast horizon and vast sky, 360-degree panorama... Xinjiang is outdoor, open-air, and vast – a liberation of one's field of vision. In an open environment, we look for focal points – a tree, a person, a mountain, an oasis, moving clouds. Being on the road in Xinjiang puts you in a vast space between earth and sky.

6 摄影：张宏

摄影：双元

阿尔泰山
The Altay Mountains

阿尔泰山脉的大部分在境外，中国境内的阿尔泰山，是她伸向东方的脑袋。若把中国比成雄鸡，那个高高翘起的"鸡尾巴"，就是阿尔泰山。这里是新疆降水最多、植被最好的地方，也是新疆最重要的牧场和"肉库"。阿尔泰山自古以来盛产黄金，又称"金山"。

Most of the Altay Mountain Range lies outside China's borders. The part within China is the head of the range, extending eastwards. If China is seen as a rooster, then the high, upturned "tail" would be the Altay Mountains. This is the area with the most precipitation and the densest vegetation in Xinjiang. It is also the most important region for animal husbandry in Xinjiang. As the mountain has yielded gold since ancient times, it is also known as the "golden mountain".

新疆的落差
Extremes in Xinjiang

世界第二高点和第二低点均在新疆，乔戈里峰比世界最高峰珠穆朗玛峰只低 200 多米，艾丁湖的最低点只比世界最低点死海略高一些，新疆的地理落差达到 8765 米。高与低、冷与热、荒漠与绿洲……鲜明的对比与反差彰显新疆的魅力。

The world's second highest and second lowest points are in Xinjiang, with K2 being only 200 metres lower than Mount Qomolangma, and Aiding Lake being only slightly higher than the Dead Sea. The altitude range in Xinjiang is 8,765 metres. High and low, hot and cold, desert and oasis – these stark contrasts show the beauty of Xinjiang.

7

摄影：双元

准噶尔盆地
The Junggar Basin

准噶尔盆地的核心部分是古尔班通古特沙漠。这里曾是芨芨草、梭梭和骆驼刺的世界。历史上，这里是传统的游牧区，现在有水和地势平缓的土地，早已开发成连片的农业区，深山、浅山和盆地深处半荒漠的地方才是牧区。牧区和农区交相混杂，有相对发达的交通线和密集的城镇，这是它突出的特点。

The Gurbantunggut Desert is the central part of the Junggar Basin. The area is dominated by Splendid achantherum (*Achantherum splendens*), sacsaoul, and cane thorn. Historically, this was a nomadic area. With mild geographic features, it has now become an agricultural region. Only mountains high and low, and basin areas of wilderness provide space for pasture. Pasturing areas and agricultural areas are intermixed with one another, crisscrossed by relatively developed transit corridors and dotted with large settlements.

神木园
The Mysterious Garden

在阿克苏地区温宿县的戈壁滩上，独独有一片占地近千亩的茂盛森林，叫神木园。里头有一群怪树，一群不守"树规"的树，有的长出了龙头、马头或者野兽的身子，有的卧着长、躺着长、蹲着长、坐着长，似乎怎么舒服怎么怪就怎么生长。

In the Gobi desert in Wensu County, Aksu, there is a forest of almost 700,000 square metres, called the "mysterious garden". Within there are a number of odd trees that don't follow the rules of normal trees. Some have dragon or horse heads, or the bodies of beasts. Some are lying or crouching, sitting down – all manner of odd shapes appear according to the tree's preferences.

丰富奇特的地貌景观
Rich and Varied Scenery

新疆地貌之丰富奇特，一个没有真正涉足其间的人很难想象。新疆旅游资源类型有 56 种，全国第一。高原、盆地、山脉、湖泊、草原、河流、沙漠、戈壁、森林、田野，多种景观独特地组合在一起。冰峰与火洲共存，瀚海与绿洲为邻。所谓"一日看尽长安花"，恐怕只有在新疆才能领略如此多彩迷人的景观。

The scenery of Xinjiang is rich and varied, hard to fully conceptualise for someone who has not visited. Xinjiang has 56 types of tourism resources, first in all of China. Highland, basins, mountain ranges, lakes, grasslands, rivers, deserts, the Gobi, forest, fields and other kinds of scenery come together here. Icy peaks and fiery basins coexist, and vast deserts meet with lush oases. Xinjiang is truly one of the few rare places that can be said to "have it all".

天山
The Tianshan Mountains

天山是新疆之书的书脊。它与昆仑山和阿尔泰山隔"盆"遥相呼应，东到新疆的东大门哈密，西至伊犁入哈萨克斯坦，绵延数千公里，占有最重的分量，在新疆的历史地理中位置显赫。2013 年 6 月，中国新疆天山列入联合国教科文组织世界自然遗产名录。

The Tianshan Mountains are Xinjiang's backbone. Bordering a large geographic basin respectively with the Kunlun and Altay mountain ranges, they extend for thousands of kilometres to Kumul (Hami) in the east, Yili and then on into Kazakhstan in the west. They are the largest mountains and occupy an important position in Xinjiang's geographic history. In June 2013, the Tianshan Mountains were designated as a UNESCO World Natural Heritage Site.

摄影：双元

昆仑山　摄影·黄永中

摄影：双元

塔里木河
The Tarim River

沿塔里木盆地四周的河流，共孕育出百余块绿洲，大一点的有上万平方公里，而小的不足一平方公里。正是这大大小小的绿洲，负载着历史上的绿洲城郭以及今天的南疆。

The rivers of the Tarim Basin feed in total more than one hundred oases, with the larger oases spanning more than 10,000 square kilometres, and the smaller ones less than one square kilometre. It was these large and small oases that supported the historical oasis kingdoms, and that continue to sustain present-day southern Xinjiang.

万山之祖：昆仑山
The Kunlun Range

在古代传说中，昆仑山是中华民族文明的发祥地，很多神话故事都与昆仑有关。昆仑是中华民族的神山圣域，是一座精神之山，素有"万山之祖"之称。昆仑山西起帕米尔高原东部，横贯新疆、西藏间，伸延至青海境内，全长约 2500 公里。

Ancient legends posit that Mount Kunlun is the original site of Chinese culture, and many tales have something to do with this. The mountain is revered in Chinese culture, and is held to be "the ancestor of all mountains". The Kunlun Range rises from the eastern portion of the Pamir Plateau in the west, and extends through the borders between Xinjiang and Tibet to Qinghai, for a total length of around 2,500 kilometres.

古尔班通古特沙漠
The Gurbantunggut Desert

古尔班通古特沙漠留给我的印象是一望无际的敞亮，我对它太熟悉了，却几乎没办法说出它。我十几岁时，经常在半夜赶车进沙漠拉梭梭柴，牛车穿过黑黑的雪野，村子离沙漠七八里路，连成一片的沙丘在雪野尽头隆起，感觉像走向一堵墙。

The Gurbantunggut Desert is a clear expanse stretching as far as the eye can see. I am familiar with it, yet can't describe it. When I was a teenager, I frequently drove a cart into the desert to collect firewood at midnight. As the ox-cart passed through the fields of snow in the dark, with my village being seven or eight miles from the desert, I would come upon a range of sand dunes sticking up in the snowy landscape as I made my approach – I always felt like I was walking toward a wall.

塔克拉玛干沙漠之谜
The Mystery of the Taklimakan Desert

在塔克拉玛干空旷而令人迷惑的天空下，那曾经的狼烟、商旅跟着历史走远了，留下的是被流沙埋没的古城。残墙断壁的废墟、骆驼的白骨和枯立于风中的胡杨，这些似乎是上帝设置的一个"谜"。现在，几条沙漠公路穿行而过，石油基地以及现代文明续写着新的历史。

Under the vast, captivating sky of the Taklimakan, against the backdrop of signal fires, merchant caravans made their long excursions, leaving behind cities buried in the sand. The traces of ruined walls and the sun-bleached bones of camels and starkly resolute poplars – they appear as a riddle left by a higher being. These desert expanses are now crisscrossed by modern highways, with petrochemicals and modern culture carving a new history into the land.

摄影：双元

摄影：双元

镶着雪山边儿的草原
Grasslands in the Snow

新疆的草原，有一位在内蒙古生活过的朋友做了这样的比较，他说："内蒙的草原更辽阔，更无遮碍，但是它不像新疆的草原这样镶着边儿——镶着雪山的边儿！"

One of my friends who had lived in Inner Mongolia made this comparison about Xinjiang's grasslands: "Those in Inner Mongolia are broader and more unobstructed, but we certainly don't have them interspersed with huge snow-capped mountains!"

新疆的河
Xinjiang's Rivers

叶尔羌河保留了一副古代河流的面貌，它宽阔的河床里流泻的仿佛不是水，而是永无休止的、奔腾拥挤的骆驼群；额尔齐斯河有着令人惊异的风采，它的充沛和纯净近乎神话，它的浪涛如同众多大块的碧玉倾泻翻滚；塔里木河，那是一支忧伤的歌，它以伤感的情调告别一个又一个绿洲，然后义无反顾地走进沙漠。

The Yarkant River has the appearance of an ancient waterway. Its wide riverbed seems to be filled with not water but a never-ending flock of jostling, bouncing camels. The Ertix River has a remarkable appearance, with both the amount and clarity of water being almost legendary. Its flow resembles a moving stream of deep jade. The Tarim River resembles a sorrowful song, its mourning tone bidding farewell to each oasis in succession, and then continuing resolutely into the desert.

小草与大草

Grasses

在草原民族眼中，小草是生命之根，是美的原色。在新疆，草显出了它的大。东西长 270 公里、南北宽 136 公里的巴音布鲁克大草原，还有享有东方普罗旺斯之称的伊犁河谷大片的薰衣草田，是这种大的最好诠释。天苍苍、野茫茫的世界里，草是苍茫与浩大的，盛得下所有的雄心壮志、英雄气概与浪漫情怀。

To the nomads of the grasslands, grass is the root of life and the colour of beauty. In Xinjiang, the grass shows its might. The Bayanbulak Prairie, extending 270 kilometres east-west and 136 kilometres north-south, contains the lavender fields of the Yili River Valley, known as the Provence of the Orient – a good way of understanding its size. In our vast world, grass is boundless and massive, capable of playing host to all our ambitions, heroism, and romantic feelings.

摄影：刘元

薰衣草神秘之旅
An Enchanting Journey

躺在一望无际的紫蓝色的薰衣草花田里，回首过去，或者飘向未来，现实，被一种幽深的东西消解了。幽深是色彩，也是沁人的香气。在伊犁河谷，在西域的阳光下，薰衣草是神秘的，也是明丽的，真实的，体现了生命的不可知与美。去伊犁河谷开启一段芳香之旅，在紫蓝色的神秘中漂一会儿吧！

Laying in the endless purple of a lavender field, looking back or towards the future we see reality dispelled by a deep and serene entity – colour, and fragrance. In the Yili River Valley, under the western sun, lavender is mystical, beautiful and real – it has an amazing beauty. If you have the chance, you should definitely visit this legendary purple paradise.

摄影：张宏

塔河边的月亮湾
Crescent Bay

沙雅，宽阔的塔里木河，时常有鸟群从水面上飞起来，白色的，是鹭鸶。大大的月亮形河湾中间有一个狭长的岛，岛上长着的胡杨，一直延伸到了河道中。十月，黄与绿交错，在浅蓝色的水中交相辉映。没有嘈杂的人声，没有指示牌——一个还没有被命名的地方，只有纯净的水与树，只有野鹿、黄羊、鱼和鸟。

In Shaya County, around the Tarim River, white birds frequently fly up from the surface – these are egrets. In a large, crescent-shaped bend of the river, there is a long, narrow island upon which diversiform-leaved poplars extend their reaches into the river. In October, green and yellow intersect, and are reflected in the light blue of the waters. Without the sounds of humans, nor signs to guide you, in this still unnamed place, there are only clear water and trees, deer, gazelles, fish, and birds.

摄影：黄永中

苍茫尽处是繁华
A Bustling, Vast Space

夏日，乘车奔驰在南疆的大地上，天地洪荒，几百里的大漠戈壁让你灰心绝望。这样的经历，很多第一次到新疆的人都有。但是，往往在你失望之际，一片绿色已经迎面而来——田畴交错，流水如银，白杨参天，牛羊成群。然后是交错的房舍，来来往往的人，大大小小的清真寺伸向广阔无垠的天空。

During the summer, driving around the chaotic landscapes of southern Xinjiang, your mood might sink after hundreds of miles of the Gobi desert. This is something that many first-timers in Xinjiang experience. However, when you're almost at the point of despair, a patch of green will appear. Fields intersect with silvery rivers, poplars reach towards the sky, and lambs and oxen rove in flocks. People move between houses, and the spires of mosques, large and small, point at the heavens.

绿洲的夏天
Summer Oasis

当炽热的阳光让冰川融化，第一滴下坠的水珠叩响冰壁，绿洲的夏天就聆听到了久违的呼告。在新疆这个神奇的地方，所有绿洲的田亩，并不祈盼天降甘霖，却都在祈祷阳光更强烈、更持久些，因为只有阳光可以让季节激情横溢，只有阳光可以让吝啬的冰峰像抛撒金钱般慷慨地施舍冰川之水。

When the hot light of the sun begins to melt the ice and the first drop of water knocks like a pearl against the wall, the long-awaited call that heralds the summer in the oasis is heard. In a mystical place like Xinjiang, all the fields in each oasis do not long for water from the heavens, but for stronger sunlight that last for a longer time, as only the sun can make the season a good one, only the sun can squeeze any water out of the miserly icy mountains that supply it.

脱离庸常之美
Unusual
Beauty

原始、粗犷、浩瀚、苍茫、奢华、磅礴、精致、艳丽，把这些词都用在一个地方，可能只有新疆了。三千年死而不倒的胡杨与新生者艳丽的枝叶，浩瀚的沙漠戈壁与蓝宝石一样的湖泊，树林、野花与阳光下熠熠的冰山……冲击着你所有的视觉经验和审美模式，最后，必然有一些新东西在你心中闪烁，让你脱离庸常。

Primitive, rough, vast, expansive, luxurious, majestic, fine, beautiful – to use all these words to describe a single place may only be possible in Xinjiang. 3,000-year-old diversiform-leaved poplars and fresh leaves on new branches, the vast expanses of the Gobi Desert and the emerald lakes, forest, wildflowers and the shimmering ice-capped peaks… All your senses will be dazzled with this all-around beauty. Every time something new flashes before your eyes, you exit the realm of mundanity.

绿色宝库
A Treasure-
Trove of
Green

阿尔泰山植被丰富，从海拔 4000 多米的友谊峰到海拔 1000 多米的山间草原，垂直分布的植物种类有 2000 余种，其中 17 种属濒危物种，212 种为该地所特有。从西伯利亚延伸到中国的唯一一片泰加林，生长着西伯利亚松、冷杉、云杉、欧洲山杨等，丰富的植被使阿尔泰山享有"绿色宝库"的美誉。

The Altay Mountains have a rich vegetative cover, from the 4,000-metre-high Friendship Peak to the mountainous grasslands at a kilometre above sea level. The vertical distribution of more than 2,000 kinds of plants includes 17 endangered species, and 212 endemic species. Extending from Siberia to China's only taiga forest, Siberian pines, firs, spruces, trembling poplars and other plants together give the Altay Range its name of a "treasure-trove of green".

摄影：张宏

摄影：张宏

白桦林的眼泪
Tears of a
Birch Forest

在阿尔泰山脉绵长的褶皱间，在额尔齐斯河大大小小的支流和浩浩汤汤的主河道两岸，白桦树自由自在地生长着。夏天，白色的枝干，绿色的树叶，枝干上大大小小的眼睛，让白桦林有自己的表情。据说每年四月份后，白桦树"眼睛"里会流出眼泪，人们称之为"情人的眼泪"。

In the folds of the long Altay Range, silver birches grow freely along the banks of the vast Ertix River and its tributaries, large and small. In the summer, the white branches with green leaves upon them, combined with the large and small "eyes" on the branches, give the trees their own expressions. It is said that every year after April, the eyes of these trees cry – what people call "lover's tears".

把新疆带回家
Take Xinjiang
Home

那些自然优美的风景，优雅的手工制作，甘醇的美酒，典雅的玉器，都是时光的化身。把一个物品带回家，就是把一段时光带回家，把一个地方带回家，把一个季节的色彩与醇香带回家，把一些轻风与诗意带回家——每一个季节，你都可以从新疆带回一些你喜欢的东西，至于能带多少，那就是你的能耐了。

Naturally beautiful scenery, excellent handicrafts, high-quality liquor, beautiful jade – these are all incarnations of time. Taking an object home is taking a piece of time home. Taking a location home with you in your mind is taking the colours and fragrances of a season hoe with you. Taking the soft breeze and poetic feelings of a place with you – in all seasons you can enjoy the things you like about Xinjiang; how much you bring is up to you.

19

绿洲
Oasis

绿洲是大漠与戈壁之间一个独立的、自成系统的"诺亚方舟"。它们多呈带状分布在河流以及有冰雪融水灌溉的山麓地带，大小不一。塔里木盆地和准噶尔盆地边缘，是新疆绿洲分布最密集的地区。

Oases are autonomous systems in the middle of the Gobi Desert, resembling a kind of "Noah's Ark". They mostly exist as bands along rivers, where melt water fills areas at the feet of mountains for features of various sizes. The densest concentrations of oases in Xinjiang are at the edges of the Tarim Basin and the Junggar Basin.

摄影：双元

文明的交汇地
Cultural Nexus

季羡林说新疆和敦煌是世界上唯一的四大文化体系交汇的地区，也有人说塔里木盆地是一个"文明的大墓地"。这里曾使用过的语言多达二十几种，这里出土的文物收藏在全球十多个国家的博物馆里。丝绸之路从长安到地中海，一路都是点和线的关系，只有到了塔里木盆地，才变成了一个面。

Prof. Ji Xianlin describes Xinjiang and Dunhuang as the only places on the planet in which all four of the great classical civilisations interacted, with some others saying the Tarim Basin is a "cultural graveyard". More than twenty languages have been used in this area, and artefacts from more than 10 kingdoms have been unearthed and are displayed in museums in the region. The Silk Road extended from Chang'an (present-day Xi'an) to the Mediterranean Sea, its entire route comprising a series of what are geometrically points and lines – only in the Tarim Basin did it feature a whole area.

草原与小马驹
Animals on the Prairie

巴音布鲁克大草原上的朋友对我说：现在小马驹已经出生，到处可以听到那稚嫩的叫声，每到六月，到处都是马驹的身影，它们吃奶，或者跟在妈妈的身后闲逛，或者与同伴嬉戏追逐。六月的草原，让人激动，像那些长调和冬不拉的旋律。

A friend on the Bayanbulak Prairie told me: with little horses out to roam, you can hear their silly cries throughout the landscape. Every year in June, little horses are everywhere, drinking milk or following their mothers, or playing with their companions. The grasslands in June are exciting, like the music of the Tamboura.

摄影：刘元

博格达峰
Bogda Peak

天山是我们最容易亲近的山，它是西部山脉众神之中比较亲近人间的一位。天清气朗的时候，可以遥望见它的影子，云丝雪线，半空处横亘着一脉凝重而有质感的蓝色烟雾。海拔五千多米的博格达峰是众神中的小弟弟，也是天山之父派来观察守望乌鲁木齐的少年王子，它蓝袍镶金，白帽抹红，英俊伟岸。

Mount Tianshan is the easiest mountain to approach, as it is one of the closer mountains to human settlement in the western mountain range. When the skies are clear, we can see its far-off silhouette, and against rain and clouds it stretches across half the sky. The mountain range is covered by a deep blue haze that has a solid quality to it.

大地的颂词
Geographic Eulogy

在新疆的旷野，你闭上眼睛，听听辽远天空下的声音。微风拂过白桦林，溪流撞击巉岩，蝉鸣划破夜空，夜鸟低翔，人声高亢抑或低回，原始而又奢华的自然，别有一种热烈与慷慨、温柔与浪漫，这是新疆大地上的颂词。

When you close your eyes amidst the vast fields of Xinjiang, you hear the far-off sounds of nature. As wind combs through the birch forests, rivers flow and strike against precipitous rocks, cicadas and birds make their calls, night birds fly low, and human voices call out high or echo low. The nature, both primitive and luxurious, has a liberal ardour and a warm romance – what a eulogy to Xinjiang!

摄影：双元

摄影：张宏

温宿大峡谷
Grand Wensu
Canyon

温宿大峡谷是中国西部最美的丹霞地貌奇景。峡谷口是平整而干枯的河床，河床两边是红褐色的山，仿佛置身于一个红色的"场"中，一个激情的场。还有一层层的蓝、白、黄、绿在流动、翻滚，形成一波波的浪。谷内群峰林立、沟壑纵横，犹如迷宫。视野时而开阔，时而闭塞，峰回路转处，别有新天地。

The Wensu Canyon is one of the most beautiful Danxia landforms featuring Western China. Its entrance is a flat and dry riverbed, flanked by reddish-brown cliffs, almost resembling a kind of "red square", a kind of exciting venue. There are also layers of blue, white, yellow and green, rolling together like rumbling waves. There are numerous peaks within the valleys, with ravines and gullies criss-crossing as if in a maze. The field of view is wide at times and narrow at others – each turn around a bend takes you to a new landscape.

花开震四野
Say "Bloom"

新疆的花，是春与夏的临界点。那些花积攒了两个季节的能量，它们的开放就不简单是开放了，那一枚枚花蕾，铆足了劲，憋红了脸，喊一声"开吧"，就一起亮开嗓喉，震耳欲聋的花的叫喊，经久回荡在四野和大山。

Flowers in Xinjiang appear at the boundary between spring and summer. When they've gathered the energy of the two seasons, they do not simply open, but rather the buds, having mustered their strength, red-faced from exertion shout "bloom", and roar together as they burst open with a deafening roar that echoes throughout the land.

硅化木园
Petrified Forest

新疆奇台县硅化木园位于准噶尔盆地东部戈壁腹地人迹罕至的荒丘沟壑之中。侏罗纪时代，这里森林参天、湖泊荡漾、恐龙结队，生长着银杏、苏铁、松柏……而亿万年后，这些森林变成了坚硬的含硅铁的树化石，树皮、年轮完好如初，蕴藏着地球演变的信息，是罕见的世界奇珍。

The petrified forest in Qitai County is situated in the eastern part of hinterland of the Junggar Basin, where traces of human existence are quite rare among the barren hillocks and gullies. During the Jurassic period forests towered, lake waters rippled, and dinosaurs roamed in packs. Gingko, cycads, pines and cypresses grew here… A hundred million years later, these forests have been transformed into petrified wood and bark, retaining their original forms after all this time, containing information about the evolution of our planet – a rare world treasure.

花开如礼炮
A Floral Salute

把新疆花朵的绽放称之为爆炸亦不为过，那轰轰隆隆滚过田野的巨响，是花蕾大片大片爆开带来的，杏花白色的巨响，桃花粉色的轰鸣，沙枣花金黄的澎湃，形成礼炮的交响。烽火弥漫处，杏花的苦味、桃花的甜味、沙枣花的浓郁香味混合成经久不散的焰火。

Describing the blooming of flowers in Xinjiang as an explosion isn't overdoing it – when they burst open across the fields, blossoms bring bursting waves of colour to the landscape – white apricot blossoms, a roar of pink from the peach contingent, a surge of yellow in the form of the flowers of the narrow-leaved oleaster. The flames of war surge as the bitter scent of the apricots, the sweetness of the peaches and the fragrance of the oleaster blend to create an intense flame.

不黏腻的新疆
Feeling Good

一个人在夏天流一身汗并不是什么难事，而流一身汗并保持通体的干爽，却不是一件易事。只有新疆的夏天可以让你痛快地大汗淋漓，又让你适宜地永葆清爽，决不黏黏糊糊，决不拖泥带水，就仿佛真性情的新疆人，该承诺的一定承诺，该回绝的必定回绝，不留一点遗憾。

Sweating profusely in summer is nothing out of the ordinary, but keeping the body clean and dry while sweating is no mean feat. Only in Xinjiang's summer heat can you sweat a lot and still feel fresh and clean rather than sticky and dusty all over. This is like the people of Xinjiang itself – that what must be promised will be, and that which should be refused will definitely be, leaving no room for regrets.

摄影：张宏

多变的云
Capricious
Clouds

新疆的云很不老实，刚刚还是晴空万里，不一会儿就会发怒发狂，让人措手不及。但是，通常情况下它们清高而又傲慢，走走停停，悠闲自得，望都不望你一眼。人捉摸不透它，连天气预报也没弄懂它。

The clouds of Xinjiang aren't well-behaved, and can easily go from calm to wild in a quick moment, surprising onlookers. However, under normal circumstances, they are high and lofty, drifting and pausing, unhurried, and unconcerned. Humans, as well as the weather report both find themselves unable to grasp them.

塔吉克族人　摄影：黄永中

帕米尔高原上的塔吉克族人
Tajik on the Pamir Plateau

帕米尔是上帝在自己触手可及的地方给人类放置的一只摇篮。塔吉克族人就是生活在这摇篮中的婴孩。他们祖祖辈辈以放牧为生，草原就是家，天空就是屋顶，过着恬淡而宁静的生活。

Some people think of Pamir as a place where a deity touched the earth, creating a cradle for humanity, which would make the Tajik people the infants that grew up in this cradle. They have been herders since ancient times, and call the grasslands their home. Their ceilings are the skies, and their lives are simple and calm.

昭苏草原之春
Spring in Zhaosu

"人间四月芳菲尽，昭苏桃花始盛开。"那泛滥的色彩似乎是对你目光的一次挑逗，黄色的、粉色的、蓝色的、紫色的花朵会一直延伸下去再延伸下去。即使你的目光变成一匹野马，也难以追逐到这些色彩。如果不是那些低垂的云朵、久而不散的彩虹的陪伴，那么你的目光与想象可能会迷失在这无尽的色彩之中。

"When fragrances are in full swing in April, the peach trees of Zhaosu blossom." The colours play with your eyes, with parades of yellow, pink, blue, purple flowers extending as far as the eyes can see. Even if your gaze were a horse it would still have a hard time chasing them all down. Were it not for the low-hanging clouds and plentiful rainbows, your sight and mind could very well be lost in the endless sea of colour.

江布拉克
Jiangburak

江布拉克一词为哈萨克语，意为圣泉或生命之泉。它位于新疆奇台县半截沟镇南部山区，壮观的万亩麦田、神奇的怪坡、神秘怪石圈、响坡、仙人洞、五哥泉以及夫妻松等都颇具看点。雪峰、高原、群山、林海、山泉、湖泊、草地、鲜花、牛羊、毡房……囊括了原始的自然生态和独特的高山草原风光。

Jiangburak is a Kazakh word which means "sacred spring" or "spring of life". Situated in the mountains of the southern region of Banjiegou Township in Qitai County, the area has magnificent fields, mysterious slopes, mystical rings of odd rocks, the famous "singing slopes", a sage's cave, the Wuge Springs and the "couple pines" among other sites. Snowy peaks, highlands, mountain ranges, immense forests, mountain springs, lakes, grasslands, flowers, oxen, lambs and yurts… All of these things exist in a pristine natural state and accent the unique beauty of the high grasslands.

镌刻誓言
Carving
Promises

不要把誓言拓在沙漠上，因为有风；也不要把誓言写在冰上，因为有太阳。在新疆，誓言被镌于岩石上，它会成为天山岩画的一部分，变为永恒；或者把它刻于白杨树干上，随着时间的流逝，誓言被不断放大。

Don't write your promises in the sand as they'll be blown away; don't write them on ice as the sun will eventually melt it. In Xinjiang, promises are carved on stones, becoming part of a rock painting – this way they are permanent. Or, you can carve your promise into a poplar and as the tree grows it will become bigger and bigger.

收获的季节
Harvest
Seasons

放眼新疆秋天的大野，在付出与收获这一古老的命题中，所有人都会得出新的结论：播种的是跳蚤，收获的可能是龙种；播种的是芝麻，收获的可能是西瓜。在新疆肥沃的土地上只要你舍得投入，淌出大汗，不必拿出血本，回报就往往大大超乎你的想象。

Looking at the autumn fields in Xinjiang, everyone has their own conclusion that they make in the age-old discussion of effort and reward: planting fleas can yield dragons, planting sesame seeds can yield watermelons. With Xinjiang's fertile soil, anyone willing to make the effort and sweat a bit can reap large benefits.

摄影：双元

摄影：双元

天山天池
Tianshan Tianchi

天山天池古称"瑶池"，位于天山博格达峰下阜康县境内，是距今 200 余万年前第四纪大冰川活动中形成的冰碛湖，三面环山，北面为一座天然堤坝。天池湖面略呈半月形，是世界著名的高山湖泊之一。传说天池是西王母梳妆台上的银镜，又说是西王母的沐浴池，孙悟空偷吃蟠桃、大闹天宫均出于此。

Originally called the "Abode of Immortals", Tianshan Tianchi ("Heavenly Lake in the Heavenly Mountains") is situated beneath the Bogda Peak of the Tianshan Mountains, within the borders of Fukang County. A morainic lake (drift-dam lake), it was formed through glacial activity more than two million years ago during the Quaternary Period, and is encircled by mountains on three sides, with its north side dammed by a natural barrier, and is half-moon-shaped. It is one of the highest mountain lakes in the world. Legend holds that it was the silver mirror on the dressing table of the Queen Mother of the West, or her bathtub, or the site at which the Monkey King (protagonist in the classic novel *Journey to the West*) stole and ate the peach of immortality.

草原
Grasslands

在新疆，草原是介于森林和沙漠戈壁之间的一种形态。那些毛茸茸的绿草，无数单一个体集聚而成的大社会，从一叶草开始的故事，到整个大草原仍未能结束。

In Xinjiang, grasslands are the boundary between the forests and deserts, covered in countless blades of shaggy grass. The story that starts with one blade of grass continues throughout the land.

摄影 双元

魔鬼城雅丹地貌
Yardang Landform

雅丹地貌是风的杰作，时间的遗赠。风是一位雕刻大师，把荒原上裸露的土丘、山体雕琢得奇形怪状、千姿百态，如同中世纪的古城堡，又如惟妙惟肖的象形群雕。从魔鬼城的造型中，你可以看出各种各样的形象：人物、动物、建筑、城池、树木……

Yardang landform is an artwork carved by wind, a legacy of time. Wind is a great sculptor, carving the exposed earth of wastelands and the forms of mountains into every kind of odd shape, such as castles of medieval times, or lifelike sculptures. In the shapes of the ghost city, you can see all kinds of forms: humans, animals, buildings, cities, trees…

鱼湖
Fish Lake

鱼湖是一条细长的水带，细瘦而蜿蜒的样子，被很多路过但没有停留的人当成一条河。沙漠河是那种流着流着就会被沙子慢慢吸干的河流。但鱼湖不是河，它既不会流走也不会被沙漠吸干，虽然它就在沙漠里。这个长 12 公里、宽只有两三百米的湖，在民丰县城东北 40 公里、距沙漠公路 13 公里的 315 国道的两侧。

Fish Lake is a long body of water, slender and serpentine. Many passers-by believe it to be a river. Desert rivers withstand the constant incursion of sand which dries them out. However, Fish Lake is not a river. It neither flows away nor is dried out by the desert. This 12-kilometre-long lake is only two or three hundred metres wide, and lies 40 kilometres northeast of Minfeng County, 13 kilometres from Desert Highway 315.

草原上的游牧民族
Nomads on the Grassland

新疆历来是游牧民族的主要聚居区之一。哈萨克族、柯尔克孜族、蒙古族、塔吉克族是新疆传统的游牧民族。草原是游牧民族的家，千百年来他们沿袭着"随季节迁移，逐水草而居"的生存方式。人们在草原上围起一道栅栏，一则防止自家牛羊走散，二则标示此处为自己的"领地"，外人不能轻易进入。

Xinjiang is historically an important nomadic area. Kazakhs, Kyrgyz, Mongolian, and Tajik are the traditional nomadic peoples of Xinjiang. The prairies are their homes, and for centuries and millennia they followed the seasons, going where there was water and grass. People would construct fences to keep their livestock from wandering off, and also to mark their "territory" – outsiders could not enter rashly.

新疆夏天的绿
Summer Green in Xinjiang

新疆夏天的绿，是一种勇猛的绿。这些绿，总能在巨大苍黄的沙漠戈壁留下"吻痕"，醒目而狂野，在其他任何地方的夏天，你都不会遭遇这样的绿。

Xinjiang's green is a kind of wild green. These hues that appear as bruises against the vast expanses of greenish yellow in the desert are startling and savage. You won't encounter this kind of green anywhere else in summertime.

昭苏盆地
Zhaosu Basin

昭苏盆地由乌孙山、阿腾套山、南天山和哈萨克斯坦境内的查旦山围拢，形成一块几乎封闭的高位盆地。特殊的地理与气候，使这里远离了夏季的酷热，也远离了拥挤的人群。

The Zhaosu Basin is a high-altitude basin formed by Wusun Mountain, Atengtao Mountain, Nantian Mountain and, within the borders of Kazakhstan, Chadan Mountain. The area is characterised by special climactic and geological features, far away from the summer heat and crowded human civilisation.

摄影：双元

阳光的味道
The Flavour of Sunlight

新疆，阳光明澈而强烈，日照时间长得让人难以置信。夏至的喀什，在接近子夜时分的 23 点之后，天光才完全消失。如此漫长的日照，会令瓜果储满糖分，小伙子挺拔健朗，姑娘丰满妖娆。当然小麦也会无比优秀，鼓胀胀的麦粒，就是一颗颗微型的太阳，阳光的味道，温热而喷香，令人过齿难忘。

Sunlight in Xinjiang is bright and strong, and the length of daylight hours is almost hard to believe. In Kashgar in the summer, sunlight persists until after 11 at night. With this much sunlight each day, fruits become filled with sugar, boys grow up healthy and bright, and girls grow up well-developed and enchanting. Excellent wheat grows in this climate, with each grain being a small kernel of sunshine. The flavour and warm fragrance of sunshine is hard to forget after you have tasted it.

摄影：张宏

新疆金秋
Golden Autumn in Xinjiang

新疆秋天的色彩，有着难以言说的华美。金牧场、金草地、金田野、金湖泊、金风、金雨、金阳光，这些以黄金的基本色泽为底色，呈现出的是夺目的力量。从这些炫目的色泽中，每个人都会感受到这个季节的分量。

The beauty of the colours in Xinjiang is hard to describe. Golden pastures, golden plains, golden fields, golden lakes, golden wind, golden rain, golden sunlight – these colours all have a lustrous gold as their base, and a captivating power. We feel the full brunt of autumn when we are dazzled by these colours.

冲出塔克拉玛干
Out of Taklimakan

塔克拉玛干，维吾尔语意为"进去出不来的地方"。它位于塔里木盆地腹地，总面积约 33 万平方公里，是中国最大的沙漠，世界第二大流动沙漠，被称为"死亡之海"。沙漠里沙丘绵延，受风的影响，沙丘时常移动。1995 年中国第一条沙漠公路，南北贯穿塔克拉玛干大沙漠，全长 522 公里。

Taklimakan means, in the Uyghur language, "a place you cannot exit after entering". Located in the hinterland of the Tarim Basin, with an area of approximately 330,000 square kilometres, it is China's largest desert, the second largest rolling desert in the world, and has the nickname "the sea of death". The dunes extend for vast distances and move frequently due to the action of the wind. In 1995, China's first desert highway was constructed, running north-south through the Taklimakan Desert, with a total length of 522 kilometres.

哈密瓜
Hami Melon

去新疆游玩，不可不尝的是哈密瓜。哈密瓜甜香味美、营养丰富，有"瓜中之王"的美称。八月，在新疆，当阳光将石头炙烤得生烟时，空气中弥漫的全是哈密瓜的气息，香甜得浓稠婉转，令人迷醉。用一把英吉沙小刀将哈密瓜剖成月牙的形状，金灿灿的小船可以把你渡到甜蜜的彼岸。

You can't miss out on Hami Melon (Cucumis melo, similar to a cantaloupe). The Hami melon is sweet and fragrant, nourishing and full-bodied, and known as the "king of melons". In August, the Xinjiang sun heats the rocks so hot that they steam, and the smell of Hami melons permeates the air, fragrant, thick, and intoxicating. Cutting the melon into crescent-shaped slices with a Yengisar knife, the little golden boats will transport you to a wonderful paradise of sweetness.

狗鱼和鹰
A Pike and an Eagle

在去阿里的路上，发生了这样的一幕：一只鹰被鱼拖进水里。一只鹰，飞着飞着，在接近水面的一瞬，忽然向河中扑去。它要去啄水里的一条鱼，可那是一条大狗鱼，比鹰大得多。鱼迅速向水底游去。鹰扇起双翅欲挣脱飞走，但几番挣扎后还是被狗鱼拖入水中。水面上冒出几个气泡，随之便了无痕迹。

This scene unfolded on the way to Ali: an eagle was pulled into the water by a fish. The eagle, flying over the water, dove down, but the fish that it was trying to catch was a big pike – much heavier than the eagle. The fish quickly pulled the eagle into the water. The bird struggled but after a few flaps of its wings, it was still submerged. Disappearing into the depths, it left no trace other than a few bubbles.

丝路遗韵
The Sound
of Silk

古代丝绸之路北、中、南三条线路，仿佛是新疆大地上绵长而柔韧的琴弦，在不同的历史时期，发出时而激越、时而幽怨、时而低回、时而迸发的乐音。

The historical north, middle and south routes of the Silk Road resemble three pliable yet tough strings of a musical instrument. In different historical periods, their melodies have been intense at times, and melancholy, lilting, progressive at others.

截然不同的美
Different
Beauty

在新疆，只要你不关闭触觉和感官，就会遭遇截然不同的美：冷峻冰峰对应热烈沙漠，碧绿草原唱和苍黄戈壁，咆哮河流诱惑龟裂河床，茂密森林遥望不毛荒原，丰饶村镇对视凄清故垒，柔美湖泊反衬铁硬山岩，宽容绿洲伴唱肆虐风沙，火洲太阳辉映帕米尔峰雪，浪漫伊犁回眸古典喀什，托木尔峰俯瞰艾丁湖。

In Xinjiang if you just keep your eyes open and senses alert, you'll feel a new kind of beauty: icy peaks meeting scorching deserts, lush, deep green prairies and the green-yellow Gobi Desert. Roaring rivers contrast with cracked, dry riverbeds, and dense forests look out over desolate wasteland, rich and fertile villages contrast with ruined old cities, the soft beauty of lakes contrast with iron-hard rocks and stones. Broad oases and violent sandstorms co-exist, scorching sunlight glances off the snowy peaks of the Pamir Plateau, romantic Yili sets off ancient Kashgar, while Tomyr Peak looks down upon Aiding Lake.

摄影：双元

天山是金雕
A Golden
Eagle

天山是一只金雕，南疆和北疆是它巨大的翅膀，因此在新疆，常常有飙升的冲动，有扶摇九天的感觉。

Tianshan Mountain is a golden eagle, with northern and southern Xinjiang its wings. When it flaps its wings, all of Xinjiang feels the whirlwind.

冰山之父：
慕士塔格峰
Muztag Peak

慕士塔格峰，地处塔里木盆地西缘，东帕米尔高原东南部，被称为"冰山之父"。从任何角度看这座山峰都像是被谁刻意雕琢过似的，呈等边三角形，完全是天造地设的金字塔。慕士塔格峰有两条登山路线：西山脊和南山脊路线。西山脊路线最成熟，坡度较平缓，是登山爱好者初涉 7000 米山峰的首选。

Muztag Peak lies at the western edge of the Tarim Basin, in the southern reaches of the eastern Pamir Plateau – it is called the "king of the ice mountains". From any angle that you observe it, it appears to have been sculpted into an equilateral triangle – a natural pyramid. There are two routes through which it can be summited – the western ridge, and the southern ridge. The western ridge is the most familiar to climbers, with smoother slopes, and the best choice for mountain climbers looking to make the 7,000-metre trek to the summit.

摄影：黄永中

摄影：张宏

喀纳斯迷人的雾岚
Mist over Kanas

在喀纳斯湖，雾岚是与白桦、冷杉、变色的湖水并驾齐驱的景致，用不着特别讶异，也不用格外等待，千百年来它们就这样显现又消失——但绝不重复，在相同的一个地方，变换着形态各异的雾岚，仿佛一团永不停歇的思想，翻搅着前所未有的涡旋，是对创世的缅想，更是对终极的思忖。

On Lake Kanas, the fog, birch, firs, and multi-coloured lake water constantly reform the scenery, but there's no need to be surprised or wait around for something to happen, as this lake always continues to present these amazing sceneries that appear and disappear, although never in the same place or manner. The fog is like a train of thought that never stops moving, stirring up new vortices, reflecting upon the formation of the world, pondering the ultimate.

反差综合体
Great Contrasts

新疆把最赤贫的戈壁荒漠呈现给你，把最富有的石油、煤炭、黄金藏匿起来；最贫瘠的土地里，生长出最甜蜜的瓜果，烈日风沙中孕育出最漂亮的姑娘；最苦涩的盐碱水让人清醒，最甘冽的马奶酒又让人眩晕；狂烈的沙暴会让人粗糙，柔曼的温泉又让人细腻。新疆就是这么一个充满了反差的综合体。

Xinjiang gives you the poorest Gobi Desert, where it hides away its oil, coal and gold. The best melons grow out of the most barren soil, the most beautiful girls grow up amidst harsh wind and sun; the bitterest saltwater wakes us up and gives us clarity, the sweetest and clearest horse milk makes us dizzy; fierce sands make us coarse and gentle springs soften us. Xinjiang is a place full of contrastive experiences.

37

摄影：张宏

喀纳斯的雨
Rain over Kanas

喀纳斯湖是雨的制造工厂，尤其是在秋天，湖区的天空像是经年使用、破损不堪的盆底，时不时就滴漏起来。当然，看起来也是毫无缘由却更常见的，是突如其来的过路雨。下这样的雨人不要跑，往往是还没有找到躲雨的地方，它就戛然一下停住了，像是统一听了谁的口令，又好像什么都没发生。

Lake Kanas is a rain factory, especially in autumn, when the sky resembles a clean basin that occasionally leaks water. Of course, often and seemingly for no reason, rain bursts forth. There's no need to run from this kind of rain as it will stop before one can find shelter, as if it has been ordered to stop – everything goes back to normal quickly.

沿着一条河流的方向
Along the River

我们去寻访一片河滩，准确地说，是要寻访一条河流，一条名叫额敏河的河流。可它在哪里呢？起初是一些树木的遮挡，继而是一座村庄，几间破败的砖房前，消隐在另一个时代的标语依稀可见。我并不以为自己走错了方向，只是固执地认为，或许那一条河流，一不小心，就会出现在一个村庄和一排房子的后面。

We are looking for a riverbank – more precisely, we are looking for a specific river called the Emin River. Where is it? First there are some trees blocking us, then a village, then some ruined houses, and then a blacked-out slogan from another era. We don't think that we've taken a wrong turn – we just firmly believe that the river may suddenly appear behind a village and a row of houses.

洁身自好的白桦
Trees with True Integrity

图瓦人说，白桦是非常洁身自好的一种树，她选择在洁净的水边生长。因此，断定一条水系是否优良，看它的岸边是否有白桦驻足就可以下结论。在额尔齐斯河畔，白桦生长得亭亭玉立、英姿勃发，诠释着这条水系的优秀。

The Tuva people say that birches are trees with true integrity, and only pick clean places to grow. Thus, if one wants to evaluate the quality of a waterway, simply look if there are birches growing along it. Along the banks of the Ertix River, birch trees grow stalwart and strong, handsome in figure – this shows that the water is of excellent quality.

白桦林里许个愿
Make a Wish to a Birch

在喀纳斯，白桦林又叫情人林。据图瓦人说：情侣如果想要白头偕老，就去白桦树下许个愿吧；如果你想爱人一辈子只爱你一个，你就用红丝带蒙住白桦树的一只眼睛，那么爱人的眼睛里就会只有你！

In Kanas, birch forests are known as "lover's forests". The Tuva people say that if a couple of lovers want to grow old happily together, they need only to make a wish under a birch tree. If you want someone to only love you, use a strip of cloth to "blindfold" a birch tree, and that person will only have eyes for you.

摄影：双元

摄影：黄永中

喀什噶尔的夜晚
Night in Kashgar

喀什噶尔的夜晚让人兴奋，空气里弥散着夹竹桃、无花果、葡萄、石榴以及各种艾草的香甜味，烤羊肉飘出的浓郁烟香，馕坑里散发的小麦香气，婉转的歌声和吐曼河浑浊流水的低语声互相唱和。这挟带着各种芳香的尘土，悬浮、超越、升起、降落。

Night in Kashgar is exciting, the air filled with the fragrance of rosebay, figs, grapes, pomegranates and all kinds of atemesia. The thick scent of roasted lamb and bread baking in the oven, along with the mild notes of songs and the rolling of the Tuman River accompany each other in the air. All kinds of fragrant dust float, dart, rise and fall in the night atmosphere.

大河向北流
Flow to the North

额尔齐斯河汹涌的波浪像草原上奔腾的野马，信马由缰，那激昂澎湃的涛声犹如马的嘶鸣。这是一条流向北面的河，当她注入北冰洋时，国人看不见，就像出塞的王昭君，去而不返。我欣赏她的个性，当众多的河流成为母亲河，成为华夏儿女的乳液，她却默默地向北，一直向北。

The tempestuous waves upon the Ertix River resemble a wild horse running on the plain, dashing forward without guidance or restraint, the surging waves sounding like a horse's whinny. This is a north-flowing river, unseen by us when it enters the Arctic Ocean – leaving and not coming back, like the famous Wang Zhaojun. I admire its character – while many rivers come together as tributaries to larger flows inside Xinjiang, the Irtysh flows alone onwards, towards the north.

大海子
The Great Sea

大海子是乌伦古湖的俗称，也叫福海，是乌伦古河从阿尔泰山流下之后的尾闾湖。河变成湖就像大地的一个拥抱，湖叫作海就像一个蓝色的幻梦。当它呈现在面前时，我真的把它当作大海了。这浩如烟海、波光粼粼的水域，不就是海吗？不经意间，你可以看到鱼在湖里自由地吃着水藻，呼吸着阿尔泰山独有的空气。

"The Great Sea" is a nickname for Ulungur Lake; also called the Lucky Sea, it is a lake which receives water from the Altay Mountains via the Ulungur River. Where the river becomes a lake resembles an embrace of the earth, and calling it a sea is a blue dream. When it appears in front of me, I truly see it as a sea. This vast, twinkling expanse of water should be thus called. One can even see fish eating algae, breathing Altay's unique air.

摄影：双元

大西洋的最后一滴眼泪：赛里木湖
Sayram Lake

赛里木湖是新疆最美的湖泊之一，被誉为天山深处的蓝宝石。然而关于它的一个最精彩的说法是"大西洋的最后一滴眼泪"——它是大西洋暖湿气流向东吹拂最远到达的地方。

Sayram Lake is one of Xinjiang's most beautiful lakes, and has been called the sapphire of the Tianshan Mountains. It has also been called the "last tear of the Atlantic Ocean" – it is the farthest inland area that receives moisture from the Atlantic.

夏尔希里
Xia'erxili

长在夏尔希里的草是有福的，这里的每一棵草，都活出自由的样子。不像别处的草，春天刚发芽就被羊啃掉。草在一个春天忙着发芽，忙到秋天依旧是草根。夏尔希里的每棵草都开花，每朵花都结果，在漫长的西北风里，草木的种子远播到广袤的土地上。

Growing up in Xia'erxili is fortunate – there is a type of grass here that always grows in a free manner. Unlike the grass elsewhere, which is eaten away by sheep as soon as it sprouts; here, the grass continues to sprout all spring, all the way until autumn when it still only exists as roots. Every plant will bloom, every flower will produce seeds, and in the long-lasting northwesterly wind, the seeds will be flung far away to spread.

来者不拒的 新疆
Welcoming Xinjiang

自古以来，新疆来者不拒地接纳了各类倒霉的人、穷困的人、饥饿的人、逃难的人、没有身份的人，新疆给了他们喘息的茶水或悔过的苦酒……

Xinjiang has long been a place that accepted people who were down on their luck, the poor, the hungry, refugees, people without identity – Xinjiang gives them tea to refresh, or liquor to repent.

传统的交通 工具
Traditional Transit

新疆传统的交通工具，主要依靠马、驴、驼、牛等畜力。草原民族主要依靠马，而生活在塔里木盆地绿洲带的农耕民族则依靠驴、马、牛等，沙漠边缘的人多用骆驼，帕米尔高原的人们则使用牦牛，塔里木河两岸也用独木舟。

Traditional forms of transportation in Xinjiang are mainly powered by animals such as horses, donkeys, camels and cows. Grassland nomads mainly rely on horses, and the residents of the Tarim Basin who engage in agriculture rely on donkeys, horses, cows and the like. Those who live at the edge of the desert use camels, and those of the Pamir Plateau use yaks. Those who live on the banks of the Tarim River have canoes.

摄影：黄永中

可可托海
The Koktokay Sea

位于新疆阿勒泰富蕴县的可可托海，像一只眼睛，它眼眶很阔，绵延几百里。它睫毛很长，茂密如丛林。它眼珠很亮，其实真正让它光射四方的是它的蕴藏丰富的宝藏。

The Koktokay Sea, located in Fuyun County of Altay, Xinjiang, resembles an eye, with a wide orbit of a few hundred kilometres. It has long eyelashes, those of dense forests. Its pupil is bright – that which makes it shine so brightly is its true treasure.

魔鬼城
Ghost City

魔鬼城位于克拉玛依市乌尔禾区，蒙古族称它"苏鲁木哈克"，哈萨克族称呼它"沙依坦克尔西"，都是"鬼山"的意思。从科学角度讲，"城"里当然没有鬼，只是这里地处风口，每当风起，飞沙走石，天昏地暗，怪影迷离，大风在凄厉地盘旋呼号，有如鬼哭狼嚎。若目光惨淡，更显鬼影幢幢，阴森恐怖。

Located in the Urho District of Karamay, these mountains are known as "sulmuhaq" in Mongolian and "shaitan kersi" in Kazakh, both words meaning "devil's mountain". From a scientific perspective, although the "city" has no ghosts in it, as wind blows through the mountains, it kicks up dust and sand, darkening the skies and ground for an eerie appearance. Strong winds produce a mournful sound, like the cries of ghosts. Moonlight only adds to the eerie effect, casting frightening and flickering shadows.

摄影：张宏

摄影：汤祥

梦幻神仙湾
A Dreamy Bay

白茫茫的氤氲之气摇曳在这一池黛蓝之上，使人不禁猜想，它是从湖面升腾而起，还是从云端流泻下来的？透过薄雾，一片绚烂的色彩泼洒在山上。我突然变得有些纠结，这喀纳斯的神仙湾，真像留驻人间的仙境，引得你想不眨眼睛贪婪地看，又想闭目冥思，步入梦幻。

Thick white mist flickers over a dark blue lake, which makes people wonder: is it rising from the lake, or is it descended clouds? Through the mist, a splash of gorgeous colour appears on the mountain. I suddenly start to feel that Kanas' Fairy Bay is like an entrapping paradise, making you want to keep your eyes open to watch, or close them to slip into dreams.

"野兔子"之地
Wild Rabbits

乌尔禾，蒙古语，一说是野兔子之意。传说当年成吉思汗大军路过此地，士兵发现草丛中野兔众多，惊喜地喊出"乌尔禾"。另一种说法是"套子"的意思，乌尔禾兔子多，抓野兔下套子就行了。

"Urho", in Mongolian, means "wild rabbit". Legend has it that when Genghis Khan's army passed through the area, a soldier saw a large number of rabbits in the area and exclaimed "Urho!" Another explanation says that the word means "trap", as traps are used to catch the numerous wild rabbits in the area.

卧牛石
Rocks and Ox

天空澄明，阳光和煦，阿勒泰小东沟，克兰河水欢快地奔流。河床中乱石穿空，怪石嶙峋。一头劳作了一天的"卧牛"舒适地躺在不息的流水中，喝上几口清水，舒活舒活筋骨……啊，疲劳尽消！

Under a clear sky and warm sun, the Kelan River runs happily along in Xiaodonggou, Altay. The river is studded with tumbling rocks and jagged protruding stones. An ox, tired after a day's labour, comfortably lies in the water, drinking from the river and relaxing.

摄影：汤祥

阿尔金山
Altun

从若羌到阿尔金山很远，说是路又不像路，进山以后一直在乱石中颠簸，一条沟很长，除了沟里偶尔能见到一些零星的植物，两岸的群山上几乎见不到一块植被，沟中的水若有若无。山，静得出奇，再往上走就看到雪了。阿尔金山是我国目前最大的自然保护区，总面积 4.5 万平方公里，平均海拔 4500 米以上。

It's a long way from Ruoqiang to Altun, with the road sometimes not even resembling a road. Once one enters the mountains, there are stones everywhere, and in a long ravine one can occasionally see some sporadic plants, with almost no vegetation on the two banks of the mountain range. Water may or may not be present. The mountains are surprisingly quiet. Walking further up one can see snow. Altun is currently the largest nature reserve in China, with a total area of 45,000 square kilometres, and an average elevation of 4,500 metres above sea level.

蒙王府热气泉
The Hot Springs

和布克赛尔蒙古自治县有个蒙王府热气泉，在此居住的土尔扈特部族的人都称其为健身骨、治百病的"仙气"泉。泉周边的雅丹地貌，景观独特，色泽鲜艳。冬季，大气蒸腾，一道道热气冲出地面，很像史诗《江格尔》里描绘的大雾蒸腾、降下甘露、解救英雄的地方。

Hoboksar Mongolian Autonomous County has a hot spring – the Mongolian Palace Hot Springs, which the Torghut tribe call the "saintly spring" for its health benefits. The surrounding yardang landforms are vibrant with beautiful scenery. In winter, steam rises and forces its way up through the ground – just like in the epic *Jiangger*, in which steam condenses into mist that saves the hero.

星星峡
Xingxingxia

星星峡到底是一条怎样的峡谷？我每次经过都像在睡梦中一样，一觉醒来却是哈密，星星峡只是一个梦。星星峡没有大峡谷，没有湍急的河流，这里只有戈壁的风和石头。星星峡是一个镇子，一个关隘，它是西出阳关进入新疆第一个有人烟的地方。对于新疆人而言星星峡就是一堵院墙，过了院墙就算是出疆了。

What kind of valley is Xingxingxia ("starry gorge")? Every time I pass through it, it's like a dream, and when I wake up in Hami I feel like it wasn't even real. Xingxingxia has no large valley and no rapid rivers, only the wind of the Gobi Desert and stones. Xingxingxia is a village, a pass, and the first place where humans are seen in Xinjiang. The people of Xinjiang say Xingxingxia is a wall, and once you cross it, you have left Xinjiang.

草原花
Grassland
Flowers

这是一个无比灿烂的季节，牧人骑着马，游人也骑着马，草原上有洁白的羊群，也有盛开的花。我有时感到自己的笨拙，怎么也画不出一幅画，因为草原太大了。有草原的地方就有花，它一直开放在我心里。

This is a truly brilliant season, as herders ride horses, travellers do too, as flocks of sheep roam and flowers open everywhere. Sometimes, I feel a bit clumsy, and can't make a painting, as the grasslands are too vast. There are flowers on all the grasslands, and they are cherished in my memory.

怪石沟
Guaishigou

位于博乐市东北的怪石沟，不如说是怪石山，怪石在山上，沟借山而出名。一条小溪从沟底流过，梭梭、沙棘懒散地长在它的两旁，似乎有意告诉游人，不要看沟，还是看看这里的石头吧。我不知该给这些石头如何定义，它就是石头，本色又出色的石头，很像京剧的脸谱。

Situated in Guaishigou ("odd stone ravine") in the northeast of Bole City, the area should be called "Odd Stone Mountain", as the mountain has the stones, and the ravine simply derives its name from them. A small stream flows at the bottom, with sacsaoul and seabuckthorn growing on both sides, as if to tell travellers to move their eyes from the ravine to the rocks. I don't know how to define these rocks. They're just rocks – real and outstanding rocks, resembling the facial make-up in Beijing opera.

摄影：双元

醉爱
Intoxicated Love

我知道自己醉了，在哈萨克族人家，面对主人端上的羊头，我把羊耳朵给了一个巴郎，然后我喝了一碗又一碗酒。走出帐房，满眼的花开，有一只蜜蜂闻到了酒香，竟把我当作了花蕊，我告诉它，还是去采花吧！蜜蜂飞了，花还开着，中午的骄阳正照在草原上。

I know I'm already drunk. At a Kazakh's house, I took the ear from the lamb's head on the table and gave it to a boy, and then I drank a bowl of liquor, and then another. Walking outside, my eyesight was blurred, a bee mistook my scent for honey, and thought I was a flower. I told it, go find some flowers! The bee flew away to the flowers still open, as the blazing afternoon sun shone down over the grasslands.

冬天里的塔里木
Tarim in Winter

冬天，塔里木盆地上的胡杨树像一个个干柴老人，树叶已经落光了，剩下了硬硬的骨头。没有风时，一片万里无云的晴空，就像被吸尘器吸过一样，没有水分，也没有一丝云朵。地上的沙丘犹如农民喜晒的粮食，黄黄的，一堆又一堆，望不到边，也望不到头。

In winter, the poplars in the Tarim Basin resemble so many matchsticks – all leaves have fallen, and only the hard bones remain. At times without wind, the sky is completely cloudless, as if it's been vacuumed of all water. The sand dunes look like grains being sunned by farmers, yellow, numerous, boundless, and endless.

古尔图
Gurt

古尔图是蒙古语"桥"之意，我没有发现桥，却走进了一片胡杨林。那林子很大，秋天里，太阳挂在高高的蓝天上，没有干燥的热，风里便有一丝丝温暖。据说这片原始的森林有 80 万亩，里面有着全世界最大的梭梭林，它曾经是蒙古王爷的避暑地。

"Gurt" is Mongolian for "bridge". I didn't find a bridge, but walked into a poplar forest which was quite large. In the autumn, the sun hung high in the blue sky, without a dry heat, but a slight warmth in the wind. This old-growth forest covers over 533 square kilometres, and within has the world's largest sacsaoul forest. It was previously the Mongolian king's summer retreat.

台特玛湖
Lake Taitema

一望无际的水面，把沙漠沉到了湖底，有几只鸟像在水面上弹奏一把大琴，没有震耳欲聋的音响，无声中却有着悦耳的旋律。台特玛湖，这个早已被人们遗忘的湖泊，忽然重现在塔里木，让人的心灵为之震撼。

An endless water scene buries the desert in the lake. Birds make noise on the lake surface but no echo appears. In the silence there are some pleasant melodies. Lake Taitema was long forgotten, and then suddenly reappeared in Tarim – a startling occurrence for sure.

新疆扉页：吐鲁番

Turpan: The Title Page in the Book of Xinjiang

吐鲁番是一个随手可取的、袖珍的新疆，一个首先翻到的新疆的扉页，一个具备了基本元素、被哲学家和游客概括出关键词的新疆。吐鲁番的海拔，中国最低；吐鲁番的气温，中国最热；吐鲁番的葡萄，中国最香甜。

Turpan is a hand-sized, pocket Xinjiang; the title page you'll turn to in the book of Xinjiang. It possesses the fundamental elements, and has been pointed out by philosophers and travellers alike as a "keyword" in the vocabulary of Xinjiang. Turpan has the lowest elevation and the hottest temperatures in China. Its grapes are the best in all China.

白哈巴

Baihaba

白哈巴靠近中哈边境，是图瓦人聚居的古老村落，颇具欧式村寨风情。晨曦初露，阳光轻洒，外观古朴的小木楞屋间，炊烟袅袅升起，与迷人的晨雾纠缠一起，升腾缭绕，勾画出一幅生动、闲适的农家晨炊图。希望这种恬静祥和，永远也不要被打破。

Baihaba lies near the Chinese-Kazakh border, and it is an old village in which Tuva people gather. It has a European feel. As dawn breaks and sunlight spreads, smoke rises from the wooden cottages, and mixes with the morning mist, coiling up as it rises to paint a picture of a lively and pleasant rural morning cooking scene. One hopes this pleasant scene will never be disturbed.

摄影：汤祥

历史・传承

History and Traditions

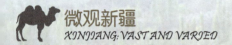

露天博物馆：吐鲁番
Turpan: An Open-Air Museum

吐鲁番是世界上最大的露天考古博物馆。交河故城、高昌故城、阿斯塔那古墓群、千佛洞，作为记忆残片的壁画以及写在桑皮纸上的摩尼教残卷，红色灰烬般的火焰山、蛮荒的世界第二低地艾丁湖，博物馆里的木乃伊和巨犀化石……它们是时光慷慨的馈赠，散发着岁月和尘土的气息。

Turpan is the largest open-air archaeological museum in the world. The ancient Jiaohe City and Gaochang City, Astana Tombs, and Thousand Buddhist Grottoes, as well as ancient murals, Moni scrolls carved on mulberry bark, the burning red fiery mountain, the world's second lowest point at Aiding Lake, the mummies and giant petrified life forms – these remnants have been scattered by time throughout the area.

彩陶之路
The Road of Coloured Pottery

听过彩陶之路吗？从六七千年前开始，中原人就带着彩陶技艺，越沙漠踏戈壁，寻天山翻冰川，至汉代止于巴尔喀什湖，上演了一出东西八千里、上下五千年的历史剧。剧情复杂，结构宏大，引人入胜。

Have you heard of the road of coloured pottery? From six or seven thousand years ago, the people of the Central Plains produced coloured pottery, taking the art across deserts and over the glaciers of the Tianshan Mountains to even Lake Balkash in the Han Dynasty. The path spanned four thousand kilometres and five thousand years of history. The plot is complicated, the construction grand, and the story alluring.

摄影：黄永中

五星出东方利中国

China Will Rise

1995 年 10 月 26 日，中日尼雅考察队开掘新疆民丰县尼雅古墓群 8 号墓，出土大批珍贵文物，其中一块织锦护膊尤为光辉灿烂、耀人眼目，青底白色赫然织就八个汉隶文字：五星出东方利中国。人们说它的出土预示着中华民族复兴梦想将实现。这款织锦现收藏在新疆维吾尔自治区考古研究所。

On October 26, 1995, a Sino-Japanese investigative team excavated the No. 8 Tomb at the Niya Burial Site in Minfeng County, unearthing a large number of precious cultural relics, among them a brilliant brocaded arm guard with a black background and white designs that impressively feature eight Chinese characters, "when the five stars in the east appear, China will rise". People say that the object's unearthing is proof that China will become glorious. The object is stored in the Xinjiang Uyghur Autonomous Region's Institute of Archaeology.

伏羲女娲图

Fuxi and Nüwa

画，以白、红、黄、黑四色描绘，人首蛇身，伏羲左手执矩，女娲右手持规。二人上体相拥，下体相缠。因其与人类生物遗传结构——脱氧核糖核酸分子的双螺旋线的结构非常相似，被国际社会题名为"化生万物"。

The painting is composed of white, red, yellow and black, featuring human heads upon snake bodies. Fu Xi holds a quadrature in his left hand, and Nüwa holds a rule in her right hand. The two figures embrace each other, their bodies intertwining. Their bodies resemble deoxyribonucleic acid, the building block of human life and so many other living things.

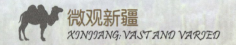
九龙壁
A Nine-Dragon Wall

20 世纪 80 年代，新疆阜康县出土了大型古生物化石。九个完整的古脊椎动物骨架，保存在一块岩壁上，被形象地称为九龙壁，化石轮廓逼真，形状各异，再现了三叠纪时期副肯氏兽群的生活方式。

In the 1980s, a large amount of petrified artefacts were unearthed in Fukang County in Xinjiang. Nine complete vertebrate paleontological specimens were found in the form of petrified skeletons, preserved in a rock wall – this wall came to be known as the "Nine Dragon Wall" (an important mythical concept in Chinese culture). The petrified forms are quite lifelike, and appear in various postures, representing the lives of parakannemeyeria in the Triassic period.

阿斯塔那古墓群
The Astana Tombs

阿斯塔那古墓群距吐鲁番市 40 多公里，是古代高昌王国的公共墓地，被称为"高昌的历史活档案、吐鲁番地区的地下博物馆"。那里埋葬的以汉族人为主，也有车师、突厥、匈奴、高车等少数民族居民；既有达官贵族也有普通百姓。可见，当时高昌王国的主体民族是汉族，而且各民族之间、官民之间非常平等。

Located 40 kilometres from Turpan City, the Astana Tombs are a public tomb site of the ancient Kocha kingdom, and are said to be both a record of the life of the Kocha as well as an underground museum in Turpan. Most of the persons buried within are Chinese, but there are also people from the Gushi, Turk, Xiongnu, Kocha and other ethnic tribes, including both high ranking officials and common people. It can be seen that the major ethnic constituent of the Kocha was Han Chinese people, and that within and between each ethnic group there was a high degree of equality.

波马古墓之谜
Riddle of the Poma Tomb

1997 年 10 月，昭苏波马修路工的巨大铁铲，铲出了金光乍泄的一幕：千年墓主金衣裹体。然其被破坏殆尽，劫后余生尚得一堆金罐银杯。其中一件镶嵌红宝石的黄金面具，奢华无比，庄严生动。面具的主人是谁？属于哪一个部落？惊天之谜给考古学界带来巨大兴奋。

In October 1997, during highway construction work in Poma, Zhaosu, an excavator unearthed a splendid tomb: the millennium-old owner of the tomb was wrapped in gold cloth. It had decayed extensively, leaving behind a pile of golden jars and silver cups. Among them was a golden mask inlaid with rubies, and an extremely luxurious and valuable artefact. Who did the mask belong to? Which tribe did he belong to? This riddle continues to puzzle archaeologists today.

八窍头骨
Orifices and Bones

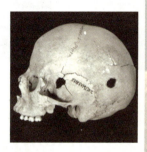

人的头骨上有七窍，可在新疆伊犁河流域的乌孙墓、吐鲁番盆地的姑师墓等多处史前墓地的考古发掘中，人们发现一些头骨上有神秘的第八个孔洞，圆形或方形，无序排列。是用来防腐？赶时髦？或者是某种巫术行为？谁也说不清。

In Chinese, people are said to have seven orifices – the eyes, ears, nostrils and nose. However, in the Wusun tomb site of the Yili River Valley and the tombs of the Gushi in the Turpan Basin, excavations have found an extra hole in the skulls of burial subjects, sometimes round and sometimes square, with no apparent definite order or placement. Was it used for antiseptic reasons, for fashion, or some kind of ritual or witchcraft? Nobody can be sure.

轮台城
Luntai City

在去往乌鲁木齐南山的路上，有一座古城遗址，据说是当年的轮台城。戍楼西望烟尘黑，汉兵屯在轮台北，唐代边塞诗人岑参曾在这里生活了三年。如今，戍楼不再，烟尘已散，但大唐时代的边塞诗却留存了下来，大唐的博大与包容也留存了下来。在天山明月之下，豪放与阴柔，早已融入了新生者的血液。

On the road to Nanshan in Urumqi there are the ruins of an old city, said to be Luntai City. Scenes from the lookout tower of Luntai are famous in Chinese poetry, and Tang Dynasty poet Cen Shen lived there for three years. Today, the lookout tower is gone and the smoke and dust have scattered, but the Tang Dynasty poems remain, and the feelings of vastness and inclusivity still remain today. Under the moonlight of the Tianshan Mountains, the bold and unconstrained mingle with the tender and soft for a new-born bloodline.

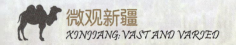
小河墓地
The Xiaohe
Tomb Site

小河墓地位于罗布泊地区孔雀河下游河谷南约 60 公里的罗布沙漠中，东距楼兰古城遗址 175 公里。小河墓地整体由数层上下叠压的墓葬及其他遗存构成，墓地沙山上密密麻麻矗立着 140 多根多棱形、圆形、桨形的胡杨木桩。小河墓地神秘的建筑被称为"死神的立柱殿堂"。

The Xiaohe ("little river") Tomb Site is located in a valley of the lower reaches of the Kongqi River, in the Lop Nor region, 60 kilometres into the desert. It lies 175 kilometres east of the ruins of the city of Loulan. The Xiaohe site has a number of layers of tombs stacked upon each other as well as other architectural remnants, and there are more than 140 rhomboid, round and remiform wooden pillars made of poplar wood stuck close together in the desert. This mysterious burial site has been called "The Palace of Pillars of the God of Death".

中国最早的佛窟
Buddhist
Caves

在明屋塔格悬岩陡壁上的克孜尔千佛洞，层层相叠，绵延 3.2 公里，是新疆最大的佛教文化遗址。它开凿于公元 3 世纪至 13 世纪，是我国最早的石窟，共有 236 个洞，现存壁画约 1 万平方米，是仅次于敦煌壁画的艺术宝库。没有人知道，第一个来到这里的佛教徒是谁，在什么时间，来自哪儿……

On the steep cliff walls of the Kizil Thousand Buddha Grottoes, layer after layer overlap for a length of 3.2 kilometres – it is the largest Buddhist relic site in Xinjiang. The caves were cut from the 3rd to 13th century, and are the earliest man-made grottoes in China. There are 236 caves with murals covering about 10,000 square metres, one-upped only by the Dunhuang Caves. Nobody knows who the first disciple to visit was, nor when and where he was from.

三道海子巨石堆
A Pile of Giant Stones

阿勒泰青河县的深山谷底，有一个山样大小的人工石堆，在那里伫立了三四千年。它在三道海子之间耸立着，构造和形制像一轮太阳。据说，这是一座巨大的太阳神殿，山水互映，神殿突兀，是游牧民族构想的天堂之境。

Among the steep mountains and deep valleys of Qinghe County in Altay, there is a pile of giant stones that has stood for three or four thousand years. It towers in the Sandao Haizi region, and resembles a sun. It's said that this was an altar to the Sun God, situated where mountain and water meet, and was a monument constructed by ancient nomadic herders.

完美废墟：交河故城
Perfect Remains: The Ancient Jiaohe City

交河故城位于吐鲁番市以西 10 公里的雅儿乃孜沟村。它是世界上最大、最古老的的生土建筑城市。故城长约 1650 米，最宽处约 300 米。它建在一个约 30 米高的岛状悬崖平台上，一道河水分流环绕城下，形成天然的护城河，四周崖岸壁立，形势险要，易守难攻。交河故城是一座有重要历史价值的城堡，被称为"东方庞贝"。

The ancient Jiaohe City is located ten kilometres west of Turpan City, in Yarnaz Village. It is the largest and oldest adobe city in the world, with a length of 1,650 metres, and a width of 300 metres at its widest point, constructed upon a 30-metre high mesa. A river forks around the two sides, surrounding it and forming a natural moat. It is surrounded by high, precipitous cliffs on both sides, making it very hard to attack. The ancient Jiaohe City is of important historic value, and is known as the "Pompeii of the East".

佛教圣地：苏巴什故城
Subas Old City

1700 年前，佛教在龟兹占有绝对统治地位，政教合一使龟兹王朝成为西域最繁华的佛教胜地。在今库车县城东北约 23 公里的苏巴什故城，为魏晋时代佛寺遗址。库车河穿城而过，将其分为两半，故有东寺、西寺之称。后秦名僧鸠摩罗什、唐代名僧玄奘曾在此讲经。龟兹国当时有寺庙 100 多座，僧人 5000 多名。

1700 years ago, Buddhism in Kocha held a position of absolute administrative rule, with the theocratic kingdom being one of the most developed sites of Buddhism in the Western Region. In today's Kuqa County, approximately 23 kilometres to the northeast, is the Subas Old City, which is the remnants of a Buddhist temple from the Wei and Jin Dynasties. The Kuqa River cuts through it, dividing it into two halves – the East Temple and West Temple. The famous monk of the Latter Qin Dynasty, Kumarajiva, and the Tang Dynasty monk Xuanzang both preached sermons here. During the time of the Kocha Kingdom, there were more than 100 temples and 5,000 monks.

恐龙沟
Dinosaur Gulley

恐龙沟位于准噶尔盆地东部的奇台县，是世界范围内恐龙化石最集中、种类最多、保存最完整和个体最大的一个地区。这里至少生活过 10 种以上的恐龙，化石种类自白垩纪早期到侏罗纪上统、中统、下统，基本贯穿整个恐龙的地史分布。在此可以遥想恐龙在毁灭前的灼炼之痛，体验生物大灭绝后的空寞与荒茫。

Konglonggou, or "dinosaur gulley", located in the eastern reaches of the Junggar Basin, in Qitai County, is one of the most concentrated, most diverse and most complete sites of its kind in the world. More than 10 varieties of dinosaurs have been discovered here, with petrified specimens ranging from the early cretaceous to the reaches of the Jurassic period, more or less covering all of dinosaur history. From here we can imagine the pain of the extinction event and the desolation after its occurrence.

新疆曾是一片汪洋
Xinjiang Was a Sea

新疆这块巨型的疆域，是这个世界距海洋最远的陆地。然而，据《地史学》考证，远在 5000 万年前，新疆却是一片汪洋大海，镶嵌在新疆很多山崖上的贝壳就是明证。其中有两座巨型岛屿，那就是今天的塔里木盆地和准噶尔盆地。

The immense area of Xinjiang is the farthest region from the sea in the world. However, according to *Historical Geology*, 50 million years ago, Xinjiang was a large ocean, with sea shells on many peaks in the region proving this. It also had two enormous islands – the modern-day Tarim and Junggar basins.

世界上最早的毛皮滑雪板
The Earliest Skis

2005 年，一位牧民在离阿勒泰市区 30 多公里的汗德尕特蒙古民族乡敦德布拉克发现了一处岩画。画中，4 人跟在牛马后边，3 人踩在毛皮滑雪板上，手持长棍。岩画属于旧时器时代晚期，也就是说，距今约 1.2 万年或更早，阿勒泰山地居民已发明了滑雪板。敦德布拉克岩画是人类对滑雪活动的最早记录。

In 2005, a herder found a petroglyph in the Mongolian village of Khandgat 30km outside of Altay City, in Dundbulak. In the painting, four human figures follow a horse, and three stand on leather sleds, holding long poles in their hands. The petroglyph dates from the late Palaeolithic period, that is to say, 12,000 or more years ago, the residents of Altay had discovered a form of skiing. The Dundbulak Petrogyph is the earliest record of human skiing activity.

**生殖崇拜：
康家石门子
岩画**

An Old Rock
Painting

呼图壁县的深山里有一幅闻名世界的岩画——康家石门子岩画。岩画里满绘极度夸张的男女交欢图，它与山体河谷互为一体，散发出浓浓的巫术味道。岩画直白地展现了三千多年前天山沟谷居民的所思所想。

Deep within the mountains of Hutubi County, there is one of the famous petroglyphs in the world – the Kang Shimenzi Petroglyph. It's an extremely exaggerated depiction of sexual intercourse, integrated into the mountain and river landscape that exudes a bewitching feel. This petroglyph gives us a clear view into what the valley residents of 3,000 years ago had on their minds.

骆驼石

The Camel
Rock

从和什托罗盖镇前往和丰县城的路边上，有一似骆驼造型的风蚀台地。台地旁边有中亚罕见的超大型旧石器制造场，乃目前所知新疆历史的起笔之处。

On the road from Heshituoluogai Township to Hefeng County town, there is a wind-eroded mesa that resembles a camel. Next to the mesa is a Palaeolithic manufacturing site, quite a rare find in Central Asia – as far as we can tell, it is the starting point of history in Xinjiang.

王国
The Kingdom

司马迁《史记》中提及西域三十六国。这些王国均为游牧民族所建，虽然在规模上明显带有部落痕迹，但它们都是独立的，各王国都有国王，有军队，具备对外发起战争和防备敌人入侵的能力。他们的城邦都建在极富战略意义的地方，比如车师国，就选择了一个被两条河环护的高地作为城邦。

Sima Qian mentions the thirty-six kingdoms of the Western Region in his *Historical Records*. These kingdoms were all constructed by nomadic peoples, and even though they showed vestiges of tribal society, they were independent kingdoms with their own rules, armies, and the ability to conduct and defend against outside invasions. Their cities were built upon sites that had strategic significance, such as the Cheshi, who built their city upon a plateau surrounded by two rivers.

解忧公主
Princess Jieyou

乌孙国是西汉时期由游牧民族在今新疆北部伊犁河流域建立的。汉武帝太初二年（前103），解忧公主奉命赴西域，嫁与乌孙王，被封为右夫人。她积极参与政事，致力于兴国安邦，乌孙国出现前所未有的兴盛局面。解忧公主受到人们的爱戴，人们称赞她：汉家公主的美貌赛过天鹅，爱民如子的美德天下传颂。

The Wusun Kingdom was established in the river valley of Yili, Northern Xinjiang, during the Western Han Dynasty. In 103 B.C., Emperor Wu of the Han Dynasty married Princess Jieyou to the Wusun King to strengthen their bond. She participated energetically in administrative affairs and helped the kingdom prosper to an extent it never had before. The princess was loved and admired, and she was praised for being beautiful, morally upright, and loving of her people.

怪异胡须墓
Odd Graves

你见过这样古怪的墓葬吗？古墓封堆向东延伸出南北相对、长数十米到数百米不等的弧形石条阵，像山羊的胡须。新疆托里县的这些胡须墓是两千多年前草原民族的一种特殊祭祀遗存。关于胡须墓，还有很多未解之谜。

Have you seen an odd burial site like this? The tombs extend eastwards, opposing each other North-South. Arcs of stones extend from dozens to almost a hundred metres along the landscape, like a goat's beard. Tombs of this kind exist in Xinjiang's Tuoli County, a relic of the special burial rituals of the residents of the grasslands. There are still many as yet unanswered questions about tombs of this kind.

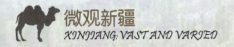
微观新疆

XINJIANG: VAST AND VARIED

夏塔古道
The Xiata
Passage

夏塔古道是早年人们穿越天山的重要通道之一，在昭苏境内。沿夏塔峡谷盘旋而上，经过木扎尔特冰川，可直抵南疆阿克苏温宿县境，全长 70 余公里。古道蜿蜒崎岖，地势险要，狭窄之处仅能供人畜通过。现在古道已近于荒废。当时的商旅、军队从这里走过时所留下的脚印与喘息已渐渐被岁月抹去了。

The Xiata Ancient Passage was one of the major passes through the Tianshan Mountains used by ancient peoples. It lies within the borders of Zhaosu County. Winding through the pass takes one over the Muzart Glacier, directly to the border of Aksu's Wensu County, in Southern Xinjiang. The total length of the pass is more than 70 kilometres. The old passage is winding and rugged, with dangerous landforms and narrow passages that allow only people and beasts to cross. The passage has already fallen out of use. The footsteps and breath of the soldiers and merchants who passed through in times past have gradually been worn away by time.

《福乐智慧》
Fortune,
Happiness
and Wisdom

《福乐智慧》是一部回鹘文长篇诗作，也是重要的哲学、伦理学著作。其内容主要表述治国之理及作者的哲学、道德思想。诗中四个人物：日出国王、月圆大臣、贤明大臣和觉醒隐士，分别象征正义、幸运、智慧和知足。诗作作者为 11 世纪维吾尔族诗人、思想家、政治活动家玉素甫·哈斯·哈吉甫。

Fortune, Happiness and Wisdom is a long poem in the old Uyghur script, and an important philosophical and ethical work. It mainly expounds upon administration and the author's own philosophy and thoughts on morality. There are four characters in the poem: the Sunrise King, the Secretary of the Moon, Secretary of Sagacity, and the Awakened Recluse, which symbolise justice, happiness, wisdom and contentment respectively. The author was the 11th century Uyghur poet, thinker, and political activist Yusuf Khaas Hajib.

驿站与巴扎
Post Station
and Bazaar

从部落到氏族，从氏族到国家，交流与融合，使人类一步步走到今天。历史上，新疆这片土地是两个大洲的桥梁，是驿站，是巴扎，是文明的会所。在丝绸的窸窣声中，在瓷器的温润光泽下，在葡萄和香料音乐般的氤氲气氛里，世界，一点点地变得丰富滋润起来。

From tribes to clans and clans to states, interaction and blending between groups of humans brought mankind to where it is today. Historically, Xinjiang has been a bridge between two continents, a post station, a bazaar and a cultured meeting place. Amidst the rustle of silk, the lustre of porcelain, the enshrouding musical fragrance of grapes and perfume, the world was enriched ever so little by little.

摄影：韩连赟

草原石人
Stone People

在新疆广阔的昭苏草原上散布着大大小小的石人，那些散落的石人，经历过多少次战争、灾难以及人群的繁衍与死亡？没人知道。上千年的风蚀雨打，多少个日月与朝代的更迭，并没有改变它的默守伫立。低垂变换的浮云、来去匆忙的风、寻找家园的鸟，在掠过这茫茫草原的时候掠过它。

On the vast plains of Zhaosu in Xinjiang there are strewn "stone people" of various sizes. One must wonder, through how many wars, disasters and human activities have these figures survived? Nobody knows. Millennia of wind and rain-driven erosion, and the coming suns and moons of various dynasties did nothing to change their silent positions. The low-hanging clouds, swift winds, and migrating birds all passed over these figures when they passed over these plains.

陶器上的巫觋
Wizards on a Jar

哈密天山北路墓地出土的一件彩陶罐的双耳上，绘有两个奇怪的男女，是一对巫觋。男女三角构图、张开枝状大手、头插翎羽，仿佛置身巫术现场。该彩陶距今有 3500 年历史。

On the handles of a coloured pottery jar unearthed at the Tianshan North Road Tomb in Qumul, there are two odd human figures – a man and a woman. They are shamans. Their composition is triangular, with their dendritic hands spread open, heads adorned with feathers, as if they are in the middle of a ritual. This pottery vessel is at least 3,500 years old.

63

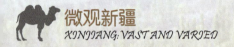
锡伯族西迁
The Xibe
Migration

1764 年，为了维护边疆稳定，1000 多名骁勇善战的锡伯族官兵举行完祭祖大典后，带着乾隆帝 60 年回故乡的承诺，携 3000 多名家眷从盛京（今沈阳）出发，到新疆伊犁地区屯垦戍地。西迁的一年多时间里，有 350 个婴儿出生，从出生起他们稚嫩的肩膀就担负起了守边固防的重任，被称为世界上最小的兵。

In 1764, in order to maintain border stability, more than 1,000 fierce Xibe warriors, after a large official ceremony, made good on an agreement with the Qianlong Emperor and took more than 3,000 family members with them, heading out from Shengjing (modern-day Shenyang) towards a troop station in the Yili Region of Xinjiang. In a more than year-long journey towards the west, they carried 350 infants with them – from birth they were tasked with the responsibility of border defence, and thus were called the world's youngest warriors.

丝路商人
Merchants on
the Silk Road

丝绸之路，某种意义上是商人们踏出来的，他们在其所处的时代，用艰苦跋涉换取了经济利益。商人们对丝绸之路兴旺发达做出的贡献功不可没，但他们在历史中的面孔却是模糊的。在这一点上，商人们给历史留下了空白。

Much of the significance of the Silk Road derives from those merchants who tread it. As they made their arduous journeys upon it, they extracted value from it. Although they made a very important contribution to the prosperity of the route, their likenesses are unclear to us – in this respect they left blank pages in the books of history.

摄影：黄永中

有天马的地方
Heavenly Horses

两千多年前，汉武帝为寻求汗血宝马派张骞出使西域。有宝马的地方，必然有骁勇的骑士。汉朝为联合乌孙以击败匈奴，将汉宗室公主细君、解忧远嫁到乌孙。从那时起，新疆与中原便被一脉割不断的血缘相连。当时昭苏草原是乌孙的领地，更是宝马的故乡。如今每年 7 月，天马国际旅游节在昭苏开幕。

More than 2,000 years ago, Emperor Wu of the Han Dynasty dispatched Zhang Qian to the Western Regions to attain Akhal-teke horses. Where there are great horses there must also be great riders. In order to unify the Han Dynasty with the Wusun Kingdom and defeat the Huns, a Han consort was married off to the Wusun. From then on, the bloodlines of the Central Plains region and Xinjiang have been inextricably linked. The Zhaosu Grasslands were the territory of the Wusun at the time, and the home of the Akhal-teke horses. To this day every year in July there is a Heavenly Horse International Travel Fair in Zhaosu.

一炮成功
Easy Work

19 世纪 70 年代，中亚浩罕国军事头目阿古柏入侵新疆。左宗棠奉命督师西征，清军在六道湾山梁上架起大炮，朝乌鲁木齐北门只开一炮，阿古柏侵略军即闻风而逃，清军轻松收复失地。坐落在乌鲁木齐水磨沟风景区的一炮成功炮台见证了这段历史。

In the 1870s, the Kokand leader Yaqub Beg of the Central Asia invaded Xinjiang. General Tso Tsung-t'ang ordered a supervisory expedition, through which the Qing army installed large artillery at the ridge of Liudaowan Mountain. They only fired one shot at the north gate of Urumqi, and the invading army fled, allowing the Qing forces to easily retake the lost land. A cannon still stands in the Urumqi Shuimogou Scenic Area as a testament to this victory.

左公柳
General Tso

丝绸之路沿线茂密的左公柳，是新疆的一张历史名片。左公即左宗棠，19 世纪 70 年代，左宗棠奉命西征，讨伐入侵的阿古柏。在征战中，深感茫茫戈壁没有绿荫的困苦，便率军植树造林。大军人人随身携带柳树苗，一路走一路栽，形成了一道连绵数千里、绿如帷幄的塞外奇观。

Beside the Silk Road stand the General Tso Willows, a card in the pages of the books of history of Xinjiang. In the 1870s, General Tso dispatched an expeditionary army to repel invaders, and lamented the lack of trees and shade in the Gobi Desert. For this reason, he had his army plant trees. The army carried seedlings with them, and planted them alongside routes to create a long corridor of dense shade cover that is pleasant to look at.

和布克塞东归雕塑 摄影：双元

土尔扈特部东归

The Torghut Return

早在明朝末年（1628），土尔扈特人为了寻找新的生存环境，离开新疆塔尔巴哈台故土，来到伏尔加河下游、里海之滨，建立起土尔扈特汗国。乾隆三十六年（1771），土尔扈特部首领渥巴锡为摆脱沙俄压迫，率部众冲破沙俄重重截击，历经千辛万苦，返回故土。

In 1628, during the late Ming Dynasty, the Torghut people left their homeland in Tarbagatay, Xinjiang, to find a new space to live in. They arrived at the lower reaches of the Volga River, where they established the Torghut Khanate. In 1771, the Torghut leader Ubashi, in order to get free from Tsarist Russian oppression, led his people to break through Russian interceptions and returned to their homeland after untold hardships.

老铁匠
An Old Master

坎土曼巴扎，是喀什著名的传统铁艺集市，至今仍有一批传统的铁匠传承着古老的工艺。维吾尔语把铁匠称为铁木尔其，这位老师傅出身于铁匠世家，身体依然健壮，和家人开了一家铁艺铺子。铁锤叮当、铁花四溅中锤炼出的是铁木尔其不曾流逝的美誉。

The Kantuman Bazaar is a traditional market for ironware in Kashgar, and even now has craftsmen practising the craft in the traditional manner. It is a craft passed down through generations. The master in this photo stays strong even in old age, running his family business. The clang and spark of his workshop are the proverbs he leaves behind for future generations.

摄影：王晖

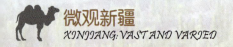

塔兰奇
Taranchi

清朝末年，一支背负着绿洲农耕文化行囊的移民，带着耕作技术来到广阔的游牧区，从南疆绿洲之地远徙伊犁，成为这里的播种者，带来了边境农商的振兴。他们被称为塔兰奇——一支特殊的维吾尔族人。

Towards the end of the Qing Dynasty, a migration occurred from Southern Xinjiang to Yili in the north, the participants being very well equipped with agricultural knowledge. Arriving in the north, they applied their skills and knowledge to make the area prosper in both agriculture and business. They became known as the Taranchi – a special branch of the Uyghur people.

尼雅城
Niya Ancient City

西域三十六国精绝国国都尼雅，沉睡在塔克拉玛干沙漠深处上千年，没有人扰动它的平静。1901 年，考古学家斯坦因找到了这个古城。城里的人像是遭遇了什么变故，突然跑得一个都不剩了。有人撂下刚做的一锅饭，有人撂下正在劳作的农具，有人撂下刚摊开的书，也有人来不及解开栓在门框上的狗。这一切都是谜。

The resplendent capital of the Thirty-Six Kingdoms, Niya, had lain for more than a millennium in rest in the Taklimakan Desert, nobody disturbing its quiet. In 1901, archaeologist Marc Aurel Stein discovered the remains of the ancient city. Some kind of incident had occurred, and the residents of the city had fled suddenly. People left behind food in pots, tools in the fields, open books, and some of them had no time to release their guard dogs. We have no idea why.

罗布人村寨
Lop Nur Villages

罗布人村寨位于尉犁县，方圆 72 平方公里，有 20 余户人家，是中国西部地域面积最大的村庄之一。中国最大的沙漠、最长的内陆河、最大的绿色走廊和丝绸之路在这里交汇。现在村寨是后人复原的图景，木屋、图腾、水塘……它们在沙漠中低吟。太阳是罗布人崇拜的神灵，太阳把沙漠烤得炽热，太阳下只有这个村寨。

The Lop Nur Stockaded Village is located in Yuli County, and covers more than 72 square kilometres, with more than 20 families. In Western China it is the largest in terms of area. China's largest desert, longest inland river, largest green corridor and the Silk Road all meet here. The area has been restored in terms of views, huts, totems, and ponds. They quietly signal their existence in the desert. The sun was worshiped by the Lop Nur people, which heated the desert and for them shined only on this village.

摄影：于辉

铜匠世家
Copper Work

喀什老街传来富有节奏的叮当声，循声走去，看到一位老铜匠正专注于自己的工作。周遭满是做好的和正在加工的铜器，有器形较大的铜锅、铜盆、铜火锅，也有做工精巧的阿不都壶、茶壶。喀什的铜器制作工艺，在这叮当悦耳的锤声中传承了上百年，并以家庭式作坊的形式延续至今，散发出灿烂的吉祥之光。

The old streets of Kashgar feature the constant rhythmic clang of metal work everywhere – one sees a coppersmith concentrating on his work. All around are copper wares, both finished and still being worked on. There are large pots, basins, cookers, and smaller, more precisely crafted items such as abdullah pots and teapots. The copper industry of Kashgar and the melodies it generates are part of a century-old tradition, and the family workshops operate even today – a truly brilliant part of the city's history.

神秘米兰城
Mysterious
Milan

米兰，听起来很浪漫、很艺术的一个名字。但此新疆米兰，非彼意大利名城，这是一座淹没于沙漠荒原的历史古城，西汉时为楼兰国的伊循城，唐代被吐蕃占领。那里存留的古戍堡遗址，在无尽苍凉中透露出千年沉淀的神秘。

"Milan" is a romantic-sounding, artistic name. However, the Milan of Xinjiang isn't an Italian city, but rather a historical city buried in the desert sand. It was the city of Yixun in the Loulan Kingdom during the time of the Western Han Dynasty, and was absorbed by the Tubo regime during the Tang Dynasty. The remains of the city reveal secrets among the desolation.

69

达里雅布依：塔克拉玛干沙漠的肚脐
Daliyabuyi

达里雅布依在塔克拉玛干沙漠的腹地，因其与世隔绝而鲜为人知，被中外考古探险家称为世外桃源。它曾有过一个地名叫通古斯巴孜特（意思是野猪上吊）的地方。虽然在目前使用的中国地图上找不到这个地名，然而，它在国际上，特别是在地理、历史、考古界的知名度并不亚于楼兰遗址、交河故城。

Daliyabuyi lies in the heartland of the Taklimakan Desert. As it was little-known for a long time due to its isolation, it has been called the "lost paradise" by archaeologists. It also has the traditional name of "Tunggusbazit", meaning "a place where wild boars are hung". Even though this name isn't found on Chinese maps, in international circles in terms of geology, history and archaeology, it's as well known as Loulan and the ancient Jiaohe City.

唐王城
Tangwang City

我看到唐王城时，一轮并不温暖的太阳挂在高空，风很大，城的遗址紧贴在一座山下，什么都没有，破墙和瓦砾显示这里好像来过许多人，却没有记住他们的名字。我沿着山腰走了很远，天空静得只有风声。

As I looked upon the Tangwang City, a cold sun hung in the sky overhead. The wind was strong, the remains of the city sit at the foot of the mountain, and broken walls and rubble show that many people must have come here, but their names were never recorded. I walked along the mountain side quite a distance, the only sound in the sky being the wind.

"吉卜赛人"村落
The Gypsy Village

位于疏勒县以南47公里的罕南力克镇的协合力村，距喀什市约60公里。村民们有自己独特的生活方式，不爱种地，喜欢流浪，游走四方，靠乞讨、卖药草和看手相为生。他们的生活是吉卜赛式的。他们的村庄，只是漂泊回来后停息和落脚的一个大本营。

Located 47 kilometres south of Shule is Xieheli Village, in Hanerik Township, about 60 kilometres away from Kashgar. The residents have a unique lifestyle. They don't sow crops, and instead roam about, relying on begging, selling herbs, and palm-reading to support themselves. Their lifestyle resembles that of Gipsies. Their village is not much more than a camp at which they can settle for a while after coming back from their wanderings.

小木匠
A Young Carpenter

小木匠十四岁，家住喀什的吾斯塘博依，一条以制作和销售维吾尔传统手工艺品而著称的千年古街。他和哥哥一起随父母经营木制品店，一家人分工合作，他锯砍刨凿，哥哥打磨剜刻，爸爸是师傅，妈妈管售卖。他希望日后成为一名技艺高超的大师傅。在抢斧走凿、扬锤拉锯中，他的梦想很具体，很扎实。

A young carpenter of 14 years of age lives on Wustanbowie Street in Kashgar, a street with a thousand years of history of producing and selling traditional crafts. He and his brother run the shop with their father – a family working together. He cuts and planes wood, while his brother sands and carves. Their father is the master, and their mother is the merchant. He hopes to become a highly skilled master one day. In his daily carpentry activities, he has a real, solid dream.

摄影：王晖

摄影：王晖

笼屉匠人
Fine
Craftsmanship

构成喀什老城味道的因素之一，是这里的老手艺还依然流淌在老城血脉之中。喀什传统的木质笼屉，需要圈笼、拴扎、刨光、打眼、缝扣、上笼布等全套工序，纯天然原材料，全流程手工制作。想想看，圈笼用柳木，缝扣用麻绳，笼布用棉布，蒸出的食物是不是有种将自然融于美食的独特味道？

One of the components of the flavour of old Kashgar is the traditional craftwork that still runs in the blood of the city. The traditional wooden food steamers, with all their skilled craftsmanship, precision fashioning and use of natural materials are a start-to-finish work of art. Seeing that the cages use willow wood, the stitching uses jute rope, the cover uses cotton cloth, we can say that the food they produce is a fusion of natural beauty and special taste.

楼兰姑娘
Loulan Girl

20 世纪 80 年代，一具欧罗巴特征美女干尸的出现，使楼兰再次轰动了世界，一曲《楼兰姑娘》唱遍大江南北。神秘沉睡的楼兰姑娘，引得无数人对那传说中太阳落山的地方充满了向往。

In the 1980s, the mummified remains of a European-seeming female were discovered, which brought Loulan into the international spotlight again. A song, *Loulan Girl*, became quite popular all over China. The story of this "Loulan girl" caused many interested parties to take a journey to the site.

剃头匠

A Fancy
Shave?

在南疆的巴扎，传统的维吾尔族剃头匠并未被时髦的理发师代替。传统的营生工具，一副剃头挑子、几把剃刀、一块磨刀石，还有火炉和脸盆，这些准备停当，就可以开工了。这里不需要花里胡哨的技艺，最传统的理发、剃须、修面已能满足主顾的需求。服务者和被服务者享受的都是一种简单坦然的生活。

In the bazaars of Southern Xinjiang, the traditional Uyghur head-shavers have not been replaced by modern fashions. The traditional tools are a wooden pole, razor blades, a knife sharpener and an oven and water basin. These are all one needs to set up a shop. No flashy techniques are required – simply being able to style hair, cut, and shave faces is all one needs to do. The providers and customers of the service both enjoy a simple, frank life.

摄影：韩连赟

巴斯拜捐飞机
I'm Gonna Buy You a Plane

在抗美援朝战争中，积贫积弱的中国，以个人名义为志愿军捐献飞机的只有两人，一位是著名豫剧表演艺术家常香玉，另一位就是新疆哈萨克族同胞巴斯拜。为了购进最先进的喷气式战斗机，他拿出了400匹马、100头牛、4000只羊和100两黄金。

During the Korean War, as China was impoverished, it turned to the charity of its citizens to support the Chinese People's Volunteer Army's war effort – only two individuals donated a plane. One was the famous Henan opera performer Chang Xiangyu, and the other was Basibai, a Kazakh from Xinjiang. In order to purchase the most modern jet fighter of the time, he sold four hundred horses, one hundred heads of cattle, four thousand sheep and 100 taels of gold.

蒲昌古城
Puchang

蒲昌古城位于库尔勒以南，距离库尔勒市约200多公里。古城东西长297米，南北长328米，占地近1万平方米。登上城墙，哨位、射击孔依然完好。到底这里发生过多少战争，不得而知，而今天这里已没有战火的硝烟。

The ancient city of Puchang is located in the south of Korla, more than 200 kilometres south of the Korla metropolitan area. The city is 297 metres east-west, and 328 metres north-south, for a footprint of almost 10,000 square metres. The top of the city wall was a great place for sentries and archers to execute their duties. Although numerous battles must have occurred here, we can't know the details as the gunsmoke has long since faded.

宗教・民俗
Religion and Folklore

一方水土
一方人
You Are What
You Eat

一个人能长成什么样子，和他肚子里装着什么东西有直接关系。被舌头供养的身体，或魁岸或猥琐，或粗猛或秀顾，全是那一方水土的反映。不要指望新疆草原上骑马的汉子长成西子湖畔的灵秀小生，当然你也不要指望南方的男人一顿能吃下一只羊。

What kind of person you grow into is related to what you eat. Whether one turns out stalwart or wretched, rough or elegant depends on the soil and water of where the food is grown. Don't expect the strong riders of the Xinjiang grasslands to turn out like the lithe beauties of the West Lake in Hangzhou, and don't expect a southern Chinese man to eat an entire lamb in one sitting.

巴扎
Bazaar

巴扎是集市，又不完全等于集市。巴扎也是养育维吾尔族人的地方，有谚语说：巴扎是父亲，巴扎是母亲。并不是每个人在巴扎上都做生意或买东西。有时候，逛巴扎更像个节日，女人在巴扎上展示自己的美丽，年轻小伙子是为了看漂亮古丽。也有人是为了见见熟人，握握手，说几句话。

A bazaar is a market, but not quite like those of other cultures. A bazaar is where the Uyghurs grow up. As a saying goes, the bazaar is the mother and the father. Not everyone there does business or goes shopping. Sometimes, walking around a bazaar is a kind of holiday, with women showing off their beauty and boys flocking there to see the display. Some people prefer to meet with friends, shake hands and exchange kind words.

摄影：徐纯

摄影：黄永中

麻扎
Mazar

麻扎狭义是指伊斯兰教圣裔或贤者的坟墓，有圣地之意，是伊斯兰教教民晋谒之地。阿拉伯语原意为晋谒之地。如喀什的阿帕克和加麻扎（即香妃墓）、阿图什的沙图克·波格拉汗麻扎、英吉沙的乌尔德麻扎、吐鲁番的阿尔发达麻扎、霍城的秃黑鲁帖木儿汗麻扎等，都有定期的宗教活动。

A mazar is, in the narrow sense of the term, the tomb of an Islamic sage or saint. The word means "sacred place", and mazars are places where adherents congregate – this is the meaning of the term in Arabic. The Apak Hoja Mazar (Tomb of the Fragrant Concubine) in Kashgar, the Shatuk Bogela Khan Mazar in Artux, the Uld Mazar in Yengisar, the Arfad Mazar in Turpan, and the Tuheilu Temur Khan Mazar in Huocheng all have regular religious activities.

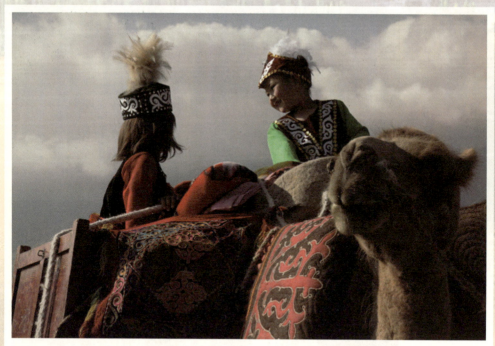

摄影：韩连赟

转场
Livestock Transfer

转场是北疆一道独特的风景。春季，牧民赶着牛羊进入夏牧场；秋末，他们又向冬牧场迁徙，这被称作转场。转场路上打头的往往是家庭主妇，最后驮的是漂亮的花毡，最快乐的当然是孩子。

"Livestock transfer" is a unique scene in Northern Xinjiang. In the spring, herders drive their flocks into summer pastures, and at the end of the fall drive them away to winter pastures.This kind of activity is called "livestock transfer". Leading the pack is always the woman of the house, and the last animal always bears a felt blanket upon it – a great place to sit if you are a child.

西迁节
Migration to the West

1764 年农历 4 月 18 日，东北地区 4000 多名锡伯族军民奉旨离开故乡，移驻新疆伊犁。经过一年零五个月的艰苦跋涉，终于到达伊犁，从此在伊犁扎根，屯垦戍边，为保卫边疆立下了汗马功劳。每年农历 4 月 18 日便成了新疆锡伯族人的西迁节。

On the 18th day of the 4th lunar month of 1764, a group of 4,000 ethnic Xibe soldiers from the northeastern region departed their homes under imperial order for Yili, Xinjiang. After one year and 5 months of arduous trekking, they arrived at Yili and set down roots, protecting the border area and distinguishing themselves in battle. Every year on the 18th day of the 4th lunar month, the Xibe people in Xinjiang celebrate their migration to the west.

冰雪中的温暖

幽蓝的天空下，炊烟从小木屋里袅袅升起；茫茫冰湖上，哈萨克族人、图瓦人的活动一个接着一个。周围是雪蘑菇和蓝玻璃一样涓涓而去的河水，一家人围火而坐倾听冬不拉，屋外偶尔滑过的马拉爬犁，一起构成了北疆天空下冰雪世界中独特的幸福。

Smoke rises from a small wooden hut against the backdrop of a blue sky, and the Tuva and Kazakhs conduct their activities on the vast iced lake. River water flows like winter mushrooms and blue glass, and a family sits around a fire listening to the tamboura, and occasionally a horse-drawn sled passes by – these pieces make up the snowy wonderland of Northern Xinjiang.

摄影：韩连赟

盛开的花朵：
新疆女子

Girls in
Xinjiang

新疆女子多取名古丽。古丽是花儿、花朵的意思。新疆自古以来交汇着各种血液，盛开着各种女人生命的花朵，花儿品种齐全，丰富多彩，因而自成一番格调。

Many girls in Xinjiang are named Guli, which means flower or petals. Xinjiang is an area that has historically seen a high degree of ethnic intermixing, and the flowers of Xinjiang come in all manners, types, and colours, forming a wonderful bouquet.

摄影：韩连赟

摄影：韩连赟

吐峪沟
Tuyugou

吐峪沟是吐鲁番鄯善县的一个古村落，是佛教文明与伊斯兰教文明交汇的典型。走进吐峪沟就是走进千年以前，此间无物不古，唯人为新。古树、院落、泥墙、木门、雕花的门窗和床架，土坯砌成的临河的院栏，都使人错乱古今，以为一盏油灯是阿拉丁神灯，一块花毯是阿拉伯飞毯，恍乎走进《一千零一夜》的故事。

Tuyugou is a village in Shanshan County, Turpan, and a site of intersection of Islam and Buddhism. Approaching this area, one walks into a millennium of history. Everything in this area is ancient, with only the people being young. Old trees, courtyards, adobe walls, wood doors, wooden window frames carved with flowers, riverside barriers built with earthen bricks – all these mix past and present, making you believe it is a genie springing from an oil lamp, or a flying carpet with an Arab seated upon it, as if it were a scene from *Arabian Nights*.

骑手醉伏在马背上
Sleep it off on the Horseback

一位哈萨克族作家讲起一个令人动情的瞬间：马匹与羊群在草原上移动，却不见骑手。走近了才发现，骑手原来伏在马背上。嘈杂声让他抬起身子，醉眼迷离，有一种惬意，一种悠然，也有一种苍茫与忧伤。

A Kazakh author described a touching moment: horses and sheep moving across the prairie without a rider in sight. Approaching closer, he discovered that the rider lay on the back of a horse. A sharp sound caused him to wake up, eyes blurry, with a look that blended satisfaction, leisure and somehow boundless sadness.

81

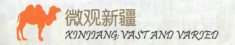

游牧挽歌

An Elegy for Nomadism

游牧是一种与现代概念截然不同的生存方式，离我们很近，又恍若隔世，散发着人类童年的记忆。因为陌生，不免对其充满诗意的想象，但诗意抵挡不住不合理人为活动导致的草原退化，抵挡不住年轻人对城市的向往，抵挡不住游牧生活在现代社会的衰落。唯其如此，才更令人怀恋，无奈感伤如一曲飘荡的挽歌。

Nomadism is a lifestyle that is conceptually quite different from modern life – close by, yet separated by the ages. It is a memory of when we were younger as a race. Its strangeness to us inspires us to think of it poetically, but these poems can't stop illogical people from destroying grasslands with modern activities, with young people leaving for cities, and the decline of a nomadic lifestyle in the context of modern society. In this way, the songs we sing for this disappearing way of life become elegiac.

圣佑庙

The Temple of Divine Protection

圣佑庙位于新疆昭苏县城内，是当地蒙古族牧民求神祈祷的场所。最初建在察汗乌逊乡，后经多次迁址，1889 年在昭苏洪那海重新选址。清光绪二十年至二十四年（1894—1898），由北京来的建筑名师及工匠兴建，是新疆现存最完整的一座藏传佛教寺院。1984 年，十世班禅活佛额尔德尼·确吉坚赞曾来此参禅。

The Temple of Divine Protection is located within the borders of Zhaosu County, Xinjiang. It is a site where local Mongolian nomads pray to their deities. First constructed in Qipchak, Wusun and then moved many times later. In 1889 a new site was selected at Hongnahai, Zhaosu, and it was rebuilt between 1894 and 1898 with assistance from famous architects and builders from Beijing. It is the most complete Tibetan Buddhist temple in Xinjiang. In 1984, the Tenth Panchen Lama visited this temple.

摄影：双元

给洗手水
Hand-washing Water

去维吾尔族朋友家做客，主人会在就餐前拿出"阿不都"（洗手壶）叫你洗手，并用"其不拉其"（接水盆）接水。主人会给每人倒水三下，洗手三下。维吾尔族洗手必须是冲洗，他们认为盛在脸盆中的水是"死水"，是不洁的。洗手时一定要两手环绕洗，洗手后千万不要甩水，迅速接过主人递上的毛巾把手擦干。

When visiting Uyghur homes as a guest, the host will take out an "Abdo" (hand-washing pot) and ask you to wash your hands before a meal, using a "Qiblaq" (water basin) to catch the water. The host will pour the water for each guest three times. Uyghurs wash their hands with running water, as they believe water in a basin is "dead water" and unclean. When washing one's hands one must wash the front and back of both, taking care not to splash water. After washing, the host hands a towel for a guest to quickly dry his hands with.

萨满乐舞
Shaman Dances

1000 多年前，许多属于阿尔泰语系的古老游牧部族为了获得诸神的善待，逐渐兴起了崇拜自然诸神的萨满教——巫师在鼓声中且歌且舞，以此和部落神灵沟通。千年的时光之后，神和巫各归其位。新疆锡伯族人和维吾尔族人的萨满乐舞中，古老的招魂歌充满了烟火气，人们在其中聆听自然，释放自我。

More than a thousand years ago, a number of Altaic-speaking tribes, in order to gain the favour of various gods, gradually became adherents of shamanistic religions – shamans sang and danced to the beat of drums, and communicated spiritually with the tribespeople. Over a millennium later, these gods and wizards returned to their respective places. The shamanistic dances of the Xibe and the Uyghur people, as well as the associate songs are filled with the spiritual smoke and fire of times past – one loses oneself when listening.

时间是一笔糊涂账
Through Time

阿勒泰的游牧民族，自古以来，用文字写诗歌，却很少用它去记时间、历史。时间在这里是一笔糊涂账，有的只是模糊的传说。

The Altaic nomads have since time immemorial used writing to record their songs, but rarely to record events or history. Time here is an unclear phenomenon, and the only stories we have are blurry legends.

新疆女人
Xinjiang's Ladies

新疆女人，只有在冬天的时候才表现出柔美的一面。她们的面庞像窖藏的苹果，馥郁而酡红，她们的裙裾仿若风中的旗帜猎猎飞扬。她们会用一个冬天的时间为自己的男人煮一壶提神长劲的奶茶，会把冬天当作自己的责任。对冬天来说，她们是熊熊的火；对她们来说，冬天是一张可以让男人舒筋展骨的大炕。

The true beauty of the women of Xinjiang appears in the winter. Their faces resemble cached apples, perfumed and red. Their dresses resemble flags fluttering in the wind. They use the winter to brew excellent milk tea for their male companions, taking the winter as a time of responsibility. To winter, the women are a blazing fire, and to them, the winter is a good time for their loved ones to relax.

永不谢幕的民族博览会
Never-ending Meetings

新疆这个在亚洲中部被高山环峙的大舞台，历史上曾上演过各民族演绎的剧目，真是你方唱罢，我又登台。今天，新疆仍是一个多民族聚居的地区，这里生活着 55 个民族，其中汉、维吾尔、哈萨克等 13 个民族为世居民族。可以毫不夸张地说，新疆是中亚腹地永不谢幕的民族博览会。

Xinjiang is a stage in Central Asia ringed by high mountains, upon which many peoples have historically played their part – you sing, and I'll dance. In the present day, Xinjiang is still an area in which many peoples meet, with 55 different ethnicities, including Han, Uyghur, Kazakh and thirteen other major groups. It's no exaggeration to say that Xinjiang is a Central Asian multi-ethnic conference that never concludes.

进城的靴子
Boots and Customs

在南疆进城路上，常常会看到这样的情形，不少赤脚的维吾尔族老乡在尘土中暴走，而靴子却挂在他们的肩头。这是因为他们觉得在尘土和砾石上走路太费靴子。走到城边了，找一处有渠水的地方，洗干净了脚，再换上一尘不染的漂亮皮靴。进城的靴子代表着乡下人对城市的极大敬畏和尊重。

On the roads to cities in Southern Xinjiang, it's a common sight to see Uyghurs, running in the dust, with their boots hung over their shoulders. This is because they think that walking in the dust and rubble is too hard on their boots. When they reach the city, they can wash their feet and put on their clean boots – this is how they show their respect for the city when entering from the countryside.

**新疆姑娘的
小辫子**

Take it
Seriously

对待新疆姑娘，想法如果像小辫子那么多，肯定会失败。这不是一个量的问题，而是一个质的问题，一个时间的问题。有人用一生来等待一句话，或用一生去验证一个眼神。在这里，信诺就是时间，谁不曾拥有这样的时间，谁就不会拥有真正的爱情。

If one pursues a Xinjiang girl with many many ideas, one will inevitably fail. This isn't a question of quantity, but rather quality. Some people wait a lifetime to hear a certain sentence or to verify a look in another's eyes. Here, trust is time, and those who are unwilling to wait will never have true love.

摄影：黄永中

宰牲
Sacrifice

在新疆，屠宰一只羊是一件平常但不寻常的事，宰牲前会有一个简单的仪式，请阿訇念经，为其超度亡灵，也抚慰一下屠宰者不安的灵魂。就算是生活在新疆的汉族人，在屠宰一只羊时，也会嘴里念叨一番：不是我心狠，是老天爷定下的规矩，让你升天，我来帮助你。

In Xinjiang, the slaughter of a lamb is a commonplace occurrence. There is a simple ceremony beforehand, in which an imam reads a few passages from the Quran, for the beast about to die, and to calm the butcher's soul. The Han Chinese of Xinjiang also say a few words before slaughtering a lamb: "It's not that I'm savage, but rather that these are the rules laid down by god. You need to go to heaven, and I'll help you go there."

塔吉克族墓葬
Tajik Tombs

新疆塔吉克族的墓葬颇具象征意义。他们常常将墓场砌成马鞍的形状，这是对逝者的赞誉，对一名骑手的肯定，骑马去天堂也许要快些。

The tombs of Xinjiang Kazakhs have quite a deal of symbolic significance. They are usually carved into the shape of a saddle – this is a kind of respect for the deceased, confirming their status as a rider and hoping they will reach heaven faster on a horseback.

摄影：韩连赟

摄影：黄永中

刀郎人
Dolan

刀郎意为一堆一堆或分堆聚居的人。刀郎人的先民以渔猎为生，其渊源众说纷纭：一说是源自塔里木盆地的原住民；另一说是突厥高车部多览葛人的后裔，与回鹘同源；还有一说为塔里木原住民与蒙古族后裔的融合。刀郎人大多居住在麦盖提、巴楚、阿瓦提和莎车等地，沿叶尔羌河流域有一个独特的刀郎文化区。

"Dolan" means "the people who live in clusters". The predecessors of Dolan were hunters and fishers, and there are many stories as to where they come from. One says that they come from the Tarim Basin and are the original inhabitants, and another says that they are the descendants of the Turk and Kocha peoples, and have the same origins as the Uyghurs. Another explanation is that they are the descendants of Tarim peoples who mixed with Mongolians. Most Dolan people live in Markit, Bachu, Awati and Yarkant and the surrounding area. They have their own unique culture.

拍打无花果
Beating the Fig

生活在新疆的穆斯林在吃无花果时保持了这样一个习惯：要将成熟的果子包在无花果叶子里，认真拍打三次，然后再吃。传统的说法是：拍打既是惩罚，也在提醒拍打者必须怀有一颗羞愧之心。

The Muslims of Xinjiang have maintained a custom when eating a fig: wrap the ripe fig in fig leaves, then hit it soundly three times, and then eat it. The tradition states that the beating is a punishment, which also reminds the beater to have a sense of shame.

托包克游戏
Tobuk: A Traditional Game

托包克游戏是流传于南疆维吾尔族中的一种游戏，一旦玩起来就不能停下来，伴随一生。道具是羊的髌骨，又叫羊髀矢。两个人玩，自己的羊髀矢刻上记号，交给对方。以后的时间里，对方一要，就得拿出来。拿不出来，输。拿出来，对方输。有时游戏约定二十年或者五六十年，有的人一生能输掉 50 只羊。

Tobuk is a traditional game among the Uyghurs of Southern Xinjiang – once the play has started, it can't be stopped. The equipment is a lamb's kneecap. Two players play, with each player carving a sigil on his own kneecap, and giving it to the opponent. Afterwards, either player must produce the kneecap upon request – failure to be able to do so at any point in time loses the game, and vice versa. The allotted time for the game can be twenty, or even fifty or sixty years, some people losing as many as fifty lambs in a lifetime.

深埋在沙石下面的冰块
Ice Blocks Buried in the Desert Sand

沙漠里的盛夏，没有冰箱，你仍然能喝上冰镇葡萄汁和酸牛奶。你无法想象，一块巨大的冰从何而来。那时，民间储存冰有种土法子。在冬天结冰的河面上，取下冰块，深埋在沙漠底部，上面盖上苇草和沙土，在夏季最炎热的时候再挖出来。

Even though there are no refrigerators in the hot summer desert, you can still drink ice-cold grape juice and yoghurt. You may be wondering where the huge block of ice would come from. Actually people there have invented a way to store ice. When the rivers freeze in the winter, they cut ice blocks out and bury them deep in the desert sand, covering them with reeds and sand, and then digging them up in hot summer when needed.

雪山的力量
The Power of Snow-capped Mountains

图瓦人觉得雪山比什么都强大，一年四季始终是那么洁白，从来都不因为什么而改变。他们喜欢望雪山，每次望完雪山，他们都觉得自己获得了一种力量。他们说：活着，这事情那事情的，心里的力量用着用着就不够了，只好从雪山上取一些力量，装到心里去，人就活得好了。

The Tuva people think that nothing is mightier than the snow-capped mountains, able to stay white all year long, never changing. They enjoy looking at them, feeling that they get a kind of power each time they look upon one. They say that one needs power to cope with all the trials of human life, and thus we can boost our reserves by taking a bit from these mountains.

马与蒙古族人
Mongolians
and Horses

生活在新疆和生活在内蒙古的蒙古族人有着相同的生活习惯。马是他们的忠实伙伴。一个蒙古族男孩长到一定的年龄必须拥有一匹马。马是蒙古族男人的象征，他们往往要驯服性子最烈的马，让它成为自己的坐骑，相伴一生。马背上有一个蒙古族男人的一切，他们在马背上思考，饮酒，唱歌，和情人接吻。

Mongolians in Xinjiang and those in Inner Mongolia have similar customs. The horse is a faithful partner for them. Once a Mongolian male reaches a certain age, he must have a horse. The horse is a symbol of masculinity among Mongolians, and they pick the best horses for domestication to ride, spending their lives together. They do everything on horseback, from thinking to drinking, to singing, to kissing their lovers.

摄影：韩连赟

山的表情
Mountains and Expressions

在塔吉克族群居的村落中，山是无法回避的神壁。人们把灵魂寄托于山脉，把祖先交付给群峰。生存者的目光年复一年地从天上落到山上，日复一日地接受着与大山共生共荣的现状。

In Tajik communities, mountains are an unavoidable spiritual barrier. People give over their souls to the mountains, turning their ancestors over to mountain peaks. Survivors come down year after year from the heavens, and maintain a symbiotic and harmonious relationship with the mountains.

漂泊的克里雅人
The Kerians

新疆和田地区于田县的塔克拉玛干沙漠腹地，克里雅人分散居住在克里雅河下游的 110 多万亩胡杨、红柳丛林里。克里雅人说维吾尔语，不耕种，以牧羊为生。克里雅在维吾尔语中是飘移不定的意思。一个克里雅人就是一个王国，一个属于孤独与漂泊的王国。一片胡杨林，一口水井，一群羊，就是这个王国的所有财富。

Yutian County, located within the Hotan area of the Taklimakan Desert, is an area in which the Kerian people live, spread out over 730 square kilometres of poplars and willows. The Kerians speak Uyghur, and don't plant crops; instead, they raise sheep. "Keria" in the Uyghur language means "drifting". A Kerian is a kingdom – his own, independent, drifting entity. A poplar forest, a water source, a lamb – these are the kingdom's resources.

摄影：黄永中

摄影：韩连赟

哈萨克族摇床礼
Cradle Ceremony

哈萨克族在婴儿出生 40 天的时候，会举办摇床礼。摇篮，是一个用木头做的船形小床。在游牧转场中也便于放在马背上，所以摇床就成了哈萨克族人生之初第一个启蒙的怀抱。摇床礼这天，要宰牲，邀请邻里妇女孩子参加，请德高望重的老妇把孩子放入摇床。放摇床前用火在摇床上绕三圈，有驱邪之意。

40 days after a Kazakh baby is born, a "cradle ceremony" is performed. The cradle is a boat-shaped bed fashioned of wood, suitable for carrying on horseback in a nomadic setting, and for this reason it has become the first setting in which a Kazakh grows up. On the day of the ceremony, an animal is sacrificed, and mothers and children are invited. An old mother of high prestige is invited to place the baby in the cradle. Before placing the baby inside, three rings of fire are lit around the cradle, to ward off evil.

卸落在地的马鞍
Saddle on the Ground

在新疆，如果在草原上的一个小山坡或树林旁有一副卸落在地的马鞍，说明有一对情人已从马背上下来，正在附近的角落里幽会，卸落在地的马鞍提醒路人这个地方已被他们占有，请勿打扰。

In Xinjiang, if one finds a saddle on the ground near a slope or wooded patch, it means that a pair of lovers are trysting nearby – the saddle is a marker to show others that the space is occupied and that privacy is required.

锡伯族人的婚礼
Xibe Weddings

在锡伯族人的传统婚俗中，有指腹为婚的蛋蛋婚，入赘式的招女婿和童养媳式的小姐婚等多种婚姻形式，现今则主要是自由恋爱结婚。锡伯族的婚礼过程一般要经过说亲、许亲、订亲、迎亲四个阶段。婚礼进行时要唱婚礼歌、嫁女歌、婆亲歌、丁巴歌，一场婚礼一般举行 3 天。

In Xibe marriage traditions, there are marriages in which two couples arrange to have their children married before they are born, marriages in which a young girl is married off to another family while still a child to grow up and live with her future husband, and other kinds of arrangements. Most marriages now, however, are love marriages. The four stages are those of matchmaking, acceptance of a proposal, engagement, and finally entry into the husband's family. Weddings involve songs and dances and generally last for three days.

摄影：韩连赟

维吾尔族巴扎上的"毕德克"
Bidek: A Middleman

毕德克就是经纪人。在现今的巴扎贸易中仍保留了古老生意场上的一些习俗，比如仍活跃于巴扎牛马市上的毕德克。他把买方和卖方说得都很满意，解决了交易中的很多利益矛盾。之后，毕德克从满意的买卖方那里收取中间费。

A bidek is a middleman, a traditional role which persists in modern-day bazaars. Areas such as horse and cattle markets continue to employ their services – they help the buyer and seller reach an agreement, and resolve many conflicts of interests in the deals. Once their task is completed, they receive a fee from both parties.

馕高于一切
Nang above All

作家王蒙说：我在巴彦岱看到维族同胞怎样对待粮食，特别感动。他们告诉我，世界上最伟大的东西就是馕，馕高于一切。一个农民，哪怕一个很小的孩子，走在街上吃着吃着有一块馕掉下来了，要还能吃，就把它拿起来弄干净再吃下去，不能再吃了，怎么办？挖一个坑，把馕埋起来，馕是不能随便丢弃的。

Author Wang Meng said: In Bayandai when I saw how our Uyghur comrades treat food, I was very moved. They tell me that the greatest thing in the world is a Nang bread, that it is above all others. When a villager, even a small child, walking along the road drops a piece of Nang he is eating, he will not simply leave it there – if it can still be eaten, he will wipe it off and do so, and if it cannot be saved he will dig a small hole in the ground and bury it there – Nang cannot be carelessly discarded.

刀郎人狩猎遗俗
Dolan Hunters

刀郎人居于塔克拉玛干的边缘，这里沙丘连绵，荒滩遍地，胡杨、红柳、灌木、杂草丛生。历史上的刀郎人以狩猎放牧为主，虽然后来农业生产逐渐发展起来了，但人们仍保留了原始状态下的放牧、狩猎习俗。在他们的舞蹈中亦有明显的狩猎文化遗迹。

The Dolan people live on the edges of the Taklimakan Desert, where dunes are numerous and desolate sands everywhere. Poplars, willows, and various bushes grow here. The Dolan were historically hunters, although they later gradually turned to agriculture, while still preserving their original habits and customs of hunting. There are still clear traces of a hunting culture in their dances.

摄影：韩连赟

维吾尔族民居

Nice Homes

生活在绿洲上的维吾尔族人，喜欢把家布置得像个小园林。小院里种着葡萄、石榴、苹果、无花果等果木，居室深藏绿荫之中，有的还把小渠水引入小院。葡萄架下有待客的大床，建筑装饰精美华丽，配上院子里的小溪流水、林荫花卉。对于生活在戈壁荒原边缘的维吾尔族人来说，家就是十分惬意的天堂。

Uyghurs living at oases enjoy decorating their houses like small gardens, with courtyards containing grapes, pomegranates, apples, figs and other fruiting trees, bathing their homes in green and shade, some of which incorporate a small stream. Grape trellises have large beds for guests underneath them, and the buildings are decorated beautifully, combined with flowing water and dense shade, for a wonderful effect – a paradise to the Uyghurs living on the edges of these wastelands.

摄影：韩连赟

土尔扈特蒙古族人的见面礼
Saying Hi

土尔扈特蒙古族人相遇一定下马互致问候。传统的礼仪里，朋友相见互敬鼻烟壶，现在敬烟。家中来客，如是约定的客人，应带酒出迎，把其中的长者扶下马，为客人敬下马酒，敬献哈达。客人接酒后要唱祝词。喝了敬酒，把客人让进毡房，坐定后宾主相互问候，互道家人平安的吉祥语，然后上奶茶、煮肉、敬酒……

When Torghuts and Mongolians meet, they will dismount from their horses and exchange greetings. In traditional ceremonies, people would meet with snuff bottles, whereas now cigarettes are used. If an invited party comes to one's home, alcohol should be brought out, elders should be helped from their horses, and a toast should be conducted. After the drink is completed, felicitations should be sung. Once formalities are completed, the guests are taken into a yurt and pleasantries are exchanged, and then milk tea, boiled meats, and alcohol are enjoyed.

塔吉克族人的播种节
Sowing Seeds

在田野，人们将备好的优质种子交给村里的长者，先有一农妇点燃一盆火放在中间，人们祈祷。这时长者把种子撒向蓝天，撒向大地，撒向幸福的人们，周围的人纷纷掀起自己的衣襟，让这幸福的种子落入怀中，然后播入自己的土地。此时，请一老妇坐在火盆边，人们围绕她表演翻地播种的游戏。

In the field, people give the best seeds to the elders, and then a farmwife lights a fire in a basin, and the people pray. At this time the elders throw the seeds in the air, to the ground, and towards the lucky people, who open the lapels of their jackets to allow these lucky seeds to enter their own clothing. People make a game of gathering around the sower of seeds as she makes a display of turning the soil and planting them.

鸠摩罗什
Kumarajiva

鸠摩罗什出生在古代西域的龟兹国，前秦建元十八年（382）苻坚遣吕光攻焉耆，灭龟兹，劫鸠摩罗什至凉州。后秦时，他到长安组织了规模宏大的译场，主持佛经翻译。他圆寂前发下誓言：我所译出的经典如果不失佛意，那么肉身尽化后舌头不会焦烂。大师圆寂后以火焚尸，烟销骨碎，他柔软的舌头果然完好无损！

Kumarajiva was born in the western kingdom of Kocha in 382, during the Former Qin Dynasty; Fu Jian sent Lü Kuang to attack Yanqi, destroy Kocha, and take Kumarajiva to Liangzhou. In the Latter Qin, he went to Chang'an and established a large-scale translation academy to translate Buddhist scriptures. Before passing away, he promised: if my translated scriptures retain their meaning, then after my physical body decays, my tongue shall remain. After he was cremated, his bones were pulverised, but his tongue remained unharmed.

95

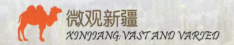
独特的起名方式
Naming Names

"您贵姓？""免贵姓肉。"这是初次和维吾尔族朋友见面时的对话，看到我困惑的神情，朋友大笑，他叫肉孜·依明，拿汉族姓名的命名方式和我开了个玩笑。维吾尔族名字构成很有特点，是自己名字加上父亲的名字，肉孜是他的名字，依明是父亲的名字。原来，维吾尔族没有姓的概念，采取父子连名的起名方式。

I've been confused when asking the names of my Uygur friends as they sometimes make jokes that I don't understand. Their naming conventions are quite different from Chinese names. Uyghur surnames are patronymic, where the name of one's father becomes the surname of the child – completely different from that of Chinese or Western tradition.

萨满教
Shamanism

在新疆的维吾尔、哈萨克、柯尔克孜、蒙古、锡伯、乌孜别克等少数民族中，至今仍可见到萨满教的遗存。萨满，维吾尔语称巴克西。萨满教信仰万物有灵，崇拜祖灵麻扎。在拉甫乔克的萨满活动中，人们用手鼓为巴克西伴奏。

One still sees remnants of shamanism among the Uyghurs, Kazakhs, Kyrgyz, Mongols, Xibe, Uzbeks and other ethnic groups in Xinjiang. The shamans are called "baksi" in Uyghur; they believe that all things have spirits, and worship ancestors at their mausoleums. In the shamanistic activities of Lafqiak, people beat finger drums to provide rhythmic accompaniment.

摄影：韩连赞

不想伤害，也不想掩埋
Respectful Distance

在和田洛浦70公里开外的塔克拉玛干沙漠里，见到了热瓦克佛寺。佛寺被青色的沙子围拢，处于低洼处。奇怪的是，沙漠一直在随风游走，却避开了佛寺。看来，沙漠对它是有情感的，不想伤害，也不想掩埋。

The Rewak Temple lies 70 km to the east of Lop, in Hotan. The temple is surrounded by dark sand, and is situated in a depression. Strangely, the sands blow all around the desert yet avoid the temple – we can see that even the sand has emotions, and doesn't want to harm or bury the temple.

维吾尔族的见面礼
Pleasantries

维吾尔族是一个非常讲究礼仪的民族。见面礼、待客礼都较讲究。朋友、长者相见要把右手抚在左胸部，点头、屈身鞠躬，问：艾沙拉姆，艾里库姆（愿主降福于您，祝您平安）！对方也做同样的动作，说：外里克姆，艾里库姆（同样祝您平安）！然后上前握手、拥抱，问候对方家人、子女平安。

Uyghurs are very much in to rituals – meeting others, receiving guests and the like. When friends and elders see each other, they place their right hand on the left of their chest, nod, dip their heads and say "peace be upon you", to which the other responds "and upon you, too". Afterwards, they shake hands, hug and ask about the other's family and health.

坚硬的树瘤
Burrs on Trees

新疆的蒙古族牧民很喜欢树上坚硬的树瘤，认为这是树神赐予的礼物。他们取下树瘤雕刻一种叫沙吾勒的杯子。渴了，用它喝茶。饿了，里面放上酥油、炒面，兑入奶子就是一碗香喷喷的饭。需要钉木楔或敲打硬物时，它又成为一个方便而实用的榔头！

The Mongolian herders of Xinjiang like the hard burrs on trees, as they see them as gifts from the arboreal world. They take them from the trees and carve them into cups. When thirsty, they can be used to drink tea. When hungry, they can be filled with butter, fried noodles and milk for an excellent meal. When affixed to a staff, they can even function as hammers.

观蹄印识羊
Resilience

在新疆，一位蒙古族老人告诉我：庄稼地里的庄稼被羊吃了会留下脚印，看脚印就知道是绵羊或山羊吃的。山羊的蹄子又粗又宽，而绵羊的蹄子又窄又细。我后来观察了一下，还真如此！

In Xinjiang, an old Mongolian told me: when crops are eaten away in the field, one can tell whether they were eaten by a lamb or a goat by looking at the footprints left. Goats have rough, wide hooves, and lambs have narrow, fine hooves. I took a look myself, and it was true.

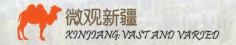

蒙古族人不吃马肉
No Horse Meat for Mongolians

马在蒙古族人中是受尊重的动物。如果是一匹赛马，即使老到驮不动任何东西了，主人也不会宰杀它。如果老死了，主人会把它的头和四只蹄子剁下来，送到高高的山顶上去。其余的部分，就抛散在干净的荒野里，让狼和鹰吃掉。蒙古族这一习俗使我们懂得：人，应该有所敬畏，不能什么都吃，什么都做。

Among the Mongolians, horses have a respected place. When a racehorse gets old, even if it can't move, its owner won't slaughter it. If it dies of old age, its head and limbs will be cut off, and transported to a high mountain peak. The remaining parts will be scattered in a clean, barren place for wolves and eagles to eat. We understand this custom among the Mongolians: humans should have respect, and not eat everything that comes along.

骨头游戏
The Bone Game

新疆蒙古族在家宴上有一种比力量的骨头游戏。就是吃光了叫达楞玛合（羊的肩胛骨）的肉，拿羊的肩胛骨来当角力的道具。第一关是用食指和中指打掉肩胛骨上端凸起的骨头，第二关是用中指打掉下端扇形的一块，第三关是捏碎剩下的肩胛骨。胜出的人被看作最有力量的勇士。

There is a game among Mongolians in Xinjiang used to test strength – when all the meat on a lamb's shoulder blade has been eaten, the bone is used as a contest of strength. The first is to use the index and idle finger to knock off the protrusion on the top of the bone; the second is to use the middle finger to knock off the fan-shaped piece at the bottom of the bone, and the third is to twist the remaining bone in two. The victor is viewed as the strongest warrior.

天然饮品白桦树液
Natural Drinks

每年五月前后，布尔津的俄罗斯族人会到白桦林采集树液。他们在白桦的树干上，钻一个深约三厘米的小洞，塞进一根皮管子，甜丝丝的白桦液就汩汩地从树干里涌出来，流进小桶里。放完树液，他们在树洞上塞进一个木楔子，相当于补丁。早年的俄罗斯族人很喜欢饮用这种天然的饮品。

Every year around May, the ethnic Russians of Burqin County go to birch forests to collect sap. They drill a deep hole, around 3 centimetres deep, and into it stick a leather tube, through which the sap gurgles out into a small container. After completing the process, they stick a wooden pole into the hole to seal it up. Early Russians very much enjoyed drinking this natural drink.

拜火教
Zoroastrianism

拜火教，是在基督教流行之前中东最有影响的宗教，曾为波斯帝国的国教。三世纪中叶，拜火教经丝绸之路传入我国新疆乃至中原地区。火是人类文明的标志之一，拜火教的遗存，在新疆各民族习俗中传承下来。

Zoroastrianism was the most popular religion in the Middle East before the advent of Christianity. During the mid-third century, it spread via the Silk Road into Xinjiang and then the Central Plains region. Fire is one of the marks of human civilisation. Remnants of this religion persist today in Xinjiang.

草原上的美容
Beauty on the Prairie

那些常年生活在草原上的游牧民族，由于风吹日晒，强烈的紫外线照射，容易皮肤皴裂、过敏起痘、干燥起癣。他们会把挤好的鲜奶放上两小时，然后把上面凝浮的生奶皮抹在脸上，或者把煮熟后的酸奶产生的黄色酸水拍在脸上，可让皮肤光洁如初。

Nomads who live on the grasslands must deal with wind, sunshine and strong ultraviolet radiation, which makes their skin prone to chapping, allergic reactions and overdrying. They will let fresh milk sit for two hours, and then rub the cream on their faces, or use the whey of yoghurt, in this way restoring their skin to a nice, smooth condition.

冬季出生的孩子
Winter Children

如今在牧区，冬季的孩子出生后，人们会给孩子用温水洗澡，也有用牛奶洗的。然后，给孩子周身抹上羊油，轻轻按摩一小会儿，既可御寒，又可预防感冒。即使在牧区的医院里，也会见到牧民给孩子抹羊油的情景。这是新疆蒙古族民间流传的风俗。

Even now in nomadic regions, when a child is born in winter, it will be bathed in warm water, or in milk. Afterwards, it is rubbed with mutton tallow and gently massaged for a while – this prevents the child from being or catching cold. Even in the hospitals in these regions, one will see the mutton fat and massage practice applied. This is a traditional practice of the Mongolians in Xinjiang.

给自己接生的接生婆
Doing it Yourself

你听说过自己给自己接生孩子吗？在新疆和布克赛尔蒙古自治县，有一位名叫仙巴依尔的老人。她已经 70 多岁了。从 1964 年至今，她已经为草原上的牧民接生了 1000 多个孩子，包括自己生的两个孩子。

Have you heard of someone delivering her own child? In Xinjiang's Hoboksar Mongolian Autonomous County, there is an old woman named Xianbayier, already in her 70s. From 1964 to now she has helped nomads deliver over 1,000 children, including two of her own.

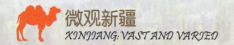
让你一次吃个够
Eating your Fill

在新疆大部分餐馆吃拌面，留下印象的除了味道，还有"让你一次吃个够"的实在劲儿。一盘面、一盘菜，是标配，面不够，叫声"老板加面"，一份免费的加面很快就摆在面前，让你不会有一碗不够、两碗吃撑的尴尬。一些拉面馆，标配之外你可以"加面"或"加汤"，外加的面和汤当然也是免费的。

When eating noodles in most restaurants in Xinjiang, aside from the taste, one also comes away with an impression of the experience – you're assured to eat your fill. Noodles and vegetables come in a standard size, but you can always call over to the proprietor to "add noodles", and another bowl of noodles will quickly appear in front of you, free of charge – there's no reason to feel awkward about wanting more. Some noodle houses will let you call for more noodles, and more soup – also both free.

自然生长的羊羔
Let Them Be

冬季是牧区产羔的季节。新疆的冬天特别冷，但放牧的人都知道，羊产了羔后，小羊羔不能放在火炉旁烤，那样的话不易长大。据说，被火烤后内脏遇热后就定形了。所以不要害怕羊羔冻死，最好让它自然生长。

Winter is the kidding season for nomads. The winter in Xinjiang is quite cold, but the herders know that the kid can't be placed next to the stove for warmth, or they won't grow large. This is because the heat will harden the innards and they will become too rigid. Thus, one needn't fear the kids will freeze to death, and instead should let them grow up naturally.

摄影：双元

塔吉克族的春节
Tajik Spring Festival

居住在新疆帕米尔高原东部的塔吉克族，春节的第一个清晨，家中的小孩儿会牵着一头黄牛走进屋子，在家里绕行一周。家中的长辈向牛背上扬撒面粉，给牛喂过面饼，再让孩子牵出屋子。接着，亲朋好友鱼贯而入，互相祝贺。妇女们会上前给来宾的左肩撒上面粉，祝福吉祥。

The Tajiks who live on the eastern portion of the Pamir Plateau in Xinjiang have a custom: on the first early morning of the Spring Festival, a child will enter the house with an ox, and walk around the house. The older members of the household will sprinkle flour on the ox's back, and feed the cow cakes, and then send the child out. Then, friends and family will file in, and congratulate each other. Mothers will sprinkle flour on the left shoulders of guests, conveying good wishes.

锡伯族人的供奉与崇拜
Xibe Beliefs

新疆的锡伯族人民因为不断迁徙，吸收了丰富的外来文化因素。他们信奉萨满教、喇嘛教，也信奉关公、周仓等神。最有趣的是锡伯家庙，本为喇嘛寺，但除了供奉三世佛、十八罗汉外，又塑有关公等偶像，同时，也供奉孔子、关帝、娘娘等神位。祭祀祖先也占有重要地位。

The Xibe people of Xinjiang have absorbed rich outside cultural influences due to successive and continuous migrations. They practise shamanism, Lamaism, and believe in other various gods. Most interestingly is the home temple of Xibe, which is a small lama temple, but in addition to the three Buddhas and eighteen arhats, there are also statues of deities like Guan Gong. At the same time, they also worship Confucius, Guan Gong, Empress Niangniang, and others. During rituals, ancestors also have an important position.

草原上的女人
Women on the Grassland

草原上的女人熟悉草的味道。含着露水味的草，含着暴风味的草，含着山土味的草，她们只要拿过来闻一下，就知道这是谁家牧场的草。谁家牧场的草是修长的，谁家牧场的草是粗壮的，谁家牧场的草是深色的，谁家牧场的草是浅色的，她们全知道。草的秘密生长在她们心里。

Women on the grassland are familiar with the fragrance of grass. Dew, strong wind, mountain soil – they only need to smell a blade and can tell you whose pasture it comes from – whose grass is long, whose grass is thick, whose grass is deep in colour, whose is light – they know the answers to all these questions. The secrets of the grass grow in their hearts.

塔吉克族的崇拜
Tajik Beliefs

居住在新疆帕米尔高原东部的塔吉克族居民普遍信仰伊斯兰教伊斯玛仪派。他们的清真寺很少。教徒不封斋，不朝觐。除部分老人每天在家中做两次礼拜外，一般群众仅在节日进行礼拜。在信仰上兼有祖先崇拜、自然崇拜和圣徒崇拜等特征。

The Tajiks in Xinjiang who live on the eastern part of the Pamir Plateau all are Isma'iliyya adherents of Islam. They have very few mosques. They do not observe Ramadan, nor make the hajj. They only worship on the holidays. They also practise ancestor worship, nature worship and saint worship.

动物崇拜
Animal Worship

许多阿尔泰语系突厥语族的神话故事都和动物崇拜有关，像天鹅、狼、熊等动物，这往往和这些民族的祖源传说有关。故事里这些民族受惠于这些动物，有些干脆就是狼或熊的后代。

A number of myths among Turkic and Altaic language speakers are related to animal worship, such as that of swans, wolves, bears and other animals. They are frequently involved in creation myths. In these stories, various peoples benefit from the actions of these animals, and in some versions humans are their descendants.

供奉宗喀巴和成吉思汗的蒙古族
Tsongkhapa and Genghis Khan

蒙古族人信奉藏传佛教，所以，在新疆的草原上，无论你迈进富裕的蒙古族人家还是破旧的蒙古包，一般都会看到居家正中上座有供奉宗喀巴的佛龛和成吉思汗的画像，像前常年供着祖鲁灯。

Mongolians believe in Tibetan Buddhism. Thus, on the grassy plains of Xinjiang, when you enter either a luxurious Mongolian's house, or a simple yurt, you will generally see a niche for a statue of the Buddha opposing the door, along with figures of Tsongkhapa and Genghis Khan, with a zulu lamp in front.

孩子出生的习俗
New Children

在新疆的蒙古族牧民家里，如果一个孩子在冬天出生了，孩子的父亲就会宰杀一只小羊。然后，在热羊皮里撒上盐，把孩子包在里面。还会在房门的一侧挂上昭告物。如果生的是男孩，就在门的右侧挂上弓箭；如果是女孩，就在门的左侧挂上红布条。

In the homes of nomadic Mongolians in Xinjiang, if a child is born in winter, the father will slaughter a lamb. Later, he will sprinkle salt on the hot lamb's skin and place the chid inside. Then, he will hang an object on the door of the house – a bow and arrow for a boy, and a strip of red cloth for a girl.

桑皮纸
Good Paper

桑皮纸，古时又称汉皮纸，曾经一度是造纸行业的主角，因为它结实而有韧性，被用于印制纸币、制作扇面、印刷书籍等。残存的清代桑皮纸文书和民国时期的桑皮纸钞票证明，过去新疆各地曾普遍使用桑皮纸。桑皮纸以桑树皮为原料制作，在新疆和田等地现仅存极少的制作作坊。

Mulberry bark paper was previously known as Han bark paper and once occupied a major position in the papermaking industry, as it was strong and ductile. It was used for paper money, paper fans, printed books, and other applications. Remaining items from the Qing Dynasty and Republican Period in the form of cheques show that mulberry bark paper was widely employed in Xinjiang. The paper is made from mulberry bark as its base material, and today, only a very small number of workshops exist in Hotan and other areas in Xinjiang.

摄影：韩连赟

巴扎天的毛驴车
Donkey Carts on the Bazaar Day

南疆的巴扎天，毛驴车是一道永远的风景。小小一辆驴车，可以拉得下一家人，看上去并不粗壮的四条细腿，却能驮动如此的重量。几乎每家都有一辆驴车。到了巴扎，驴车分离，毛驴被集中在一个地方，驴头攒动，驴嘶人吼，热闹非凡；巴扎散了的时候，驴主人会在万驴丛中一眼就找出自家的驴，绝不会出错。

Donkey carts are a sight that one will definitely see on market days in southern Xinjiang. A small cart can pull an entire family. These strong animals can pull huge amounts of weight despite looking small-legged. Once at the bazaar, the cart and animal are separated, and the donkeys are taken to an area where they can be themselves, making noise and kicking around. When the market closes, their owners easily pick them out from the large crowd of other donkeys, never making a mistake in identification.

长发是这样养成的
Haircare

维吾尔族妇女一头浓密的长发，羡煞许多爱美的女士，长期使用的护发土法是其中的奥秘之一。南疆维吾尔族妇女喜欢在洗头后，边梳理边涂抹用水融化的桃胶，也有使用沙枣胶的（维吾尔语称为伊林穆），这样可以滋养头发，并保持一个星期内不梳理头发也依旧整齐光亮。

Uyghur Women have long, thick hair that inspires envy in many fashionable ladies. They have long used local methods to maintain the beauty of their hair. In southern Xinjiang, after washing their hair, they apply peach gum to it while combing it, as well as olive oil, which they use to keep their hair lustrous and smooth – in this way they can go a week without brushing their hair and it will still stay nice.

女儿的第一次化妆
First Make-up

月亮般美丽的眉毛，是维吾尔族姑娘给人的初印象，这得归功于有"毛发粮食"之称的奥斯曼草。维吾尔族的习俗是，女儿出生七天后，母亲用奥斯曼草汁涂抹女儿双眉，并把眉心相连。这第一次化妆，有母女心心相印、女儿长大后不要远嫁的寓意。此后，姑娘坚持使用奥斯曼草眉笔滋养眉毛，修饰出动人的眉形。

Beautiful eyebrows are the first impression that Uyghur girls give to others, and this has to do with the glastum plant (*Isatis tinctoria*, or "Osman grass"). The custom is that seven days after a girl is born, her mother paints the juice of the plant upon the eyebrows, connecting them together. The first time the girl does her make-up, she does it with her mother, the implied meaning being that she will never be far from home. Afterwards, girls continue to use the grass to maintain the beauty of their eyebrows.

摄影：刘力

豪气的大床
A Big Bed

在新疆，特别是南疆地区，维吾尔族民居院落或正厅，甚或街头，都常见一种可供十几人休息的大床或土炕。体量如此巨大的的家什，既是全家休息的卧具，也是接人待客的地方。虽然它不够精巧还略显土气，但却简单朴实豪气。毛毡一铺，谈笑有高朋，往来无贵贱，尽可以叙交情、话言欢。

In Xinjiang, especially in the south, in the courtyards, main halls or even on the street in front of Uyghur homes, there is a very large bed that can accommodate a dozen or more people, either an entire family or a group of guests. Although the beds aren't exquisitely fashioned, they have a simple, solid feel. People can lay out a felt blanket and interact with friends, chill out, swap stories and socialise.

不一样的买卖
A Different Form of Commerce

在新疆买东西和内地不一样，西瓜、哈密瓜，在巴扎常论瓣论片卖。在内地习惯论斤论两的，新疆喜欢论个儿论堆儿，比方饺子、无花果；在内地习惯论个儿的，新疆反倒论斤论两，比如大件的铜锅、铜盆。这种定价方式是前辈流传下来的。

Shopping at a market in Xinjiang is different from doing so in the rest of China – when buying melons, they can be sold by unit or slice. In the rest of China, things such as dumplings and figs are sold by weight – catties or taels, whereas in Xinjiang they are sold by stack or pile. By contrast, things that are sold by unit in other places are sold by weight in Xinjiang – copper pots, copper basins and the like – these pricing schemes are descended from traditional practices.

维吾尔族女性见面礼
Meetings and Greetings

维吾尔族妇女见面时，要互相拥抱，轻贴右脸面颊，并说"萨拉木"（"祝福"的意思）；晚辈见到长者时，要先施礼；小孩见到老人时，应先尊敬地称呼老人，老人则亲吻小孩儿的脸蛋儿和额头。尊敬、亲切和友好就这样融化在人们生活中了。

When Uyghur women meet, they embrace and touch their right cheeks to each other, saying "salaam" (peace). When meeting elders, one salutes. When children see adults, they must respectfully call the "elder", and the elder kisses the child's face or forehead. Respect, cordiality and friendliness are fully integrated into these people's lives.

摄影：韩连赟

都瓦祈福
Duwa Prayers

新疆信仰伊斯兰教的少数民族习惯在饭后由长者带领做"都瓦"（一种祈福仪式）。做"都瓦"时，两手伸开并在一起，手心朝脸默祷一会儿，然后轻轻从上到下摸一下脸（这个动作表示吉祥如意），"都瓦"就完毕了。做"都瓦"时不能东张西望或起立，更不能嬉笑。待主人收拾完餐具后，客人才能离席。

After eating a meal, people who are adherents of Islam will conduct a "duwa" led by the eldest member present – it is a kind of prayer ceremony in which one extends both hands, the palms briefly faced towards the face, and then gently rubs one's own face in a downward motion representing good fortune. When conducting the duwa one may not look about, stand up, or play around. Guests can only leave their seats after the host is finished tidying up the table.

城市 · 乡村
City and Village

从马背上下来的城市
From Horseback to City

乌鲁木齐如果说有什么特点，那就是它的游牧气息。这个"优美的牧场"虽然早已成为中亚地区第二大城市，但它来自天山，来自西域，无论它的音乐、舞蹈、饮食、服饰，还是大声说话、大碗喝酒、大块吃肉、大大咧咧以及时间观念模糊的日常行为，无处不有马背上的跌宕气息。

If Urumqi can be said to have any special characteristic, then it would be its nomadic atmosphere. This "beautiful pasture", although now the second largest city in Central Asia, has everything from the Tianshan Range and the Western Region – music, dance, food and drink, loud voices, liquor drunk in big bowls, meat eaten in big chunks, carefree time management or rather lack of it, and a ubiquitous horseback feel.

二道桥
Erdao Bridge

二道桥如今已不是一座桥，而是一片街区——乌鲁木齐最著名的维吾尔族聚居区。宽泛意义的二道桥指的是从南门汗腾格里清真寺到南梁塔塔尔清真寺（洋行寺）方圆两三平方公里的范围，狭义的二道桥仅是二道桥民族农贸市场。二道桥是这个城市商业的心脏，有一种永不衰竭的活力。

Erdao Bridge is no longer a bridge, but rather a street area – the most famous Uyghur residential area in Urumqi. In a broad sense, Erdao Bridge refers to the three square-kilometre area between the Khan Tengri Mosque and the Tatar Mosque, and in the narrow sense it refers to the Erdao Bridge Traditional Market. Erdao Bridge is the heart of the business district in the city, and has an ever-running pulse.

兼容并包的乌鲁木齐
Compatible Urumqi

乌鲁木齐是复杂的，粗犷与精致，浓烈与清淡，所有的南腔北调、七情六欲，在这里都有一席之地。

Urumqi is complicated – coarse and fine, intense and mild, southern accent with northern inflection – a place where all these things can be felt.

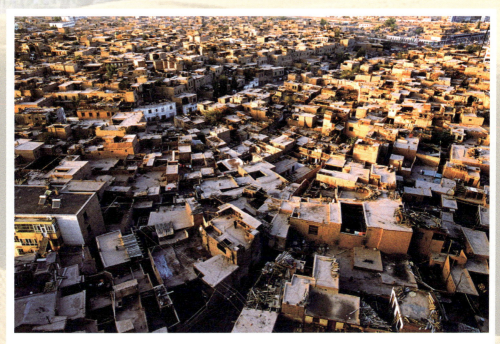

摄影：黄永中

时光的挽留
The Strings of Time

喀什老城是对时光的一次挽留。触目可见的土灰色几乎是时间本身的颜色。建筑材料是生土、土块、砖、砖坯和南疆最常见的白杨木。布局是随意的、自由的，巷子总是那么狭小、幽深，沿着它们，仿佛能走到时光的尽头去。

The old town in Kashgar is an area that encourages history to stay. A permeating earthy grey is the colour of the city. Buildings are made of earth, earthen blocks, bricks, adobe, and poplar wood, a material very common in the southern Xinjiang. The layout is capricious and free, with lanes narrow, small, deep and serene. Following them, you can almost walk into the past.

香料之城
City of Perfume

乌鲁木齐是古西域地区众多游牧民族的聚居地，也是整个古西域地区最大的香料聚集地。有人说，地域的辽远广阔与巨大的生存挑战，需要男人们时刻充满斗志，也让女人们都喜欢艳丽的服饰，喜欢能引人遐想、激情荡漾的神奇的香料。至今，它们依然是这个城市的特色之一。

Urumqi is a city where all kinds of nomads congregate, and also the largest concentration of fragrances in the ancient Western Region. People say that a vast region and strong challenge to survival lead men to be highly motivated, and women to be fond of beautiful adornments and enticing perfumes. These are characteristics of the city to this day.

马与草
Horses and Grass

在阿勒泰山夏牧场，草的深度恰好及马腹，那些漂浮在绿浪上的马匹，悠然而闲适，马的嘶鸣光芒四射，马的游动让草的颜色愈发生动。如果是匹红马，它会反衬出草的翠蓝，是水与火的效果；如果是匹白马，它会因为草色而更加飘逸，是冰与炭的统一。

In the summer pastures of Altay, the grass comes just up to the height of the waists of the horses who comfortably wade through the green waves. Their whinnies travel across the landscape, and their colour brings life to the landscape. Red horses offset the green of the grass like fire and water, and white horses look even more naturally elegant – a contradictory union like ice and coal.

悠然见南山
A View of Nanshan

南山是天山的一部分，也是乌鲁木齐的生态屏障。在唐北庭都护府时，南山即是著名的狩猎区，其后一直是西域闻名遐迩的牧场，哈萨克族牧民，蒙古族牧民，都曾在这里搭起帐篷，燃起炊烟。这里雪峰高耸，草甸青绿，林木葱郁，花草遍地，泉水幽深。游牧、农耕、定居、入城，相互交融，进退自如。

Mt. Nanshan is a part of the Tianshan Mountains, and an ecological barrier for Urumqi. During the time of the Tang Dynasty it was a famous hunting ground, and afterwards it has been a large pasture upon which both Kazakhs and Mongolians have set up tents and camps. The high snow-capped peaks, green meadows, thick forests, expanses of flowers and deep springs that make up the area lend use to nomads, farmers, residents, and cities.

沙枣花
Oleaster Flowers

有首新疆民歌《送你一束沙枣花》，好多人都听过，沙枣花的香气是新疆大地上独有的味道。那筒形的小花，像精美的小铃铛，热热闹闹地挂在树上，风一吹，摇来晃去，一串串地爆开。它的香，是种缠人的香：捂不住，收不尽，避不开。曾有人建议把乌鲁木齐种满沙枣花，让它变成一个自然香城，真是个好主意。

There is a song from Xinjiang that many people have heard, called *Let Me Give You an Oleaster Flower*. The flowers of the oleaster (*Elaeangnus angustifolia*, or "Russian olive") are a fragrant flower that is unique in Xinjiang. The tubular flowers resemble small bells, scattered upon the ground. When the wind blows they flutter about and open. Their fragrance is enticing: ineffable, provocative, and attractive. Some people have suggested planting Urumqi with these flowers all over to give the city a permeating natural fragrance – this is a great idea.

羊是长不大的婴儿
Young Sheep

羊是长不大的婴儿，永远的婴儿。它是安静的，顺从的，因为对于残暴和血腥，它是无知的。它的眼睛关闭了尘世，它的童谣传向了远方。

Sheep are ever young, and in a way, eternal infants. They are quiet, obedient, and ignorant of cruelty and violence. They close their eyes to keep out the dust, and bring themselves back to the cradle.

喀什小巷
Kashgar's Alleys

步入喀什小巷，就如同进入了时光隧道。每一个原木本色的双扇门后，都隐伏着吸引你探究的巨大诱因；每一扇雕花的窗棂里，也都催生你无尽的联想。在阴凉的过街楼下，与你擦肩而过的老者，银髯飘飘，一副高古之相，让你误以为他就是编写出千古不朽的《突厥语大辞典》的马赫穆德·喀什噶里。

Entering Kashgar's small alleys is like entering a passage through time. Behind every plain wooden double door there is a great temptation to explore. Behind every carved window lattice is the impetus to imagine wildly. Upon the cool streets shaded by buildings, one passes by a silver-bearded elder and thinks he could be Mahmoud Kashgaly, the author of the immortal *Dictionary of the Turkic Languages*.

摄影：黄永中

和田的浮尘
Hotan's Dust

尘沙不疾不徐地到来，听不到哪怕一丝声音。这些在塔克拉玛干沙漠聚合的东西，如今又被分散到每一个人眼里，一种完全被浸泡的感觉。沙土的腥味若有若无，还糅和着畜群与果树浓稠的气息，仿佛宇宙混沌的胸肺，没有一点透亮的清新，还没有开始就已老去，尚未幻想便告结束——给人更多的是一种莫名的痛感。

Sand and dust unhurriedly arrives, with a soft rustling sound. These things which gather on the Taklimakan Desert are scattered in front of everyone's eyes, as if they were completely immersed. The dust may or may not have a scent, blending with the intense characters of livestock and fruit trees, as if there were no light or clarity in the chaotic lungs of the universe – already passed before it has started, over before fantasied, giving us a kind of mysterious pain.

**飘香的城市
与女人**
Scents of the
City

因为一直面对自然的美丽与苍凉，新疆人比其他地方的人更喜欢种植花草。花草中有一些不能言说的交融于空气中的味道——乌鲁木齐就是一个有着各种香味的城市，自然，少不了和女人千丝万缕的联系。

As they constantly face both beauty and desolation, the people of Xinjiang like to plant flowers. Flowers have a certain indescribable scent that they instil the atmosphere with. Urumqi is a city that has this kind of atmosphere – natural and somehow inextricably linked with femininity.

**彩云归处是
家乡**
A Sense of
Home

由于雄踞地球之巅的帕米尔高原山路崎岖，交通极为闭塞，不易受外界影响，生活在这里的塔吉克族人一直保持着自己古老淳朴的文化传统，而这一特点在塔吉克族人的家庭道德观念与伦理、婚恋、丧葬、节日等习俗中表现尤为突出。

Due to the relatively high barrier to entry in terms of access on the Pamir Plateau, outside influence is scarce and the Tajiks who live there have maintained their simple cultural traditions – their distinctive family values and concepts of marriage, love, death, burial and holiday all reflect this.

**世界上最大
的村子**
World's
Largest
Village

塔什库尔干塔吉自治县是中国人口最少的县，而这里的勒斯卡木村可能是世界上"最大"的村子，从村界的这一头到那一头，骑一匹快马十天也未必能到。

The Taxkoragan Tajik Autonomous County is China's least-populated county, and the Lesikamu Village may be the world's "largest" village – it takes more than 10 days ride on a horse to cross from one end to the other.

喀什的遥远
Distant
Kashgar

喀什的遥远在于它在等同的时间段内制造的陌生，喀什的神秘在于它在相对的空间里由这种陌生而引发的诸多联想，而喀什的历史则是在时间和空间的向度中所能保持的清晰或模糊的背影。

Kashgar's distance lies in the curiosity it has forged in an equivalent period of time; its mystery lies in the thoughts that this curiosity has provoked in the minds of observers. Its history lies in both the existence and lack of clarity within the dimensions of time and space.

牧人
Herders

那些埋头吃草的牛羊，其认真与执着会令我们想起以同样的姿势面对草原的牧人。草原的邈远辽阔，风吹草低现出的诗意，悠长的牧歌和金雕一同在蓝天下盘旋。这些恍若和牧人们都没有太大关系，他们只是默默地面对土地，任草荣草枯，几只羊变成一群羊，几声牛哞变成牛的大合唱。

Seeing cattle and sheep grazing, heads buried in the grass, their dedication makes me think of herders in the same position. On the vast prairie, the wind blows poetically, and the long pastoral song accompanies the golden eagles spiralling in the sky. These things seem to have no great relationship with the herders, as they quietly face the ground, the state and distribution of the grass dictating the gathering of herds, the sounds the cattle make forming a chorus.

摄影：韩连赟

摄影：黄永中

没有小偷儿的县
A Place without Thieves

塔什库尔干塔吉克自治县的县城很小，用当地人形象的说法，一个馕滚在路上就能滚出城。这里生活的塔吉克族人，极其善良守规矩。塔吉克族人里没有小偷儿也没有人犯罪，这里的法院很多年没有开过庭，这里的监狱建成 30 多年没有关过一个犯人。

The Taxkoragan Tajik Autonomous County is quite small – in the words of the locals, a dropped roll of bread might roll all the way out of the town. The Tajiks who live here are quite nice and well-behaved. There are no thieves nor criminals, and the court is rarely visited. The jail was built 30 years ago, and has not yet held a prisoner.

喀什噶尔的古老街区
Kashgar's Old Streets

喀什噶尔的古老街区，大都是以具有 500 年历史的艾提尕尔清真寺为中心扇状地向外扩展。而那些被吐曼河水切割并形成台地的高埠之处，有的成了昔日王官的所在地，更多的则是商人、手工艺者聚集的街巷。现在被称为高台民居的阔孜其亚贝希，就坐落在老城东南那座高 40 多米、长 800 多米的黄土高岸上。

Most of the old streets in Kashgar radiate from the 500-year-old Id Kah Mosque, which lies at the centre of the large fanning network. The lanes on the plateau carved by the Tuman River, the site of the former palace, are mostly populated by businessmen and craftspeople. What is now known as the high cliff residential area, Koziqiyabixi lies in the southeast of the old city, and is more than 40 metres high and 800 metres long.

难懂的喀什
Enchanting
Kashgar

喀什一眼望去就与众不同，它吸引你，迷惑你，但同时又让你永远难以深入。语言、风俗、内心世界，历史文化的巨大跨度造就了喀什魅力。你可以一眼望穿乌鲁木齐的五脏六腑，但你永远无法看透喀什那双迷人的眼睛。

Kashgar is clearly different from other cities. It attracts and enchants you, but is hard to fully grasp at the same time. Language, customs, and the inner world – these are all profound. You can easily see everything there is in Urumqi, but you'll never be able to see all of Kashgar.

昭苏，一个连回忆都奢侈的地方
Zhaosu, a
Wonderful
Place

昭苏在伊犁的南面，这里的绝美不只是像海浪一样从山坡上蔓延下来的油菜花和一望无际的黄、绿、紫、红等各种色彩，还有天空。每天雨雨晴晴，天空的色彩极为丰富多变，表情时时不同。昭苏的空气是奢侈的，景色是奢侈的，甚至远离它的回忆都是奢侈的。

Zhaosu is in the south of Yili. In addition to the beauty of the slopes that roll like waves and the boundless yellow of rape blossoms and the bands of green, purple, red and other colours on the landscape, there is also the sky. With light rain every day, the sky shows all kinds of colours that may change moods at any time. The air is wonderful, the colours of the scenery are wonderful, and even the memories after one leaves are wonderful.

摄影：双元

孤独的毡房，我的家
Lonely Yurt

作家周涛说："毡房不是村落，它总是孤独的，像是在躲避什么。它总是散落在一些很远的、不容易找到的地方。"我有一个真实的注解：早年搭一个哈萨克族司机的车去伊犁，车行到巩乃斯草原，司机说要回家看看。我们跟着司机找他的家，找了将近一天也没有找到，因为没人知道他们的毡房搬到哪里去了。

Author Zhou Tao said: "Yurts don't appear in groups, they're always alone, as if they're hiding from something. They are always scattered in far-off, hard-to-find areas." I have an annotation to make: years ago, I took a ride from a Kazakh driver to Yili, and when we reached the Kunas Grasslands, the driver said he wanted to stop at his home. I just followed him, and we looked for almost a day without finding it, as nobody knew where the yurt had been moved to.

伊宁汉人街
Hanren Street

汉人街是伊宁市的标志性街道之一。名字虽叫"汉人街"却没有多少汉族人。土生土长的老伊宁人，有百分之六七十都或生或长在汉人街。在他们童年的记忆中，伊宁市就是汉人街，汉人街就是全部的伊宁市。据传最早在汉人街上做生意的是来自天津的杨柳青人。

Hanren Street in Yining is one of the most important streets in the city. The fact that it is called "Hanren" (Chinese people) Street has nothing to do with the population, because sixty or seventy percent of the ethnic locals were born or lived on this street. In their memories of their childhood years, the street made up all of Yining City, and the city was only one street. It's said that the earliest Chinese who came to do business on the street were from Tianjin.

活着的历史
Living History

新疆布满了很多已成遗迹的家园与城邦。西域三十六国留下的大都是一些历史的残片，有些被风带到了远处，有些被埋进时间的黄沙里，有些被时间溶解而成为猜想。而喀什，似乎依然是古疏勒城的样子。打馕的、修铜壶的、收古钱的、剃头的、打铁的、卖布的以及种种的叫卖声，呈现的是千年不变的街市。

Xinjiang is dotted with many ruins of homes and cities. The historical remnants of the thirty-six historical kingdoms have been spread throughout the region by the winds, some buried in the yellow sands, some worn away by time entirely. Kashgar still resembles old Shu-le. Making bread, working copper, collecting old coins, shaving heads, working iron, selling cloth and other commercial activities are still conducted in the age-old traditional manner.

摄影：黄永中

摄影：韩连赟

坎儿井
Qanat

吐鲁番是新疆绿洲文明的一个代表，它没有在地上流动的大河，却有在地下运行的坎儿井——世界上最长的井。这人工的"地下河"，浇灌了地上的生命，同时也滋润了丝路古道上一个个旅人的心，让这个中国最干的地方成为千年绿洲，出产着世界上最甜的葡萄。

Turpan is a representative of the cultured oases of Xinjiang. It lacks a flowing surface waterway, but has the world's longest system of qanat (underground waterworks). This man-made "underground river" provides all the water for above-ground life, and quenched the thirst of travellers on the Silk Road. It makes China's driest area into a millennial oasis, producing the world's best grapes.

伊犁河
Yili River

当隔一段时间没去伊犁河的时候，不经意间我发现伊犁河离我慢慢远了，她正在从我身体里慢慢地消失，直到有一天她让我的身体最后干涸。在伊犁河边漫步，最好是光着脚，踩在那些细碎的被太阳晒得滚热的石子上，一种莫名的舒服从脚掌下传来，缓缓而上，直至传遍全身。

After a period of time spent away from the Yili River, I discovered that somehow my distance to it had increased, that it had slowly vanished from being a part of me, eventually leaving me dry. When taking a walk along the river you should do it barefoot, treading along the sand and rocks that have been shone on by the sun. A comfortable feeling will come over you, warming you and penetrating your body.

南疆
Southern Xinjiang

南疆即新疆南部，自古以来就是一个多民族聚居的地区，有维吾尔、汉、塔吉克、柯尔克孜、蒙古等民族。有浓郁的人文景观，亦有古丝绸之路上留下的数不清的古城池及古墓葬、千佛洞等。

Southern Xinjiang has long been an area in which multiple ethnicities gathered, such as the Uyghur, Han, Tajik, Kyrgyz, Mongol, and other groups. There is rich cultural scenery, and a number of old cities, moats, tombs and caves left behind by the old Silk Road.

八卦城
City of Eight Trigrams

新疆的特克斯是个很奇妙的县城。整个县城面积 8 平方公里，以占地 26 亩的八卦公园为轴心，呈放射状圆形，向外辐射，并以四条环路相连，布局上有《易经》的 64 卦、386 爻。广场、宾馆、商场、街道甚至公园都是以八卦来命名。

Tex in Xinjiang is a curious county town. With an area of 8 square kilometres, it has a park covering an area of 2 hectares at its centre. Four roads radiate from its oblong centre, mirroring the 64 trigrams and 386 constituent components. The plaza, hotel, mall, streets, and even the park itself, are all part of the layout and have names that are part of the Eight Trigrams.

喀拉峻草原
Kalajun Grassland

特克斯的喀拉峻草原在夏季是一个花的世界，被称为"五花草甸"草原。百花盛开，繁花似锦，绿色的地毯上被纯朴牧民绣上了各式各样的刺绣，他们就在这地毯上放牧、生活，日出日落，生生不息。

The Kalajun Grassland in Tex is a world of flowers in the summertime, and has been called the "prairie of the five flowers". Blooms open resplendently against a carpet of green, as if the local herders had embroidered coloured designs into the blanket of the ground. Upon this verdant carpet they herd animals and conduct the doings of their daily lives, year after year.

一株野蛮的葡萄树
A Wild Grapevine

在废墟和火焰中间，只有野蛮地生长才能存活。吐鲁番是一株葡萄树，有着发达的根须和茂盛的枝叶的葡萄树。

Amidst the ruins and flames, only the savage can survive. Turpan is a grapevine, one with developed roots and thick, dense branches.

喀纳斯的野花
Wild Flowers in Kanas

蒲公英从五月一直开到六月初，接下来是金莲花，花瓣层层叠叠，一片金黄，看不到花冠下的绿叶和泥土。在喀纳斯湖畔，在那仁草原，在禾木，最多的就是这种金黄色的野花，然后是野芍药，大大的紫红色花冠。而野罂粟、刺蔷薇、大花青莲的开放，使喀纳斯的野性与温柔一同呈现在天地之间。

Dandelions bloom from May to early June, and then trollflowers spring forth, completely covering the green underneath in a blanket of yellow. Around Lake Kanas, among the grasses and small shrubs these flowers are all about, in addition to wide expanses of wild peony that cover the ground in purple. Wild poppies, roses and violets provide accompaniment, turning Kanas into a wild and gentle place between heaven and earth.

童话边城布尔津
Fairy-tale Burqin

从乌鲁木齐乘车北驰约 700 公里，大片的戈壁和贫瘠的荒原，使眼睛里充满沉闷与苍凉。当汽车进入额尔齐斯河与布尔津河的交汇处，突然一片绿洲映入眼帘，绿洲之中还有一个小城，一个掩映在绿树、鲜花和草地中的欧式小城。这就是布尔津，它的恬静与美丽让人惊讶，像儿时读过的一个童话。

Riding a car about 700 kilometres north of Urumqi, one is confronted with the dreary sight of the vast expanse of the Gobi Desert. When the car reaches the nexus of the Ertix and Burqin Rivers, a great green oasis appears, one that even contains a small city covered in verdant hues. This is Burqin, a place of astonishing beauty, like a fairy tale of one's past.

塔城上空的明媚
Oasis of Light

朋友说，我去的地方是个大城市，可我觉得哪儿也没有塔城大！当车子飞驰着离开塔城，我忍不住回过头去，整个天幕黯淡阴沉，有雷声从天边滚来，但塔城的上空却露出一片明媚的蔚蓝。我走了，整城的人都忘记了我，快快乐乐地生活在明媚之处。

My friend tells me that I am heading for a big city, but I feel nowhere is as big as Tacheng. As our car tears away from the city, I have to turn my head back and take a look – the sky goes dark and the sound of thunder rolls forth. Tacheng, however, stays in a strip of brightness. As I leave, I hope to be not forgotten by the city, as it exists in its little oasis of light.

喀什的高台民居
Old Residences

喀什高台民居，古老、神秘、幽深的巷道里，时常让你感受到一段又一段历史，那些只言片语、片瓦残泥里所存留的种种往事，已不只在人们的表情、举止、眉宇里，甚至这里的空气所散发的气息都有一种古老的味道。

In the old, mysterious, and deep alleys of the residences on the plateau in Kashgar, you feel like you're swimming in history. The language and the buildings flow around you, and you feel it all in the expressions, manners, brows and even the air around you.

摄影：王辉

摄影：韩连赞

在白哈巴的
一个小店里
A Store in Baihaba

进入一个哈萨克族人家的小店，店里有汉族人的凉皮，有俄罗斯式面包，有游牧人家的奶酪、奶茶。女主人普通话很好，聊家常，也聊外边的世界。门外，两匹枣红马安闲地走过；树上，不知名的鸟在叫；屋后，一群羊像天上的云飘在山坡上。橘黄的光从云层中洒下来，让人想起米勒的画。

When entering a Kazakh's shop, I saw there were Chinese cold noodles, Russian bread, and herder's cheese and milk tea. The female shopkeeper spoke Mandarin well and conversed on a variety of topics. Outside, two bay horses walked by leisurely, and in the trees some birds I couldn't identify chirped. Behind the building, a flock of sheep drifted over the slopes like a series of clouds. Golden light leaked in from the clouds, making me think of a painting by Jean-Francois Millet.

喀纳斯的春天
Spring in Kanas

进入六月，喀纳斯才完全跨进春天。虽然从三月开始，一种被称作顶冰花的黄色小花就开始在厚厚的积雪下发芽，但一直要经历过四、五月的温煦阳光，冰雪才慢慢融化。即使是六月，喀纳斯湖畔的树丛下和半山以上，积雪依然用硬朗的线条勾勒出一幅幅巨大的水墨山水。

Kanas only truly enters spring in June. Although in March a kind of small yellow flower begins to poke through the thick blanket of snow, it takes the sun of April and May to melt the snow cover. Even though in June, heavy flows of meltwater from the forests up the slopes of the banks of Lake Kanas still seep down the mountain slopes, entering the large pool of water below.

花儿沟
Hua'ergou

花儿沟当地人又叫它花儿台子，是一个山间大草甸，距乌鲁木齐市区 200 公里左右，是近年来山友们热衷的一条徒步线路。哈萨克族牧民在这里过着他们自在的游牧生活，六、七月，花儿沟的野花最为繁盛，人躺在花海里，会被野花淹没。野花繁密的地方，如一张超大花毯，让你不得不惊叹自然的奇妙。

Hua'ergou (flower gulley) is also called Hua'er Taizi (flower bed) by the locals – it is a grassy area between mountains, about 200 kilometres from Urumqi, and has become quite popular with travellers in recent years. Kazakh herders lead their pastoral lifestyles here, and from June to July, when the flowers are in full bloom, you can lie in a sea of blooms, almost being engulfed in it. In such an area, you'll be amazed that the ground has been wonderfully covered by a blanket of flowers.

大巴扎的色彩
Colours of the Bazaar

巴扎集中了纯粹的维吾尔族美食和传统的风俗文化。每到巴扎日，四里八乡的维吾尔族老乡几乎全家出动，赶着驴车马车，坐着乡村"巴士"来赶大巴扎，场面壮观，令人难忘。尤其是巴扎上铺天盖地的艳丽色彩和美丽的古丽更是绚丽夺目。

The bazaar is where pure Uyghur cuisine and cultural traditions are represented. Every bazaar day, Uyghurs come from all around, driving horse and donkey-driven carts, taking the village "buses" – it is a sight to see. The beautiful colours of wares laid out are of course complemented by the sight of the local beauties.

摄影：刘力

歌舞刀郎乡
The Songs of Dolan

麦盖提的刀郎后人，遗传了祖先酷爱跳舞的基因，对舞蹈如痴如狂。只要有音乐和手鼓，男女老少都能踩着节奏，跳起整齐的刀郎舞。在大巴扎一位卖琴的老汉唱起了高亢的木卡姆，那震撼心灵的歌声立刻就吸引了众多人。于是，有的拿手鼓，有的拿琴，还有两位大叔当场跳起了欢快的舞蹈。

The descendants of Dolan people in Markit have inherited a deep love for dancing. With just music and drums, males and females, young and old can find a beat and dance to it. At a bazaar, when an old seller of instruments started up a muqam (a kind of Arabic melody), it moved a throng of people to contribute their drums, zithers and dancing talents to make quite a scene.

摄影：刘力

刀郎乡的孩子
Children in Dolan

在麦盖提随意走进乡下一间不起眼的土屋，说不定主人就会很自豪地告诉你，她的孩子在上海、北京或哪个城市上学。麦盖提的孩子就像南疆的阳光，明亮而欢快。无论在哪里遇见，他们都是那样活泼大方天真可爱，他们的笑容像灿烂的花儿，绽放在叶尔羌河沿岸的田野，洋溢着幸福与安宁。

When you enter into an otherwise unremarkable earthen dwelling in Markit, you may be told proudly by its owner that her child is studying in Shanghai, Beijing, or some other large city. The children of Markit are like Xinjiang's sunlight – bright and fast. No matter where you encounter them, they are always active, natural and cute, with smiles that enchant like flowers, blossoming on the banks of the Yarkant River, overflowing with happiness and peace.

摄影：刘力

叶尔羌河流过的地方
The Flow of the Yarkant River

也许我们离开乡村太久了，也许我们已习惯了隔阂冷漠，习惯了在纷繁的都市里麻木地奔波。在南疆叶尔羌河流过的地方，感受大自然的安宁平和，感受人和自然的和谐相依，感受淳朴的民风和久违了的快乐，感受打开心窗让微笑真诚幸福的一刻……我的心里涌动着一个词——感动。

Maybe we have been away from the village for too long, or maybe we have become accustomed to the estrangement of living in a large city where one hardly knows one's neighbours. Where the Yarkant River flows in Southern Xinjiang, it feels natural and peaceful, and we exist in harmony with nature, enjoying a kind of customary simplicity that we have longed after for ages. We feel as if we can open up the windows to our hearts and laugh – I feel truly moved.

摄影：刘力

朴素的乡村婚礼
Village Weddings

维吾尔族乡村的婚礼大多很朴素，很有些"带着你的嫁妆、领着你的妹妹坐着那马车来"的味道。不过再朴素的婚礼也不能少了抓饭和音乐舞蹈。在麦盖提克孜勒阿瓦提乡我参加了一次在男方家的婚宴，因语言不通，我一直不知道新郎新娘是谁，大家的服饰都差不多，我猜想在房里不能出来的一定就是新娘了。

Traditional Uyghur weddings are for the most part quite simple, evoking themes of traditional songs about marriage. However, at these simple weddings there are large amounts of rice pilaf, music, and dancing. I participated in a wedding reception for the groom's side at Awati in Markit. Due to the language barrier, I didn't know who the bride was and who the bridegroom was. Everyone was dressed similarly – I figured the bride must be the one who couldn't come out of the room.

冬窝子
Winter Nest

在新疆，有一种严冬时牧民们所选的防寒避风的地方，叫冬窝子。冬窝子选在山坳里，没有风，天气比预想的要暖和得多。牧民就是这样智慧，天地再大，也能找到大山的肚脐眼儿，并且在这个窝窝里让自己和畜群度过寒冷的冬天。

In Xinjiang, there is a kind of place in which herders will pick to avoid the cold in times of especially harsh winters – this is called a "winter nest". The herders are able to find such a "nest" within the mountains where there is no wind, and temperatures are warmer than predicted. They are good at finding this refuge even in a large area, and wintering out until the weather warms.

塔城
Tacheng

塔城这座城市好像原野上没有院墙的一个现代村落，不会让来客感到紧张和疏远。身临其境只感觉仿佛水顺着河道流淌一样自然。塔城三面环山，西面的出口像一个长长的琴把通向远方，境内的五条河像五根晶莹通透的琴弦，你在塔城，也会变成美妙的音符。

Tacheng looks like an un-walled modern village on the grasslands, putting visitors at ease and making them feel welcome. When one approaches its limits, it feels like the water almost flows in a natural way. The city is bordered on three sides by mountains, with the exit to the east resembling the long neck of an instrument, the five streams within resembling streams upon it – in Tacheng, you become a note of music.

在麦盖提喝早茶
Morning Tea

麦盖提大清真寺旁的维吾尔族居住区，有一条小吃街。早上闲逛到这里，闻着烤包子手抓饭羊肉汤和刚出坑的馕饼的香味，正犹豫想吃什么时，几个正围坐着喝茶聊天的老汉邀请我一起喝茶。虽然我们语言不通，可我们比比画画聊得很开心。这个早晨阳光明亮，我和好客的维吾尔族老人们一起吃着早茶。

There is a Uyghur neighbourhood next to the mosque in Markit, and within there is a food street. Walking here in the morning, I could smell the cooked buns, rice pilaf, mutton soup and fresh pancakes – as I hesitated over what to eat, a group of old men sitting in a circle and drinking tea invited me to have a cup. Although we couldn't communicate via language, I had a good time with them, drinking tea in the early morning light with these hospitable old people.

摄影：刘力

摄影：双元

秋日的胡杨
Autumn Poplars

对于胡杨来说，夏，只是一个过程，混同于所有的生命中；秋，才是目标，特立独行于荒僻的一隅，绚烂而张扬。秋季，胡杨林一片金黄，一个真实的梦。塔里木河沿岸，不管是一棵胡杨还是一大片胡杨林，都是一个梦幻的世界，一切都变得温暖而华丽。很多东西，愈到老，才愈呈现出它的特别之处与独立之美。

To the poplars, summer is just a process, a part of the rest of life. Autumn is a goal, a solitary walk that skirts desolation on the route to splendour. In autumn, the polar forests are a blanket of gold, a dream come true. On the banks of the Tarim River, whether it's a single poplar or a whole forest, the atmosphere is always that of a dream world, where everything is warm and beautiful. Many things increase with age, to the point that they have reached a special kind of unique beauty.

小女孩的愿望
A Girl's Wish

牛石头草原上的小女孩斯尔琴嘟着嘴说："我连和布克赛尔都没出过呢！乌鲁木齐想都不敢想！听说，那是鸟儿都飞不到的地方。"

A young girl, Xirqin, on the Niushitou grassland, puckered her lips and said "I've never been out of Hoboksar! I don't bother to think about going to Urumqi! I've heard even birds cannot reach that place."

库车王府
Kuqa Palace

公元1758年，库车、阿克苏、拜城三地的维吾尔族头领米扎尔·鄂在平定准噶尔之乱和大小和卓叛乱中有功，乾隆皇帝授予其亲王衔，并派遣内地工匠建造了库车王府。现在的王府是根据末代"库车王"达吾提·买合苏提的回忆，在原址重建的，重建后的王府融合了中国中原地区和伊斯兰风格的建筑特色。

In 1758, Kuqa, Aksu and Baicheng were key cities in the Uyghur leader's suppression of the Junggar and Hezhuo Rebellions, and Emperor Qianlong of the Qing Dynasty not only bequeathed a title upon him, but also dispatched craftsmen and workers to build a palace at Kuqa. The current palace, according to Dawut Mahsuti, the last of the "Kuqa Monarchs", was rebuilt on the site of the original palace, and incorporated both Chinese and Islamic characteristics.

亲近沙漠的城市
A City Next to the Desert

鄯善的奇迹，在于它有一个离城市最近的沙漠，那就是库木塔格沙漠。沙漠与居住在它身边的人友好而又相互依存，不知是沙漠养育了人们钢铁汉子的性格，还是人们打开了沙漠另一面的柔情。总之，他们不离不弃，生死相依。

One of the interesting things about Shanshan is that it has a desert very close by – the Kumtag Desert. The desert and the residents of the city have friendly and mutually beneficial relationship – it's hard to say if the desert hardened the people, or they softened the desert. Either way, they are inseparable.

摄影：杨志勇

摄影：涂化章

神奇新疆
Mysterious Xinjiang

我见过一个帅气的俄罗斯语言学学者，他叫穆拉维耶夫，他来吐鲁番参加西域语言学高峰论坛，顺道参观了库木塔格沙漠。他站在沙漠旁边茂密的公园里，看着一池汩汩流淌的泉眼，对我说："你不觉得造物主很神奇吗？沙漠与清泉绿树毗邻，仅一步之遥。"或许，这就是新疆。

I saw a handsome Russian linguist named Muraviev, who came to Turpan to attend a conference on the languages of the Western Region, and also to visit the Kumtag Desert. Standing in a park on the edge of the desert, looking at a bubbling spring, he said to me: "Don't you think the Creator is odd? The desert and the oasis are right here, only steps away." Perhaps, this is a true reflection of Xinjiang.

打掌人
Making Shoes for Animals

维吾尔族历史上以游牧为主，畜力使用在南疆依然较为普遍，因此为驴、马打掌至今仍是南疆地区很接"地气"的一个手工业行当。为驴、马打掌，犹如为驴、马修脚、穿鞋。

Uyghur history is mainly that of a nomadic culture, and animal husbandry is still ubiquitous in Southern Xinjiang, where shoeing horses and donkeys is one of the most "local" professions that exists today. Making shoes for these animals is like running a pedicure studio and shoe shop for them.

罗布人
Lop Nur

作为新疆最古老的居民，罗布人曾世代生活在塔里木河下游和罗布泊一带。罗布人"不种五谷，不牧牲畜，惟以小舟捕鱼为食"。是水，哺育了质朴而独特的罗布文化。他们的命运如细小的沙粒四处散失，被塔克拉玛干风暴席卷而去。

As old residents of Xinjiang, the Lop Nur people live around the lower reaches of the Tarim River and Lop Nur itself. They neither grow crops nor herd animals, instead gaining their subsistence from the water. Their culture is formed around this water-based lifestyle. Their fate was scattered among the fine sands of the desert, and blown away by the dry wind of the Taklimakan.

摄影：麻军

龟兹
Kuqa

库车坐落于南疆塔里木盆地的西北缘，是古龟兹的都城所在地。在吐火罗语中库车是"繁华的城邦"的意思。英国史学家汤因比说，假如让我选择生活的地方，我愿意选择历史上的龟兹。库车自汉唐就成为丝绸之路的中心，世界四大文明在这里汇合。丝绸之路上接踵于道的商贾，将龟兹推向空前繁荣的黄金时代。

Modern-day Kuqa is located on the north-western reaches of the Tarmin Basin in southern Xinjiang, and was the site of the historical capital of the ancient Kocha Kingdom. In the Tocharian language, Kocha means "resplendent capital". English historian Arnold Toynbee said that if he were to pick a historical city to live in, it would be ancient Kocha. It was a central city on the Silk Road during the Han and Tang Dynasties, where the four great cultures of the world came together. The merchants who walked the Silk Road took the city into a wondrous golden age.

和田的尘土
Dust in Hotan

我要说的是和田的尘土。包裹着这座城市的尘土，来自于离她不远的塔克拉玛干大沙漠。千百年来，沙漠生态下的和田小城，早已经习惯了这个强悍邻居的造访和袭扰。只是，时间造就了她们的相处之道，也造就了一座沙漠与一座绿洲小城的睦邻关系。

Let's talk about the dust in Hotan. The sand and dust that surround the city come from the not-far-away Taklimakan Desert. For centuries, the residents have put up with the powerful assaults from their desert neighbour. Time has forged a channel between the two of them, and a good-neighbourly relationship between the residents of the oasis and the desert as well.

摄影：双元

冬天的和布克赛尔
Hoboksar in Winter

雪才下过两场，就再不下了。雪薄得可怜，风一吹，雪影子都找不到了，只有北边的赛尔群山看起来白雪皑皑，好像大雪的故乡。山里的牧民不能化雪取用，就去泉边或者山脚下的井水里取水来用。

After two snowfalls, it doesn't snow any more. The pitifully thin layer of snow upon the mountains is blown away with the lightest of winds, with only the Sar Mountains in the north appearing densely covered. The nomads in the mountains can't melt the snow for use, and thus go to springs, or wells drilled at the foot of the mountain to fulfil their needs.

丰饶的塔尔巴哈台
Plenty in Tarbagatay

六月的塔尔巴哈台山是属于浓密的青草和妍丽的百花的，野芍药、野雏菊、野罂粟的花朵在山峦间随风张望，花颜因为寂寞美艳至极。一些云一朵一朵聚集在天空，挤得奇形怪状。忽然车子一个转弯，云把持不住，一朵一朵坠落，跌进山坳，变成羊群，大口大口地啃噬着青草和花朵，汁液把羊毛都染绿了。

Tarbagatay Mountain in June is marked by dense grass and all kinds of flowers, with peony, daisies, poppies and others covering the landscape all around, the blooms looking beautiful in their isolation. Some clouds gather in the sky, forming odd shapes. A cart comes by suddenly, and the clouds are unable to hold on, dropping one after the other into the lap of the mountains, becoming sheep. They devour the tender grass and flowers, and their fur is dyed green.

133

撮影：双元

敖包特庙
Ovoot Temple

碧草依依，麻雀在马路上啄食，鹰蹲在家属楼顶。从敖包特庙出来，走着走着就走到了一片湿地草场里。天气总是格外好，天蓝得好像白云都粘不住，大朵大朵直往下掉的样子。喇嘛说，敖包特庙就像莲花心，而周围的湿地就是一瓣一瓣盛开的莲花花瓣。

The grass grows widely, sparrows peck at food on the road, and eagles stand upon rooftops. Coming out from Ovoot Temple, I walked to a wet piece of grassland. The weather was exceptionally great, with white clouds in a blue sky that seem to tumble down. The monks say Ovoot Temple is like the heart of a lotus flower, and the surrounding wetlands are the petals that unfold around it.

各民族通婚最多的地方
A Remarkable Place of Inter-ethnic Marriage

在新疆，塔城是各民族通婚最多的地方。塔城除了汉族外，有哈萨克族、锡伯族、达斡尔族、塔塔尔族、俄罗斯族等二十多个少数民族。在塔城，一大半以上的家庭都是由两个以上的民族构成，四五个民族组成的和睦家庭比比皆是，甚至还有一个七个民族组成的大家庭。

In Xinjiang, Tacheng sees most of the inter-ethnic marriages. In addition to Han there are more than 20 ethnic groups, including Kazakhs, Xibe, Daur, Tatar, Russians and others. In Tacheng, a large number of the families are multi-ethnic, with extended families comprising four or five ethnic groups, and some representing as many as seven.

旱獭
Marmots

塔尔巴哈台绥靖城，是乾隆三十一年皇帝命名的。塔尔巴哈台是蒙古语，意思是这个地方有很多旱獭。旱獭这种动物，喜欢在水草丰美、土层肥沃的地方居住。旱獭多，说明塔城是浑然天成的沃土。后来这里就简称塔城。

The Suijing City in Tarbagatay was so named by Emperor Qianlong in the 31st year of his reign of the Qing Dynasty. Tarbagatay means "a place of many marmots (tarabagans)" in Mongolian. Marmots enjoy nice scenery, good water, and fertile soil. The fact that many of them live here is a testament to the quality of the nearby natural resources, and the origin of the name.

塔城的家庭餐馆
Home Cooking

塔城农家乐有近千家。据说，这和塔城人的性格和心态有关。塔城人恋家喜乐，闲散从容，连吃饭都不愿离家太远。来了朋友，自家小院炒几个菜，摆上张桌子，小酒就喝上了。兴致上来，随手从屋里抄出个乐器，就吹拉弹唱上了。久而久之，不少家庭餐馆就出现了。

There are almost a thousand farm inns in Tacheng. It's said that this is connected to the character and disposition of the local people. Tacheng residents love their families and entertainment, and value proximity. When friends come to visit, one cooks in the courtyard, lays out a few tables, and prepares some liquor. When the time's right the musical instruments are rolled out and singing begins. As a natural result, a number of family inns have appeared in the city.

大地的工业艺术
Karamay

"克拉玛依"是维吾尔语"黑油"的译音，得名于市区东北角一群天然沥青丘——黑油山。克拉玛依是新中国成立后勘探开发的第一个大油田，这里的沙漠戈壁里，布满磕头机和管道，与红柳、梭梭、胡杨等荒漠植物相映成趣，像是大地上造就的华丽工业艺术。

"Karamay" means "black oil" in Uyghur, as there is a natural asphalt mound in the north-east of the city – "Black Oil Mountain". Karamay was site of the first oilfield to be discovered after the establishment of the New China. In the Gobi Desert here, pumping units and pipelines crisscross with tamarisks, haloxylon (sacsaoul), and poplar trees, like some kind of art executed on the very landscape itself.

精灵之城布尔津
Exquisite Burqin

布尔津，一座精巧而多汁的小城。额尔齐斯河和布尔津河荡漾着她美丽的倒影。这是阿尔泰山的诸神们选中的居住地，充满了童话世界的光泽和神秘气息。在新疆人眼里，它就是一座精灵之城。

Burqin is an exquisite little city. The Ertix and Burqin rivers reflect its beauty in their rippling surfaces. This is where the gods of the Altay Mountains live, and is full with a kind of fairy-tale like charms. In the eyes of Xinjiang people, it is a mythical place.

街道是草原的坐标
Markers of Grasslands

和丰的街道，每一条都通往草原深处。街道干净得只剩下街。雀子根本不把街当成街，蹦蹦跳跳，一群一群，啄食着看似啥也没有的街道。对它们来说，这里也是草原的一部分，几乎没有什么人和车，不过是几条石头一样硬的竖条条在草原上画了个坐标而已。人们在小城散步，无论朝哪个方向走，定会走到草原上。

The streets of Hoboksar all lead to the depth of the grassland. The thoroughfares are very neat and clean. The birds don't see them as roads at all, hopping along in groups and pecking at food. To them, this is just a part of the grassland, and without cars and people, the stones are simply a few markers upon the ground. When walking on roads in a small city, no matter which way one heads out, the grassland is the inevitable destination.

羊的冬天
Winter Sheep

到了冬天，羊的选择就小了，就剩下根茎和残叶银灰银灰地塌在荒原上，在寒风中等着羊温暖的嘴和肚子。羊用蹄子把雪踩回地下去，吃那些露出的根茎和残叶，捱过漫长的冬季。一只在草原上捱过饿的羊和一只在围栏里育肥的羊，它们的肉提供的养料是不一样的。

Choices for sheep shrink in the winter, and roots and fallen leaves become the means of sustenance for the animals during the cold season. The animals can kick up earth to reveal the remaining treasures, and survive the long winter in this way. The nutritional value from a sheep that has toughed out on the wastelands over the winter and one that has grown up in a pen is different.

摄影：双元

摄影：王晖

美少女和漂亮驹
A Girl and a Colt

阿尔阿依和舅舅在南山乌拉斯台牧场，她的工作是带游人骑马。鼓动着小姑娘兴致的，除了赚取学费，更重要的是在开学前一天能和心爱的马儿待在一起。阿尔阿依在甘沟乡读寄宿制小学，九岁的她和六岁的它，一学期后才能重逢。她在马鞍上扎起一个蝴蝶结，心里想着：亲爱的，你今天和我一样漂亮，等我回来哟。

Araray and her uncle are herders in Urastay, in the Nanshan Mountains. Her job is to take tourists on horse rides. Encouraging the girl to work is not just money she can earn for her tuition, but also being able to be with her beloved horses before school starts. She attends a boarding school in Gangou Township, and the nine-year old girl and six-year old horse will only see each other once at the end of a semester. She has tied a bow on the horse's saddle, and thinks in her heart: my beloved, today you are as pretty as me. Wait for me to come back.

安集海
Anjihai

安集海是新疆沙湾县一个小镇，以前这里以盛产大白菜出名，现在我只是看到了辣椒。在一望无际的戈壁滩上，辣椒就像红色的海。辣椒在静静地酣睡，在聆听地球心脏的跳动，南来北往的车怎么也唤不醒它们的香梦。我终于知道安集海为什么叫海了。

Anjihai is a small town in Shawan County, Xinjiang. It was previously famous for its lettuce, but now all I see is peppers. Looking across the endless Gobi Desert, the peppers are like a sea of red. As they quietly grow, listening to the heartbeat of the earth, the moving vehicles are unable to awake them from their dreams. I now understand why Anjihai is now called a "sea" (hai).

137

多浪河
Duolang River

多浪河并没有浪，她温柔得像个小姑娘，当这条河从一座城市穿过之后，城市就像沐浴出水的新娘，一条河让阿克苏走出了大漠迷沙。如今多浪河两岸成了旅游观光地带，这条观光带从上游到下游长7.7公里，河床很宽，不禁让人想起"一条大河波浪宽"的歌词。

The Duolang River ("wavy river") has no waves, and is gentle like a small girl, but after having passed through a city it looks like a newly married bride, taking Aksu out of the desert sand. In the present day tourist facilities have been built on both sides of the river, allowing people to travel a 7.7-kilometre segment where the riverbed is quite wide, making people think of romantic songs.

那花，那马，那少年
Back Then

七月乌鲁木齐南山苜蓿台，紫色的花儿漫山铺撒，花香在空气中酝酿，随着清风一阵阵弥散开来，各种生灵便沉醉在这甜滋滋的空气中了。看那马儿，嗅着花香啃两口香草，它就醉了。那马背上的少年，并不慌着催马前行，他把花儿啜在口中吮吸，于是他也醉了，神思悄然游荡在天地之间。

On the alfalfa steppe south of Urumqi, the purple flowers spread around as their scent permeates the air, ebbing and flowing with each gust of wind, spreading all manner of intoxicating sweet fragrance in the air. A horse, taking in the smells and munching at the grass, quickly becomes intoxicated. The youth on horseback does not urge it along. Sucking at a flower in his mouth, he is also intoxicated, wandering through the paradise in a quiet state of mind.

摄影：王晖

摄影：汤祥

清晨的劳作
Rising Early

新疆蒙古族人以从事畜牧业为主，或半农半牧。清晨，牧民们身着艳丽的服装，走出蒙古包，舀出清水，准备调制香喷喷的奶茶，然后开始繁忙的一天。他们脸上挂着的笑容，就像天上的太阳。

The Mongolians of Xinjiang are mainly herders, or half-agricultural half-nomadic. At dawn, they put on their beautiful clothing and exit their yurts, scooping out some clear water to make some fragrant milk tea before starting their busy days. On their faces are smiles, like the sun in the sky.

禾木印象
Impressions of Hemu

有人说禾木是被上帝遗忘的一个地方，它静静地坐落在友谊峰下喀纳斯河旁。这里没有一间砖瓦或者水泥建筑，柏油路刚到村口便戛然而止，小村庄拒绝柏油和水泥，一色的木头房子，土路上散发着牛粪味儿。这"土木"本色的小村落，在霜凝大地黄叶遍野的秋冬中，升腾起几缕炊烟，使人觉得它就像一部人间童话。

Some people say that Hemu is a place forgotten by God. It sits quietly under Friendship Peak, along the bank of the Kanas River. It doesn't have any brick or concrete structures, with the paved road stopping at the entrance to the village. The village has refused tarmac and concrete, and the smell of dung drifts between the houses, all the colour of wood. This "natural" village emits smoke from its chimneys even during the desolate fall and winter seasons, like some kind of fairy tale.

戈壁上长出的城市

Out of the Gobi

戈壁滩上长出绿草，是美好的渴望，戈壁滩上长出城市，可能会被讥笑为妄想。在新疆准噶尔盆地西南，有一座独立于戈壁的山叫"独山"，因盛产石油，在维吾尔语和哈萨克语中，被称为"玛依塔克"和"玛依套"（意思是"油山"）。20世纪50年代以来，这里发展迅速，戈壁真的长出一座新城，这就是独山子。

Seeing grass grow upon the Gobi Desert is a nice aspiration, but for a city to spring forth is an almost risible fantasy. In the southwest of the Junggar Basin in Xinjiang, there is a single solitary mountain called Mt. Dushan ("solitary mountain"), and is called "Karamay" and "Maitao" in the Uyghur and Kazakh languages respectively, both names meaning "oil mountain". After the 1950s, the area developed rapidly and the Gobi Desert saw the development of a new city – Dushanzi.

牧归

Herder's Duties

日出，牧人挥着羊鞭，带着羊群倾巢而出；日落，饱食膘肥的羊群随牧人欢快的吆喝快乐而回。牧羊是一种自由度和幸福度都不低的工作，牧人则是最喜欢唱歌的群体之一。

At sunrise, the herder takes up his whip and guides his flock from their resting place; at sunset the full lambs return home as the herder happily urges them on. Herding is a profession with a high degree of freedom and delight, and thus herders are among those who like to sing.

摄影：汤祥

**卖恰玛古的
老奶奶**
Selling Herbs

骑三轮往巴扎赶的是一位维吾尔族老奶奶，车上载的可不是白萝卜，而是被称为长寿圣果的恰玛古（蔓菁的一种）。恰玛古在维吾尔族人心中的分量就如同汉族人看待人参一样，不同的是恰玛古更"家常"，还不上火。南疆人长寿，除了喜食恰玛古之外，勤劳并充实地生活，恐怕也是原因之一，就像这位老奶奶。

An old Uyghur woman drives a cart to the bazaar, laden with not white radishes, but "the fruit of long life", which is a kind of gourd. The tuber is for the Uyghurs like ginseng is for the Chinese, with it being considered more common and refreshing. In addition to their hard work and full lives, eating this tuber may be one of the reasons for the longevity among southern Xinjiang residents, such as this old woman.

摄影：王莎

伊宁
Yining

进了伊宁市真的不想坐车了，这个花园般的城市就像一个迷人的美丽少女，那种妩媚宛若少女的一笑。我一直以为，那拉提草原和昭苏草原是伊犁的漂亮的裙裾，到了伊宁才知道，这座城市的大街上走动的少女几乎都是"阿瓦古丽"。

I didn't want to take transit as soon as I arrived in Yining – the garden city is like a beautiful young girl, and its charm is her smile. I always thought that the Nalati and Zhaosu grasslands were the city's beautiful skirt, but upon arriving at Yining I found out that most of the girls on the street were smoking hot.

乐活人生

A Melodic Life

游走在喀什街头，悠扬的弦声伴着深情的歌声把我们吸引，这是一个乐器行，墙上挂满了维吾尔族传统乐器，热瓦甫、都塔尔、弹拨尔、萨塔尔，应有尽有。弹唱者，不是别人，正是乐器的制造者兼乐器行老板。自制自卖，自弹自唱，或拨或挑，或弹或扫，你感受到的不只是音乐，同时还有维吾尔族人的乐活人生。

When walking the streets of Kashgar, the sound of melodies from a musical instrument attracts us to an instrument shop. Its walls are covered in traditional Uyghur instruments such as rawaps, dutars, tamburs, sattars, and others. The person singing and playing is in fact the maker of the instruments and the proprietor of the shop. Making and selling his own wares as he plays and sings with them, you realise what you are feeling is not just the music, but the musical lives of the Uyghurs themselves.

摄影：王晖

俄罗斯式风情

Russian Flavour

塔尔巴哈台是一个边境地区，位于新疆的西北部，简称塔城，其中塔城市是新疆距离边境线最近的城市，从市区到巴克图口岸仅有 12 公里，城市人口不到 20 万。这里大到建筑、习俗，小到面包、冰淇淋，都可以让人感受到*丝丝*俄罗斯式风情。

Tarbagatay is a border area, located in northwest Xinjiang. It's also known as Tacheng ("Ta City"), with Tacheng City itself being the city in Xinjiang closest to the border, with only 12 kilometres to the border checkpoint. The population of the city is less than 200,000. The large things like architecture and customs and smaller aspects like bread and ice cream all reflect a rich Russian flavour.

摄影：王晖

单车少年
A Lad Riding a Bike

正午过后，躲在屋里或树下歇凉是大人们不二的选择。这位阳光帅气、活力十足的单车少年可不愿闲着，他心里痒着呢。这点儿热算什么，轻快地翻身上车，他脑袋里只有一个念头，像放闸的鱼儿一样去欢快地畅游。

After noontime, the best choices are lying indoors or under the shade of a tree. This handsome lad that I see, full of energy, however, is unwilling to rest. Heat is no problem. When you can get on your bike and set out, you are as free as a fish swimming happily in a big river.

红山
Hongshan

登上红山，山色空蒙，整座城市在海市蜃楼之中。来过新疆的人都知道，乌鲁木齐这几年确实变高了，变漂亮了。有一位朋友在文中写道，站在红山望乌鲁木齐，简直就像香港一样。现在，这座城市的楼房高度已经远远超过了红山，然而这些林立的楼房，没有红山点缀，那一定是单调的。

When climbing Hongshan ("red mountain"), the scene is misty, and the entire face of the landscape appears like the mirage of a city. Those who have been to Xinjiang all know that Urumqi in recent years has grown taller and prettier. A friend wrote to me, standing on Hongshan, looking over Urumqi, is like being in Hong Kong. Now, buildings in the city are taller than Hongshan – those without views of the mountain are missing out.

143

那拉提草原
Nalati

那拉提在蒙古语中有太阳之意，传说成吉思汗西征的军队发现这片草原时，他们正遭遇风雪，饥寒交迫，这个游牧民族看到草原就像看到希望。当我看到半山上一片一片的针叶林，就像看到了当年那支军队，威武挺拔，这是远山的特色。树是山的村民，山是树的根基，而草地呢，是大地上的金毯。

Nalati means "sun" in Mongolian, and it's said that when Genghis Khan and his armies marched west, under the pressures of both cold and hunger, they found hope when they looked over this grassland. When I saw coniferous forest upon the mountain, it made me think of their army, powerful and forceful, seeing the mountain off in the distance. The trees are the residents of the mountain, the mountain is their foundation, and the grass upon it is the golden blanket covering the ground.

快乐的巴扎古丽
Having a Good Time

快乐，你说得清它是什么意思吗？在南疆的巴扎，看到这位卖香料的"巴扎古丽"花儿一样绽放的笑容，你一下就明白了。谁说快乐看不见、摸不着、留不住，它还可以传染呢，快乐其实很简单！

Can you say what happiness is? In the bazaars of southern Xinjiang, you can see smiles of the pretty girls selling incense, and you will understand. Who says that happiness is invisible, or intangible, or impossible to capture? In fact, it's infectious, and quite simple to grasp!

摄影：刘力

摄影：刘力

驾着"驴的"赶巴扎
Donkey Taxies

这是个没有谁命令就可以把维吾尔族老乡们聚拢起来的日子，主题只有一个——赶巴扎。巴扎之妙全在一个"赶"字，这里鲜有汽车的呼啸、摩托的轰鸣，偶有自行车的叮铃，常见的则是辘辘车马声。最具风情的当属"嘚儿嘚儿"而来的"驴的"，欢快地向着一个方向奔，那个简单的幸福之所——巴扎。

There is a holiday that has been established by nobody and stipulated by no law, yet can invariably gather up a large number of Uyghurs – bazaar day. People rush towards the location on cars, motorcycles and even bicycles, with horse-drawn carts also common. The most interesting are those who use donkey-taxies as a mode of transit. Everyone takes the chance when they have it to run into that most entertaining of places – the bazaar.

花树之城
City of Trees

喀什噶尔地处塔克拉玛干沙漠边缘，种树是当地维吾尔族人的传统，杏树、桃树、梨树、巴旦木、核桃树、无花果、苹果等，既防沙，也能带来可观的经济效益。因此，不管是维吾尔族人的庭院，还是田间地头、道路两旁，从三月到四月，喀什噶尔芳菲盛，千树万树烂漫开。

Kashgar borders the Taklimakan Desert, and the local Uyghurs have a custom of planting trees – apricots, peaches, pears, almonds, walnuts, figs, apples, and the like, not just to keep the sand out, but also for additional economic benefit. For this reason, whether it's in the home of a Uyghur or out in the middle of a field, along each road, from March to April, Kashgar is a fragrant place covered in the scent of myriad fruiting trees.

145

奎屯
Kuytun

奎屯，蒙古语为"寒冷"之意，尽管这个名字有些类似于东北的"村庄"，其前身确实也是一个村庄的规模，但当一个村庄变成一座城市的时候，戈壁滩上的寒风突然成了一首温柔的歌。奎屯并不寒冷，这个处于北疆金三角地带的明珠，更像一个温柔之乡，使路过者无不感到亲切。

Kuytun means "cold" in Mongolian, and although its name in Chinese resembles that of a village in the northeast of China, and it formerly resembled a village in scale. When it became a city, the cold wind from the Gobi Desert immediately turned to be a mild song. Kuytun isn't very cold, and is said to be the pearl of the Northern Xinjiang "Golden Triangle". It resembles a pleasant village, and leaves passers-by with an impression of closeness.

一种滋味：从舌尖到心田
Life's Sweet

真正的好滋味，应该是在我们的感觉里。在南疆赶巴扎的路上，我吃到了最甘甜、最美味的西瓜。一位维吾尔族老大爷，把自家的西瓜递到我手里，一位素不相识的脸颊淌汗、嗓子眼儿冒烟的"驴友"手里。那滋味，从舌尖流淌到心田，先是沁凉和甘甜，然后是熨帖和温暖。

True good flavours exist in the realm of our feelings. At the bazaars in Southern Xinjiang, I have eaten the best, sweetest watermelons. An old Uyghur man gave me a melon from his own farm, and we felt a connection, looking at each other's strange, sweaty faces. That flavour seeped into my heart, one cold and sweet, at the same time warm and friendly.

摄影：刘力

童子笑
Laughing
Children

这是一车快乐童子，刚刚和我做了"语言交换生"，我教他们普通话，他们则当我的维吾尔语老师。当我端起相机给小老师们拍照，嘴里喊出刚学到的维吾尔语"一、二、三"时，他们都笑啦！此时，镜头里的他们和镜头外的我，都简单着，明媚着，快乐着。

In a cart of happy children who I'd just been "language partners" with, me teaching them Mandarin, and them showing me some Uyghur language, I picked up my camera and told them "one, two, three" in their language – they all laughed! At this time, both them in front of the lens and me behind were all simple, bright and happy.

摄影：黄永中

147

兵团·边境
Construction and Defence

兵团生活
Military Life

兵团生活的组织程度、集中程度并不亚于城市生活，它的计划性和有序性使它和一般的乡村景观区别开来。它的时空存在虽然不像城市那样被切割成细小的碎片，但与乡村时空的自在风貌保持一定的距离。

The level of organisation of military life far exceeds that of the lives of civilians in large cities, somewhat in contrast with the rural settings in which it normally takes place. Its existence hasn't been carved up into pieces like the parcels of time and land in a large metropolis, but it still is quite distant from natural rural life.

亚军事风俗
Semi-military Customs

亚军事风俗意味什么？意味着让军人成为赤手空拳的劳动者，使农民带有"兵"或"工人"的色彩与形象，令知识分子懂得纪律和命令的重要，叫"小市民"具备集体化的意识、军事化的心理……

What is meant by "semi-military customs"? It means that the soldiers become bare-handed labourers, having the identity of both soldiers and workers, showing the intellectuals the importance of discipline and orders, and giving practical knowledge to our "young citizens" – a militarised consciousness.

边境线
The Border

新疆维吾尔自治区与蒙古、俄罗斯、哈萨克斯坦、吉尔吉斯斯坦、塔吉克斯坦、阿富汗、巴基斯坦、印度等 8 个国家接壤；陆地边境线长达 5700 多公里，占中国陆地边境线的四分之一，是中国面积最大、陆地边境线最长、毗邻国家最多的省区。

The Xinjiang Autonomous Region borders Mongolia, Russia, Kazakhstan, Kyrgyzstan, Tajikistan, Afghanistan, Pakistan and India– eight countries in total. Its land border extends for 5,700 kilometres, comprising a quarter of China's entire land border. It is the largest province or region with the longest border that borders the most countries.

家家是哨所
Watchhouses Everywhere

在中哈边境线上，有一座掩映在绿荫丛中的院落，一排平房顶上飘扬着鲜艳的五星红旗——这就是地处塔城地区农九师一六三团的民兵哨所。驻扎在边境线上的连队职工，可谓家家是哨所，人人是哨兵。

On the Kazakh Border, there is a compound which lies in the shade, a row of bungalows with five-starred red flags upon each roof. This is the site of the militia sentry post of the 163rd regiment of the Tacheng Area Ninth Agricultural Division. Of workers of the company positioned near the border, it can be said that every household is a sentry post, and everyone is a sentry.

小白杨哨所
Xiaobaiyang Watchhouse

小白杨哨所原名塔斯提哨所，位于塔城地区裕民县中哈边界，是著名军旅歌曲《小白杨》的原创地。20 世纪 70 年代，一名战士从家乡带来几棵小白杨树苗，栽在营房边。在与干旱、风沙、严寒的对抗中，有一棵小白杨顽强地活了下来，伴随着战士们守卫边疆。

The Xiaobaiyang Watchhouse was originally called the Tasti Watchhouse. Situated on the Kazakh-Chinese border in Yumin County, it is where the military song Xiaobaiyang ("small poplar") originated. In the 1970s, a soldier brought a few white poplar seedlings from his home village and planted them near the barracks. One of the poplars survived drought, wind, sand, and bitter cold and became a symbol of resoluteness to the soldiers stationed there.

八千湘女上天山
Calling for Reinforcements

20 世纪 50 年代初，为边疆的长治久安，为解决驻疆解放军的婚姻问题，王震将军给当时的湖南省委第一书记黄克诚写信，希望能在湖南招收志愿戍边的女兵。于是，从 1950 年到 1952 年的三年时间里，两批约 8000 名湘女志愿参军进疆，谱写出八千湘女上天山的历史篇章。

In the early 1950s, in order to protect the border of Xinjiang and solve gender disparity problems in the military, General Wang Zhen wrote to the First Party Secretary of Hunan Province, Huang Kecheng, asking him to recruit female volunteers for border defence. As a result, from 1950 to 1952, two rounds of about 8,000 female volunteers signed up for the military and travelled to the border region, creating thousands of interesting stories.

边防的魅力
The Allure of the Border

一位在北塔山守了十几年边防的连长转业到一座城市，好长一段时间里，他不太适应，若有所失。有一次他喝醉了酒，仿佛一觉醒来，不知身在何处。他左顾右盼，不停地说："我的士兵呢？我的羊群呢？"一个军人正是这样，他忍受不了空空荡荡、心无所归的生活，忍受不了浸透在城市旋涡中心的彻骨的寂寞。

A company commander who stood guard over the border for more than a decade at Baytik Mountain entered civilian life in a city, but had a hard time adjusting. One time, when he drank too much, it was as if he had awoken without knowing his own whereabouts. Looking about, he kept asking: "Where are my troops? Where is my flock?" Military men are like this – they can't have nothing to do or live an empty life, and may find themselves lonely and lost in a big city.

开国大典的国旗手李冠英
Standard-Bearer Li Guanying

1949 年 10 月 1 日，开国大典阅兵式上，擎着八一军旗、紧随聂荣臻总指挥身后的掌旗官是国民党军"重庆舰"的起义人员李冠英。随着岁月变迁与动荡，他从大连、兰州、乌鲁木齐波折辗转到和布克赛县，因为低调、无所求，一直不为人所知。2000 年李冠英在和布克赛去世。

On October 10, 1949, at the inaugural military parade, following commander-in-chief Nie Rongzhen was standard-bearer Li Guanying, participant in the uprising on the KMT ship Chongqing. As the years went by, he went to Dalian, Lanzhou, Urumqi and finally Hoboksar. As he was low-key and undemanding, he remained unknown. He died in 2000 in Hoboksar.

军垦第一犁
The First Ploughs for Reclamation

在新疆石河子市中心游憩广场内，有一座"军垦第一犁"雕群。20 世纪 50 年代初期，第一代新疆生产建设兵团人响应党的号召，扎根天山南北，铸剑为犁，屯垦戍边。为使后人不忘这段历史，新疆生产建设兵团人特立"军垦第一犁"雕群。该雕群于 1985 年 9 月落成。

In the park in the middle of Shihezi City, there is a group of statues called the "First Ploughs for Reclamation". In the early 1950s, the first Xinjiang Production and Construction Corps responded to the Party's call, coming from both north and south with ploughs as their weapons to expand usable land area. In order to remember them, the statues were erected in September 1985.

昭苏边境的格登碑
The Gurden Stele

格登，蒙古语"突起的后脑骨"之意。从格登山俯瞰下去，是哈萨克斯坦共和国的一个村庄，一旁的河流就是国界。格登碑仁立于格登山上，为"平定准噶尔勒铭格登山之碑"，碑文由乾隆皇帝亲撰。1871年，沙俄侵占伊犁，格登山被强行划入俄国版图。后左宗棠平息叛乱，收回伊犁的大部分失地，其中包括格登山。

"Gurden" means "protruding occipital bone" (at the back of the head), in Mongolian. Looking down from Mount Gurden, one sees a village in the Republic of Kazakhstan, with the nearby river being the national boundary. The Gurden Stele has stood for a long time upon the mountain, and bears an inscription commemorating the pacification of the Junggar, which was written by Emperor Qianlong. In 1871, when Tsarist Russia occupied Yili, Mount Gurden was drawn by the Russians into the maps of their own territory. Afterwards, when Zuo Zongtang quelled the rebellion, most of the area of Yili was recovered, including Gurden Mountain.

天山深处的英雄路：独库公路
A Road Through Tianshan

20世纪70年代，为修建独库公路，解放军某工程兵部队有168名官兵献出宝贵生命。这已不仅仅是一条路，它凝聚了太多的人类精神和自然内涵，数万人历经艰险十年成就。它的修建过程，在任何时候，都足以震慑每一名过客。小说《天山深处的大兵》讲述的就是这条路以及修路的工程兵。

In the 1970's, in the process of building the Duku Highway, an engineering corps of the PLA saw 168 soldiers sacrifice their precious lives. It is not just a road, but rather a concentration of human spirit and natural intension. It is the culmination of the hard efforts of tens of thousands of people. The process of the construction itself was quite a sight, enough to inspire awe in many passers-by. In the novel *Deep in the Tianshan Mountains*, the story of the highway and those who built it is told.

地窝子
Ground Nest

地窝子是一种半地下的简陋居所。在地面以下挖约一米深的坑，四周用土坯或砖瓦垒起约半米的矮墙，顶上用椽子、树枝、草叶、泥巴覆盖。地窝子可以抵御风沙，并且冬暖夏凉。20世纪50年代，新疆生产建设兵团很多人在地窝子里生活。不过，现在地窝子已经很难看到了。

A "ground nest" is a kind of simple, half-underground dwelling. After digging a pit approximately one metre deep, a short wall of about one-half metre is constructed around it, and then rafters, tree branches, grasses and mud are used to form a roof. It can resist wind and sand, and is cool in the summer and warm in the winter. In the 1950s, many of the members of the Xinjiang Production and Construction Corps lived in these structures, but they are hard to find today.

农工
Farmers or Workers?

兵团人，工乎？农乎？不知所云。很多农工都不记得自己是工人，干农活好手一把，话桑麻头头是道。只有到发工资时、退休时，才恍然大悟：噢，咱也是个工人。

Are members of the military corps workers, or famers? One may say it's hard to say. A lot of the farmers don't view themselves as workers, concentrating on doing their work instead. Only when they receive their salaries and retire do they realise: "oh, I am a worker after all."

肖尔布拉克
Schorburak

20世纪80年代，有个电影叫《肖尔布拉克》，讲了个汽车司机的爱情故事。其实肖尔布拉克是个地名，是兵团农四师72团所在地，新疆最有名的酒"伊力特"就出在这里。肖尔布拉克哈萨克语意思是"盐碱滩"。这个曾经的盐碱滩，被兵团人改造成田畴广阔、风景优美的酒城，它的酒香已飘溢到国内外了。

In the 1980s, a film called *Schorburak* told a love story that centred around a truck driver. In fact, Schorburak is a place name, where the 72nd Regiment of the Fourth Agricultural Division of the Xinjiang Production and Construction Corps is stationed. The most famous liquor of Xinjiang, "Yilite", is produced here. Schorburak means "salt marsh" in Kazakh, as the area previously was one. It was converted into farmland by members of the corps, and liquor produced by the city is enjoyed both in China and abroad.

我是一个兵
I Am a Soldier

"我是一个兵，来到了新疆省，领导为了照顾我，发了个老毡筒，哎嘿，拖也拖不动，走也走不成，敌人胆敢来侵犯，我就给他一毡筒……"这是20世纪五六十年代流传于兵团的改编版歌曲——《我是一个兵》。

"I'm a solider, I've come to Xinjiang, my leader takes care of me, giving me a felt tube – oh no, it can't be dragged or carried – should the enemy come, I'll hit them with this tube." These are the lyrics rewritten to a popular military song of the 1950s, called *I Am a Soldier*.

自嘲
A Self-deprecating Joke

"是军队没军费，是政府要纳税，是企业办社会，是农民入工会。"这是早年兵团人的自嘲，也是兵团党军政企合一的特殊社会组织的生动写照。

"We are a military unit, but without military fund; we are a government department, but have to pay tax; we are an enterprise, but have to work for the society; we are farmers, but we join in a trade union." This is a self-deprecating joke on the part of the military, as well as a snapshot of the structure of the interactions between the corps, the Party, the military, the government, and the enterprise.

新疆客新疆人
Guests and Locals

古书云"自外至者皆为客"。有这样一群人，来自中国各地，汇集到新疆。这些各行业的精英，为了新疆的发展、稳定、和谐而来，甘愿把汗水挥洒在新疆的热土，把论文书写进新疆的大地，把智慧奉献给新疆的民生，这个群体就是援疆干部。"三年援疆路，一生新疆情"，他们已"化客为主"，成为地道的新疆人。

Ancient books state that "all who come from afar are guests". There are people from all over China now in Xinjiang. These elites of various fields work hard on the hot land of Xinjiang to ensure its development, stability and peace, writing about the place and contributing their wisdom. These people are the cadres that support Xinjiang. "Three years working in Xinjiang and it is in you for life" – these people are generally assimilated into the local life and turn into real Xinjiang people.

白杨、红柳、雪松都知道兵团
The Military Corps Is Known by All

来新疆，车过星星峡，你就进入兵团了；走新疆，看到无垠绿洲，你就进入兵团了；游新疆，瞧见界碑边的牧群，你就进入兵团了……新疆有多大，兵团就有多大。这里的绿洲、草原、山河知道兵团，白杨、红柳、雪松也都知道兵团。

Coming to Xinjiang, when you drive through Xingxingxia (Star Gorge), you become part of the Xinjiang Production and Reconstruction Corps. Walking around in Xinjiang, when you see an oasis, you become part of the corps. Travelling in Xinjiang, when you catch sight of a flock of sheep, you become part of the corps – the corps is as large as Xinjiang is. The oases, prairies, mountains and rivers all know the corps, as do the poplars, willows, and pines.

摄影：双元

守墓的老兵
Keeping Watch over Fallen Comrades

乔尔玛独库公路筑路烈士陵园，一个老兵为战友守了二十多年陵。1980 年冬天，筑路部队被困在零下 30 度的天山深处，为与指挥部取得联系，陈俊贵奉命随班长、副班长求援。在雪山爬行了三天三夜，班长和副班长相继牺牲，陈俊贵掉下悬崖被牧民所救。为陪伴牺牲的战友，复员回乡的陈俊贵又回到这里，看守陵园。

At Cholma, there is a cemetery for those who perished during the construction of the Duku Highway, where an old soldier stood guard for more than twenty years. In the winter of 1980, the construction team was trapped deep in the mountains with temperatures dropping to 30 degrees below zero – in order to establish contact with superiors, Chen Jungui followed his squad leader and vice-squad leader to seek assistance. They trekked through the snowy mountains for 3 days and 3 nights, during which both his squad leader and vice-squad leader perished. He fell down a precipice and was rescued by herders. In order to respect his fallen comrades, after being demobilized and sent home, Chen Jungui returned to the site to hold vigil over the tombs.

兵团的维吾尔族人
Uyghurs as Corps Members

问：你哪个民族？答：维吾尔族。问：哪儿的人？答：兵团人。问：凭啥说是兵团人？答：哎！我骗你干啥？要不我给你唱段豫剧。说完，张口唱道：刘大哥说话理太偏，谁说女子不如男。男子打仗到边关，女子在家守家园……有板有眼，韵味十足。于是，问者信了。

Q: What is your ethnicity?
A: I am a Uyghur.
Q: Where are you from?
A: From the corps.
Q: As if I would believe that?
A: Why would I lie to you? Let me show you some Henan Opera:
Brother Liu is biased, saying girls aren't as good as boys.
Boys go to the border to stand guard, and girls stand guard at home...
The performance was authentic, and the questioner was convinced.

节省布料的军装
Saving Cloth

60 年前的一场对话："哎，那个人嘛太有意思了。""咋了？""衣服上领子没有，口袋也没有。""噢，兵团人嘛！"20 世纪 50 年代，新疆生产建设兵团官兵的衣服上没有领子、口袋。布料都被节省下来，捐给国家建工厂了。

A conversation 60 years ago: "Oh, that guy's too funny." "How so?" "He has neither pockets nor collar on his clothes." "Oh, he must be a member of the corps!" In the 1950s, the uniforms for the Xinjiang Production and Construction Corps were made without collars or pockets. The material was saved and donated for other construction purposes.

军垦第一哨
The First
Sentry

被誉为"军垦第一哨"的是新疆生产建设兵团某连队，这里地理位置特殊，地处特克斯河与苏木拜河交汇处。清朝曾在这里设置口岸，主要开展边境贸易与地方贸易。1963 年昭苏县、巩留县等地的苏侨遣返人员从此通过。现在由兵团民兵巡逻执勤与驻守。

Known as "the first sentry among the reclaimers", a division of the Xinjiang Production and Construction Corps is located in a geographically special place, where the Tekes and Sumubai Rivers meet. The Qing Dynasty established a border port here, in order to facilitate cross-border as well as local commerce. In 1963, the people from Zhaosu, Gongliu and other counties with Soviet ancestry passed through here. The point is now patrolled and administered by the militia of the Xinjiang Production and Construction Corps.

年轻的城
A Young City

"我到过许多地方，数这个城市最年轻"，这是艾青写给石河子的诗句。石河子原本是古老的游牧地。1950 年，中国人民解放军第 22 兵团（后改为新疆生产建设兵团），到此开荒生产。经过 60 多年的开发、建设，现在这里已经是一个中等规模的现代化城市，并成为联合国"人居环境改善良好范例城市"。

"I've been to many places, and this city is the youngest" – these are the words of a poem written by Ai Qing for the city of Shihezi. Shihezi was originally a pasture. In 1950, the 22nd Regiment of the People's Liberation Army (later the Xinjiang Production and Construction Corps) converted the land. After more than 60 years of development and construction, the city is now a mid-size modern metropolis, and was awarded the United Nations Award for Best Practices to Improve Living Environment.

**张仲瀚的
"吃喝玩乐"**
Zhang
Zhonghan

张仲瀚是新疆生产建设兵团的主要创建者之一。有人把他为兵团建设所做的贡献归结为"吃喝玩乐"。他"吃"出了乌鲁木齐著名的饭店"百花村"；"喝"出了名酒"伊力特"；"玩"出了早年兵团的"八大剧团"；"乐"，在他为文学家、艺术家们营造的宽松氛围，《边疆处处赛江南》等文艺作品从兵团走向全国。

Zhang Zhonghan was one of the major innovators of the Xinjiang Production and Construction Corps. Some people say that his contributions to the Corps are represented in four aspects: eating, drinking, theatrical performing and literary writing. In terms of "eating", he contributed a most famous restaurant "Baihuacun" in Urumqi; in "drinking", he contributed a famous liquor brand "Yilite"; in "theatrical performing", he contributed the "Eight Opera Troupes"; and in "literary writing", he created a more liberal environment for literary writers and artists, contributing many excellent art and literary works, such as *Xinjiang Is Beautiful and Plentiful,* a famous song which has spread from the Corps in Xinjiang to all other places in China.

艾青在兵团
Ai Qing and the Corps

诗人艾青在 1957 年被错划为"右派"，为保护他，王震将军邀请他到新疆。艾青一家在石河子垦区安了家，在新疆生活了十几年，1977 年回到北京。在新疆时，他创作了《年轻的城》《从南泥湾到莫索湾》等一部部力作。在那个年代，新疆建设兵团保护了一大批因政治问题而受迫害的优秀人才。

Poet Ai Qing was declared as "Rightist" in 1957, and in order to protect him, General Wang Zhen invited him to Xinjiang. He lived in the reclaimed area of Shihezi for more than a decade, returning to Beijing in 1977. While he was in Xinjiang, he wrote *Young City,* and other works. During those years, the Xinjiang Production and Reconstruction Corps protected a large number of talented people from being persecuted by political movements.

兵团中的特殊群体
Special Groups in the Corps

在那个物资极为匮乏的年代，有人说，只要在新疆，就不会饿死，就能吃饱。所以那时的新疆，特别是兵团，自流来疆、参加兵团工作的是个很大的群体，有百万之众。几十年下来，他们和老军垦一起，在保卫边疆、建设边疆中，付出了不少汗水与鲜血，他们的后代，已经成为实际意义上的新疆人。

When resources were extremely short, people say that only in Xinjiang could you have enough food to eat. For this reason, large numbers of people flowed to Xinjiang to join the Xinjiang Production and Construction Corps, with a large group of almost a million individuals coming to participate. Decades later, they reside in the reclaimed areas, protecting the borders and building the areas up with their own blood and sweat. Their descendants can already be called Xinjiangese in the true sense.

大漠"老兵村"
A Village of Old Soldiers

1949 年 12 月，解放军从阿克苏向和田进军，行程 1580 公里，徒步穿越塔克拉玛干大沙漠，创造了一个奇迹。到达和田后，有 600 多名官兵脱下军装，在昆仑山下屯垦戍边，成为建设兵团的一分子。六十多年过去，很多人将生命留在了这里，几位健在的老兵依然生活在这里，这里被誉为"老兵村"。

In December 1949, the PLA drove from Aksu to Hotan, more than 1,580 kilometres, crossing the Taklimakan Desert to effect a miracle. When arriving at Hotan, more than 600 PLA soldiers removed their uniforms and stationed themselves at the foot of the Kunlun Mountains, becoming a part of the Production and Construction Corps. More than 60 years later, many people have chosen to stay, with some of the original arrivals still inhabiting the village they built – sometimes called "a veterans' village".

图木舒克
Tumushuke

图木舒克是一个很小的城市，只有十多年的建城历史，可能在全国没有几个人知道她，许多年前她还只是新疆生产建设兵团的小海子灌区，这几年忽然之间就冒出个图木舒克市，让人惊奇，更让人感动。

Constructed only a bit more than a decade ago, Tumushuke is a very small city. There are few people who know of it in China, as up until recently it was just a small irrigated area constructed by the Xinjiang Production and Construction Corps. In just a few years a city appeared, both surprising and moving people.

沙漠绿岛：阿拉尔
Alar: A Green Island

阿拉尔的维吾尔语意思是"绿色的岛"，实际上这里并没有什么岛，以前也并不"绿"。流淌千年的阿克苏河、和田河和叶尔羌河汇流于此，她们见证了这片土地在兵团人手中由万古荒原蜕变为"人造绿洲"的旷世奇迹。

Alar means "green island" in Uyghur, even though the city has no island, and previously wasn't at all "green". The Aksu River, Hotan River and Yarkant River all meet here, and with the help of the Xinjiang Production and Construction Corps, it became a veritable man-made oasis.

红其拉甫
Khonjirap

在"世界屋脊"帕米尔高原，有一个古老、神秘、充满传奇色彩的山谷，因为严重缺氧，常年大风，气候寒冷，被人称之为"血谷"或"死亡之谷"。相传张骞出使西域时曾经过这里，唐玄奘西天取经也由此返回中国。现在这里是中国与巴基斯坦唯一的陆路口岸与通道。

On the Pamir Plateau, the "roof of the world", there is an old and mysterious mountain valley. Due to the lack of oxygen, and year-round strong winds, as well as low temperatures and humidity, it has been called "blood valley" or "the valley of death". According to legend, Zhang Qian passed through the valley on his journey to the west, and Tang Xuanzang also passed through here on his way back to China. Khonjirap is currently the only border crossing between China and Pakistan.

与边境有关

It's about the Border

新疆生产建设兵团组建于 1954 年。兵团人前往边境地区代替边民耕种、放牧、管理，称之为代耕、代牧、代管，就这样，一"代"就是半个多世纪。其实，这"代"也就是"守"——守边境，守国土，守尊严，守稳定。

The Xinjiang Production and Construction Corps was established in 1954. Its members flowed towards the border areas, farming, herding and administering for the local people. This "custodianship" was fated to go on for more than half a century. In fact, "custodianship" can be more appropriately called "protection" – of the border, of Chinese territory, of dignity, of stability.

绿色原野：可克达拉

Kekedala

"等到千里雪消融，等到草原上送来春风，可克达拉改变了模样，耶，姑娘就会来伴我的琴声。"一曲《草原之夜》让我们知道了可克达拉这个地方。可克达拉在哪儿？在伊犁，是兵团一座美丽的小镇。那美丽的夜色，那美妙的琴声，那草原上送信的邮寄员，当然，还有那令人神往的姑娘，构成了人们无限的遐想。

"After the thousand miles of snow have melted, after the winds of springs have come over the plains, Kekedala will have changed, and girls will come to accompany my music." The song *Night on the Grassland* brought Kekedala into the public consciousness. Where is Kekedala? In Yili, where it is a beautiful little village made of the corps. The beautiful night colours and alluring musical sounds, the postmen on the prairie delivering letters, and of course the breathtaking girls all make the place quite memorable.

给黄牛立的墓碑

Stele for an Ox

在博尔塔拉边防上，有一座给黄牛立的墓碑，因为它为战士拉了十几年水。还有一座给军犬"阿黄"立的墓碑，因为阿黄十三年来，昼夜护院，通风报信，巡逻探路，露宿放哨，屡建功绩，被誉为"无言战友"。

At a border station in Bortala, there is a stele erected to an ox, as it fetched water for more than a decade for troops there. There is also a stele to a military dog, "Ah Huang", as for 13 years it protected the compound, sounded alarm, went on searches, stood sentry over barracks and helped out with all kinds of tasks, winning itself the name "unspeaking comrade".

沙枣花香的女人

A Perfumed Lady

香妃是一位传奇女子，她的维吾尔名字叫伊帕尔汗。她的香味是沙枣花的味。一个香喷喷的妃子，她决不会雷同于别的美人——她是用香味来征服皇帝和世界的，同时也征服了后人的记忆和想象。

The fragrant concubine is a legendary female by the Uyghur name of Iparhan. Her fragrance was that of russian olive flowers. As a fragrant concubine, she was unique in that she used her fragrance to conquer the emperor and the world, as well as later people's memories and imaginations.

和云说话的人

Speaking to the Clouds

早上，在喀那斯图瓦村，遇见一个人靠在羊圈的栏杆上，仰头对天说话。我问翻译，翻译说："他早晨就醉了，他在说头顶的云，他让云'过去''过去'。"因为云的影子落在他家羊圈上了，刚下过雨，他想让羊圈棚上的草早些晒干。

In the morning, in a Tuva village in Kanas, I saw a person leaning against a sheep pen, head to the sky, talking to the heavens. I asked the interpreter what he was saying, and he told me "He's already drunk in the morning, and is talking to the clouds. He's telling them 'pass, pass'." As the clouds were shading his sheep pen and it had just rained, he wanted them to pass quickly so that the grass would dry more quickly.

摄影：韩连赟

**最封闭的村
庄：牙通古斯**

Most Isolated
Village

牙通古斯意思是"野猪出没的地方"，沙漠公路没有修通之前，它是中国最封闭的村庄之一。从民丰到牙通古斯村，骑骆驼要走3天。20世纪70年代，一位姓钟的江苏男子曾经流浪到此，与一位维吾尔族姑娘结了婚，成为村里的第一位汉族人。

Yatonggusi means "a place where boars appear". Before the desert highway was constructed, it was one of China's most isolated villages – it took three days on camelback from Minfeng to Yatonggusi at the time. In the 1970s, a man surnamed Zhong from Jiangsu travelled there, and married a Uyghur girl, becoming the first Han Chinese resident.

163

狼用尿解围
Fight or Flee

据北塔山牧场的牧民说，狼在无路可逃时，会用两条后腿紧夹尾巴把尿尿出，迅速甩进对手的眼睛，然后趁其慌乱之际迅速逃跑。怪不得狼平时总是紧夹着尾巴，原来是为了在身陷绝境时甩出狼尿解围。

A herder from Baytik Mountain said that when a wolf is cornered, it will use its two legs to grab its tail and urinate, and then flick it in the opponent's eyes so that it may quickly flee. This explains why wolves do this with their tails – they have a hidden weapon to use in times of desperation.

**"微型水库"
云杉**
Spruce:
A "Mini
Reservoir"

云杉是阿勒泰林区最常见的树种。一株云杉就像一把收拢的巨伞，拔地而起，直上云霄，堪称"望天树"和"摩天树"。有人曾赞美白杨的挺拔，其实云杉比白杨站得更直。云杉能活 400 岁左右，长到六七十米高。一株成熟的云杉就是一座"微型水库"，蓄水量达 2.5 吨。

The spruce is the most common tree in the Altay forests. A spruce resembles a drawn-in umbrella, stuck directly into the ground and extending into the skies. They are thus called "observer" trees or "skyscrapers". People have praised white poplars for being tall and strong, but actually spruce is even more so. Spruce can live more than 400 years, and grow to 60 or 70 metres in height. A mature spruce can be called a "mini reservoir" as it holds up to 2.5 tons of water.

老温的弟弟
Mr. Wen's Brother

在禾木的那个带门的桥跟前，有个卖工艺品的老温，老温是汉族。他讲过一个故事：一年冬天，他弟弟把一个喝醉了睡在雪地里的图瓦老汉送回家，老汉酒醒以后，把三个女儿叫到跟前，让老温的弟弟挑一个。就这样，老温的弟弟就留在了禾木，娶老汉的二女儿当了老婆。

In front of a bridge in Hemu, there is an old man named Wen – he is Han Chinese. He told a story to me: one year in winter, his brother brought a drunk Tuva man who had passed out in the snow back home. After the man regained sobriety, he called his three daughters out and told Wen's brother to pick one. Just like that, Wen and his brother stayed in Hemu, and the second daughter became his brother's wife.

奥尔德克
Ordik: A Normal Man

他是一个小人物，然而却是发现楼兰古城和小河墓地的第一功臣。在 20 世纪初外国探险队频频出入塔里木盆地的西域探险热中，他在寻找遗失于沙漠的一把铁锹时，帮助斯文·赫定发现了楼兰。也正是他，多年后又将沃尔克·贝格曼带到了传说中有一千口棺材的小河墓地。他叫奥尔德克，一名普普通通的罗布人。

He was a minor figure, yet also the meritorious man who discovered both the Loulan City and the Xiaohe Tomb Site. At the start of the 20th century, foreign expeditions entered the Tarim Basin one after another to conduct searches, and when looking for a lost spade in the desert, he helped Sven Anders Hedin to discover Loulan. It was also he who years later took Warlock Bergman to the famed site of the Xiaohe Tombs. His name was Ordik, a normal Lop Nur man.

甘英西使
The Emissary

《后汉书·西域传》载，公元 97 年班超派甘英出使大秦（古罗马），到达波斯湾而"望洋兴叹"，半途而废。康有为说中国近代文明的不发达源于甘英的怯弱。甘英西行，何故东返？是他的怯弱，是安息（波斯）商人的欺骗，是战事的影响，还是慑于海妖的传说？但客观地说，甘英西使推动了中西各国的友好交往。

In *The History of the Later Han Dynasty – Chronicles of the West*, it is written that in the year 97, Ban Chao dispatched Gan Ying to ancient Rome. He was taken aback by the site of the Persian Gulf on arrival, and gave up his journey halfway. Some have blamed his lack of resolution for a subsequent lack of progress in the development of Chinese culture. Why did he turn back from his journey to the west? Was he timid, was he cheated by Persian merchants, was it due to war, or was it because he was scared to cross the sea? Objectively speaking, he made great strides for progress in the area of Sino-Western relations.

165

摄影：黄永中

公主堡
A Home for a Princess

相传大汉的某位公主远嫁给西极的一位国王，恰逢战乱，道路不通，被困葱岭之上，可此时公主却怀孕了，既不便前行，也不能回国，只好筑城建堡于大山之巅，这就是公主堡的传说。公主之所以怀孕，传说是公主梦中与下凡的太阳神有过一宿情缘，故而塔吉克族人认定自己为"汉日天种"。

The princess of a Han emperor married the king of some far-western kingdom, but the region was war-torn, the roads impassable, and she was trapped at Congling. By this time, she was already pregnant, and couldn't move, nor return to her own kingdom. A castle was built on the peak of the mountain, and this is the legend of the princess' castle. The legend holds that the princess was impregnated after the god of the sun descended from heaven, and for this reason the Tajiks believe themselves to be descendants of the sun.

会报警的树木
Alarmed Wood

云杉木在新疆的矿井里常被用作坑木，当它快要断裂时，会提前一两个月吱吱作响，是一种心有灵犀、会发警报的树。

Spruce wood is used frequently in Xinjiang as a support material for mineshafts – it will make cracking noises a month or two before it fails structurally, which serve as a kind of early warning system.

断裂的文明
Interrupted
Civilization

4000 年前，一群神秘的人来到罗布泊地区，几百年后，他们神秘消失了。又过了 1500 年，这里再度出现了繁荣的楼兰国。文明的延续和断裂，似乎成了塔里木盆地历史的常态。

4,000 years ago, a group of mysterious figures came to the Lop Nur region, and then mysteriously disappeared. After 1,500 years, the flourishing Loulan Kingdom appeared here. The continuation and interruption of civilization seems to be a common occurrence in the history of the Tarim Basin.

"七"之谜
The Mystery
of "Seven"

小河墓地位于罗布沙漠之中，那里各种器物上充斥着对数字"七"的崇拜的痕迹。例如出土的木雕人头的鼻梁上有七道花纹，矗立的木桩上也刻着七道花纹，出土干尸佩戴的手链是七圈，每口棺材陪葬的木梳、木别针、木蛇等不多不少也是七个。数字"七"似乎大有深意，我们可借此窥视小河人精神世界的底层隐私。

The Xiaohe Tomb Site is situated in the Lop Desert, where all manner of objects remain as traces of a kind of worship of the number "seven". For example, on unearthed wooden carvings of human heads, there are seven tracks of patterns on the ridge of the nose, seven tracks of patterns upon the wooden pillars, seven bracelets upon the arms of unearthed mummies, with each coffin having wooden combs, pins and snakes – in sets of seven, too.

"酸奶"泉
Yoghurt Spring

新疆有许多古怪的地方，让人难以捉摸，在乌恰县托云乡，有一眼喝上去像酸奶的泉水。它不仅水是酸甜酸甜的，而且是彩色的，这就是大自然鬼斧神工的泉华地貌奇观。它有点像四川的黄龙，只是略小一些。

Xinjiang has a number of ancient, odd places which are hard for people to fathom. In Tuoyun Village of Wuqia County, there is a spring that seems to emit yoghurt. Not only is the liquid sweet and sour, the spring is also coloured – a true oddity sculpted by the forces of nature. It resembles the Huanglong site in Sichuan, except that it is smaller.

公主私情
Princess Tactics

唐朝时期，中原蚕种曾严禁外传。于阗王使计，向中原公主求婚。王子密语公主将蚕桑种藏于帽中，躲过层层盘查。此后蚕桑广播西域。

During the Tang Dynasty, it was forbidden to transport the silkworms of the Central Plains region elsewhere. The king of Khotan sent an emissary to the Central Plains region to ask marriage of a princess. The prince secretly had the princess conceal cocoons in her headgear, and after eluding the investigators, silkworms were successfully transported to the Western Region.

冯夫人定西域
Madam Feng

她是卑微侍女，却生性聪慧、能言善辩、成熟稳健。她以汉朝使节身份斡旋西域，传播汉文化，被西域贵族尊称为"冯夫人"。她，就是中国历史上第一位女外交家冯嫽。

She was a lowly servant girl, but quite clever, able to speak eloquently, and steady in form. She went to the Western Region under the identity of a diplomatic envoy, and promulgated Han culture, coming to be respectfully called "Madam Feng" by the peoples of the Western Region. She was the first female Chinese diplomat in history – Feng Liao.

新疆的图瓦人
The Tuva

有人说，生存于新疆白哈巴一带的图瓦人，是蒙古族的一个分支，是随成吉思汗征战欧亚的一部分图瓦士兵繁衍的后裔。图瓦人认为自己的祖先是成吉思汗，至今每家每户挂有成吉思汗画像。因为这里风景优美，所以人们称他们是居住在"神的后花园"里的人。

The Tuva are a branch of the Mongolian people. Some say that the Tuva surviving in Baihaba are a branch of the descendants of Genghis Khan's soldiers who travelled through the region. The Tuva believe themselves to be descendants of Genghis Khan, and every Tuva family in present day hangs a picture of him in their house. As the local scenery is beautiful, some people have said that they are the people who live in "heaven's garden".

狼背羊
The Wolf

北塔山牧场的一位牧民见过狼背着羊跑的场景：一只狼趁人不备，冲进羊群。狼的 4 颗长牙像刀子一样划向一只羊的脖子，羊随即倒了。狼用力把羊甩到了背上，背起来便跑。牧民们怒不可遏地追赶狼。狼跑到山坡下无力攀爬上去，才扔下羊跑了。

A herder from the pastures of Baytik Mountain told a story of a wolf running away with a sheep on its back: A wolf made a surprise attack on a flock of sheep, its four sharp teeth cutting into one of the sheep's necks like a knife. The sheep collapsed, and the wolf shouldered it, carrying it as it ran. The herder angrily pursued it, and when the wolf reached the foot of the mountain, it was unable to climb up, and had no choice but to leave its kill behind, fleeing.

草原守护神
Protector of the Grassland

在新疆阿勒泰草原和昭苏草原上，石人是不可不看的一大历史人文景观。石人是欧亚草原世界的标识，数千年来它们静穆地守护在墓前，庄严而不可侵犯。它们面向东方——那是太阳升起的方向，似乎在唤起时光缝隙里的神秘力量……

On the Altay and Zhaosu prairies of Xinjiang, stone figures are an unmissable historical site and cultural heritage. Stone figures are marks of Eurasian grassland civilisations, having held their positions on the prairies for millennia. They face the east – where the sun rises, as if they are calling on the mystical power of the gaps in time.

摄影：韩连赟

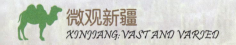
喀纳斯湖怪
The Monster of Kanas Lake

关于"湖怪"，当地传说久矣。曾有湖边饮水的牛羊被"湖怪"吞噬。这个中国湖水最深、湖光变幻莫测的喀纳斯，曾引来大量科学工作者踏勘。一个差强人意的解释是："湖怪"是学名叫"哲罗鲑"的大红鱼。

There are long-standing legends about the "lake monster". There have been purported incidents of sheep and cattle drinking at the edge of the lake being swallowed by it. The deep, dark water of Kanas Lake has long attracted many scientific researchers who come to do surveys. A passable explanation is that the "lake monster" is actually a Hucho taimen – a large, carnivorous fish that lives in deep water.

胡杨木
Poplars

罗布人使用的独木舟——卡盆，是用整棵粗大的胡杨树干掏空而制的。孔雀河古墓沟的"太阳墓"用竖埋的木桩构成太阳和放射的光芒，用的也是胡杨木。列入 2004 年中国十大考古发现的小河墓地，大量的船棺和彩绘立柱，用的也是胡杨……现在的胡杨树，则主要用于审美。

The Lop Nur people use dugout canoes – kapen. They are made out of a single, large poplar which has been carved out. The "Sun Tombs" of Old Tomb Gorge at the Konqi River use large poles driven into the ground to reflect sunlight and form the structure of the site, also from poplar trees. Added to the list of the ten greatest archaeological sites in China in 2004, the Xiaohe Tomb Site features a large number of canoe-coffins and painted poles – also poplar. Poplar trees are now mainly used for their aesthetic value.

摄影：双元

蹲在鱼身上钓鱼
Fishing on a Fish

传说，一个人有一天蹲在喀纳斯湖边的一块石头上钓鱼，一上午过去，没有钓到一条鱼。他很沮丧，回到岸上快快然准备回家。这时眼前出现的情景令他大吃一惊，那块石头突然动了，慢慢向湖中移动过去。他仔细一看，原来自己蹲了一上午的地方并非是石头，而是一条大鱼。

A story says that one day someone sat by a rock near Kanas Lake fishing, and didn't catch a fish all morning. Dejected, he returned to the bank and prepared to head home. At this time a large surprise appeared in front of him – the stone suddenly shifted, and started to move towards the water. Looking closely at the stone, he found that where he had been squatting all morning was not a rock, but a large fish.

吃羊的湖怪
Monster in the Lake

传说，有一天，一群羊在喀纳斯湖边吃草，湖的上空是蓝天白云，湖四周长满嫩绿的青草，看上去是一幅具有旷古意味的景象。突然，湖水直立溅开，一个身影模糊的东西从湖中探出身，将几只羊卷入湖中。待牧羊人赶来，湖面上只剩下一圈圈涟漪不停地扩散开，又聚拢来，剩下的羊惊恐得咩咩叫成一片。

It is said that one day, a group of lambs were grazing along the bank of Kanas Lake, as white clouds floated overhead against a blue sky, and resplendent greenery grew all around the lake – a classic scene. Suddenly, a disturbance in the lake sent water flying, and an unclear figure emerged, ensnaring several sheep and dragging them into the lake. When the herder hurried over, all that remained to see was the disturbed water, ripples spreading – the other sheep only gathered and bleated in terror.

狼哺乌孙王
Raised by a Wolf

乌孙国是东汉时期游牧民族在伊犁河流域建立的邦国。传说乌孙曾被月氏所火，逃亡匈奴。乌孙灭于月氏后，匈奴单于惊见草丛中被母狼哺乳的乌孙王子昆莫，以为神助，收养在侧。昆莫渐大，斩月氏，领其地，复辟故国。乌孙遂成为汉西域强盛的邦国。

The Wusun Kingdom was a nomadic kingdom established in the Yili River valley during the Eastern Han Dynasty. It's said that the kingdom was destroyed by the Rouzhi people, and the Wusun people fled to the Huns. After the Wusun were destroyed, Chan Yu, chief of the Huns, was surprised to see Kun Mo, prince of the Wusun, was nursed by a female wolf. Thinking this was a godsend, Chan Yu adopted Kun Mo. When he grew up, Kun Mo slaughtered the Rouzhi, recaptured Wusun territory, and re-established the kingdom. The Wusun Kingdom became one of the most powerful kingdoms in the Western Region.

天山的传说
Legend of Tianshan

传说天山是由一白一青两条巨龙变成的。白龙变成了天山后山，终年白雪皑皑，成为天山南北永不枯竭的固体水库。青龙变成了天山前山，郁郁葱葱的松林、绿草、鲜花覆盖着它，成为天山儿女优美的牧场和肥沃的农田。

Legend says that the Tianshan Mountains are composed of one white and one black dragon. The white dragon became the back mountains of the range, capped with snow all year round – the inexhaustible reservoir for both sides of the range. The black dragon became the front mountains of the range, covered in forests, grasses and flowers – a lush cradle for the sons and daughters of the range.

流星是懒汉变的
Shooting Stars Are Lazy Guys

在新疆蒙古族人的观念里，流星是不吉利的，是不祥之兆。他们认为流星是懒汉变的，这个懒汉在地上干尽坏事，被天神抓上天关在天炉里，用天火烧，要他改过。可是这个懒汉逃回地上，身上燃着的火把地上的房屋和草堆都点着了，气愤的人类又把他赶回天上。他在星星之间窜来窜去，变成了流星。

Ethnic Mongolians in Xinjiang see shooting stars as inauspicious rather than lucky. They believe they are the vestiges of a lazy guy from long ago. This jerk made all kinds of mischief and was thus locked up in the furnace of the heavens by the god of heaven, hoping to burn him and cause him to change. However, he escaped, and felt burning to the earth, where he ignited buildings and piled straw. Humans angrily sent him back up to heaven, and as the cycle repeats he continually manifests as burning stars.

狼图腾的民族
Wolf Totern

蒙古族很早就开始崇拜狼，把狼作为民族的图腾。他们从狼身上学到了最基本的生存方法，在草原上和狼相互依存。蒙古族爱狼，但也恨狼，他们会猎杀袭击家畜的狼群。从某种意义上讲，狼是蒙古族的宿命，他们活着时像狼一样与命运做斗争，死后以毡裹尸，送到野外。他们深信，只有把尸体喂狼，灵魂才能升天。

Mongolians started to worship wolves early on, taking wolves as their totemic symbol. They studied general survival skills from the wolves, and learned to coexist with them on the grasslands. Mongolians both love and hate wolves, hunting and killing packs of them. In some sense, the wolves are the fate of the Mongolians – warriors when alive, wrapped in felt when deceased, and sent out to the fields. They have deep beliefs that if their bodies are fed to wolves, they will ascend to heaven.

摄影：黄永中

百岁老人村
A Village of Centenarians

在南疆的和田有个长寿村。一天，记者去采访，走到村口，看见一个老汉在哭，记者问别人，他为啥哭？回答说是他妈训他了。记者去问老汉的妈，一个更老的老太婆，老太婆说：他现在还这么不懂事，长大以后可咋办呢？记者一打听：这个老汉已经98岁了。

There is a longevity village in Hotan, Xinjiang. One day, a reporter came to visit, and when he reached the gate, he saw an old man crying. He asked him why, and the man said he was scolded by his mother. The reporter asked the mother, an even older woman, and she said: he's still so naïve, what will he do when he grows older? He asked about the old man's age: ninety-eight.

三只虱子
Three Fleas

在牧区有一次听见这样的对话。年轻的牧民去问一个老牧民：我的羊羔为什么生下来没有精神，天天用嘴咬自己？老牧民答道：你的羊羔身上有虱子！羊生下来头顶上有三只虱子，你不信回去看。年轻的牧民回去一看，果然有三个小东西，还在动弹。

I once heard this conversation in a pasturing area: A young herder asked an old herder: "Why is the baby sheep listless after being born, and does it bite itself all the time?" The old herder replied "your little sheep have fleas! When born, there will be three fleas on the top of the head—if you don't believe me, check it out for yourself." The young herder went back to look, and sure enough, there were three small things, moving and jumping.

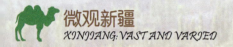

男人的喉结
A Man's Throat

哈萨克族的一则神话说：魔鬼痛恨人类，千方百计引诱和唆使人类违反上帝的旨意。他知道上帝禁止人类食用麦果，就引诱人吃麦果。女人吃完后，男人才开始吃。男人害怕被上帝发现，吃得急，卡住了嗓子，从此，男人就有了喉结。

A Kazakh legend says: demons hate humans, and always seek to lure and instigate humans to violate the rules of heaven. They know that humans are prohibited from eating the forbidden fruit, so they tempted them to do so. After a woman ate it, a man did, too. The man, afraid of being discovered by the deities, ate too quickly and the fruit became stuck in his throat, giving him his Adam's apple.

一只野鸭创造了大地
A Creation Myth

在柯尔克孜族的创世神话里，认为是一只野鸭创造了大地。它为什么创造了大地？因为它要下蛋。宇宙这么大，总该有个地方让野鸭把蛋产下来吧？总得有个承载蛋的地方吧？于是，大地形成了。

In the creation tale of the Kyrgyz people, it is believed that a wild duck created the earth. For what reason? Because it lays eggs. The universe is so big that out of need for a place for the duck to lay its egg and to bear its weight, the earth was created.

把你的儿子借我用一下
Loan Me Your Son

一个维吾尔族人的羊病了，他急忙跑到蒙古族邻居家说：把你的儿子借我用一下！我的母羊病了，羊羔没奶吃。原来，蒙古族邻居家的儿子是双胞胎，民间认为母羊不产奶，用双胞胎孩子的脚掌按摩母羊乳房二三十下，过几天羊羔就有奶吃了。

A Uyghur's sheep fell sick, and he went to his Mongolian neighbour to ask for help – "Loan me your son! My ewe is sick, and the lamb has no milk to drink." The Mongolian's son was one of two twins, and the people believe that if an ewe isn't producing milk, having a twin child use his feet to massage the ewe's teats will cause it to lactate within a few days.

"楚呼楚"泉的传说
Legend of a Spring

一位老人告诉我：塔城曾是一片荒漠，有位白眉毛神仙路过时，觉得渴了，用仙杖在地下一杵，泉水就汩汩冒出。白眉毛神仙饮完泉水，飘然而去，留下了他喝水的木碗。从此，这里就留下了一眼泉，叫"楚呼楚"（蒙古语"木碗"之意）。

An old man told me: Tacheng is a desert. Once, when a sage with white eyebrows was passing by, he felt thirsty, and drove his staff into the ground, and a spring burst forth. When he had drunk his fill, he drifted away, leaving behind his wooden drinking bowl. From this time on, the spring there has been called "chuhuchu", a Mongolian word for "wooden bowl".

爱喝酒的猫
Drunk Kitty

因为气候的优势，新疆葡萄都特别甜，很多人家会自酿葡萄酒，以供家人或是朋友品尝。在吐鲁番有一户农家，养的小猫每到酿酒的季节都会喝上一小碗，躺在葡萄藤下边晒太阳边伸懒腰。这只有美酒陪伴的猫，据说现在酒瘾不小，每天都得喝，不喝就叫个不停。

Due to an excellent climate, the grapes of Xinjiang are especially good, and many people make their own wine, for their families and friends to enjoy. A family in Turpan had a cat that would drink a bowl of wine every winemaking season, and stretch out under the grape vines, enjoying the sun. This cat, with only wine for companionship, became quite addicted, drinking every day, and crying out when there was no wine available.

反扣西瓜皮
Useful
Leftovers

新疆多沙漠戈壁，行走于沙漠戈壁的人有条不成文的规矩：吃剩的西瓜皮不能随意丢弃，必须反扣在沙土上，尽量减少水分的蒸发和尘土的侵蚀。如果有人在沙漠中迷途了，断水了，这个不起眼的西瓜皮就能救人一命。当然，留给骆驼吃也是极好的。

There is an unwritten rule in the Gobi Desert of Xinjiang – when eating a watermelon, do not simply throw away the rind, but rather put it face downwards in the sand, taking care to reduce water loss through evaporation and contamination from soil. If someone is lost on their way in the desert, and has run out of water, the watermelon rind could save their life. Of course, it is also a good option to give to camels.

大地的乳房
The Earth's
Bosom

和田古称"于阗"。它还有一个名字："大地的乳房"。这源于地乳王子的传说：没有嗣子的和田国王每天在寺院神像前祈祷。一天，突然从神像前蹦出一个俊美的男孩，可这个男孩什么奶都不喝。国王到寺院祈求，神像前的地面忽然隆起一只妇女的乳房，男孩见后立刻爬到乳房上，吃起奶来。

Hetian, called "Khotan" in ancient times, also has another name: "the earth's bosom". This comes from the legend of Gostana (meaning "bosom" in Sanskrit): the heirless king of Khotan prayed in front of a statue at the temple every day. One day, a beautiful boy jumped out before the statue, but was unwilling to be nursed. The king prayed at the temple, and a pair of breasts appeared out of the ground. The boy immediately climbed upon them and began to suck.

奇珍·异宝
Miracles and Treasures

两种光芒照耀新疆大地
Two Kinds of Light

两种光芒照耀新疆大地：阿勒泰的黄金和昆仑山的玉。

Two kinds of light illuminate Xinjiang: the gold of the Altay Mountains, and the jade of the Kunlun Mountains.

昆仑的大逻辑
Kunlun Logic

巨大的山产小小的玉，寸草不生的山产至洁至美的玉，最高最穷的山产名贵无价的玉——人间的辩证法，昆仑的大逻辑。

Giant mountains produce small pieces of jade, the beauty of the barren landscapes frozen within the stone. The highest and most barren peaks produce priceless jade – this is the dialectical method of nature, and the logic of the Kunlun Mountains.

美玉拒绝庸俗
The Natural Beauty of Jade

天然的美玉，出于石，载于水，从昆仑山的深处出发，停泊在沙滩之下，等待识玉者的慧眼。玉是美的，珍奇之物的命运自古如此。如若雕工低劣，造作扭捏，毫无美感，则是暴殄天物。一块形态自然、美质超群的奇石，被制造成凡俗之眼要求的样子，就是破坏了自然之美！

Natural jade comes from rocks and is borne by water, from deep in the Kunlun Mountains. It comes to rest upon sandy banks, waiting to be discovered by jade experts. Jade is beautiful, and thus is the fate of precious artefacts. If the carving and workmanship is of poor quality, a shoddily worked piece of jade will be in no way beautiful, and a treasure will have been destroyed. Naturally beautiful stones of great quality cannot be formed into objects simply to please the common eye – such is a distraction of natural beauty.

摄影：王斌

女性化的玉
Feminised
Jade

玉是绝对女性化的，是石头之皇后，阴柔之菁华。古人就认为，玉映月之精光而生，所以河中玉璞堆聚处，月色就加倍明亮。女性与玉天性相通，存在天然的感应。在和田，人们认为女人比男人更容易发现和找到玉。

Jade is definitely feminised, the empress of stones, the very essence of femininity. Ancients believe that jade was formed out of pure moonlight and thus places in the river where jade was found were where moonlight was bright. Femininity naturally interacts with jade's nature. In Hotan, people believe that women are better at finding and discovering jade.

精神的雕刻
Jade
Carvings

古代先民以玉治礼，并由此奠定了中华民族的主体文化——儒家文化。政治的秩序与民德的塑造，因为一块块美丽圆融的和田玉而从理念走向了现实。其后的丝绸之路，则开启了东西方的交流，我们的视野与梦想延伸向更为广大的世界，而其诗意与浪漫，则在朗朗乾坤下晕染更多的乡村、草原和城市。

Ancient peoples used jade for ceremonial purposes, and in this way established the main culture of the Chinese nation – Confucianism. Administrative structure and morality were formed, turning the harmonious beauty of Hotan jade into real-world concepts. After the Silk Road opened up communications between the east and west, our field of view and dreams both extended wider across the world, and poetry and romance touched more villages, prairies, and cities.

金山银水之地
Rivers of
Silver

谚语说："阿尔泰山七十二条沟，沟沟有黄金。"新疆的阿勒泰地区被称为"金山银水"。"阿尔泰"在蒙古语中是"金山"的意思，从汉朝开始开采金矿，至清朝，山中淘金的人曾多达 5 万。仅可可托海矿区的三号矿坑就蕴藏有包括海蓝宝石在内的七十多种矿产，被誉为世界"稀有金属天然博物馆"。

A proverb says: "The Altay Mountains have 72 gorges, and in each one there is gold." The Altay area in Xinjiang has been called the "golden mountains and silvery water". "Altay" in Mongolian means "golden mountain", and they have been mined since the Han Dynasty – in the Qing Dynasty, up to 50,000 people were involved in the activity. The No. 3 mine at Koktokay alone has hidden within it sapphires and over 70 other kinds of mineral products. It has been called a museum of rare and precious natural resources.

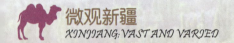

薰衣草蜂蜜
Valley of
Lavender

伊犁河谷广植薰衣草，蜜蜂却不太光顾，不是不喜欢，原因竟是薰衣草田太香了！香使得它们晕头转向，薰衣草的安神催眠作用又使它们昏昏欲睡，许多飞入薰衣草田的蜜蜂只知道瞌睡、打盹儿。所以薰衣草蜂蜜的产量很低，整个伊犁河谷一年只有两三吨，属名贵蜂蜜。打开一瓶薰衣草蜂蜜，能闻到醉人的薰衣草香味。

The Yili River Valley is covered in lavender, but the bees don't visit often – not because they don't like it, but because the scent is too strong! So strong, that it makes them dizzy. Lavender is used by the god of sleep to make them drowsy, with many bees in the area succumbing to the soporific charms. For this reason, not much lavender honey is produced, with only 2 or 3 tons coming out of the entire valley per year, making it famous and valuable. When opening a jar of lavender honey, you can smell the intoxicating fragrance of the flower.

石中美者为玉
Jade: The
Best Stones

古人有云：石中美者为玉。但我们坚信，玉不是普通的石头，这些貌似寻常的石头里，有石中的隐者，有石中最优秀的分子，有石中的王者，他们高贵沉稳、洁净润亮、丰和沉涵，又充满了灵性，但他们绝不喧哗，以石头的面目，诉说着石头以外最不可言传的一切。

The ancients said: the most beautiful of stones is jade. However, I firmly believe that jade isn't simply a stone, that when looking among rocks there are some hidden entities, some excellent specimens, some kings. They are noble, refined, clean, elegant, full of spiritualism but not noisy. They appear as stones, and say all the things that only stones could say.

摄影：王斌

摄影：李建民

天山雪莲
The Snow
Lotus

雪莲从一粒种子到一朵花，至少要历时五载。她生长、盛开，不需要掌声、赞美；她枯萎、死亡，没有遗言。她爱上高度就是爱上了遗忘，爱上了虚空的真相和缺氧的一生。

The snow lotus (*Saussaurea involucrata*) grows from a seed into a flower, a process which takes at least five years. As it grows and flourishes, it doesn't need applause or praise. When it withers and dies, nobody gives a eulogy. It loves fame, and also obscurity, the veracity of vacancy and a lifetime of anoxia.

葡萄王
Grape King

洛浦县杭桂乡有一棵300年的葡萄树，它每年结出的葡萄能供很多游人品尝。听说，它年轻的时候很"能干"，果实能让几十人吃三天三夜，现在它成了精，成了王，所有的葡萄树都成了它的子民。

There is a grape vine in Hanggui Township, Lop County which is 300 years old, and it produces enough grapes to delight many travellers each year. It is said to have been quite productive in its younger life, presenting enough grapes to feed dozens of people for three days and nights. Now, it is a spirit, a king, and all the other grape vines are its subjects.

181

玉石的时光之路
Jade Path

传说周穆王西巡，沿黄河过宁夏，到甘肃，入新疆，抵中亚，然后东返，会见西王母，欢宴于瑶池之上，然后登昆仑，视察攻玉（采玉）和琢玉部落，将玉器运往中原。从考古现场我们得知，早在殷商时期，玉器就有了复杂而精致的纹饰，其加工技艺已经非常精妙。

When King Mu of Zhou travelled to the west, he followed the Yellow River to Ningxia, then Gansu, and then Xinjiang. When he headed back east, he saw the Queen Mother of the West, enjoyed a banquet at her palace and then climbed Mount Kunlun to observe those collecting and carving jade. He had jade articles sent to the Central Plains. Archaeological research shows that as early as the Yin and Shang dynasties, jade objects were carved with complex and exquisite patterns, and that the workmanship was quite good.

五百岁无花果王
A Kingly Tree

在和田，我朝拜一棵无花果树。无言而伟大的正是这类生命，它从一棵平凡的植物变成了神灵。走进它浓重芬芳的荫庇之地，嗅到了它的气息，那气味既含有植物特有的清芬又超出了植物本身，我觉得嗅到了一位隐士或古代贤哲的气味，那是思想的气味。它掉落在地下的熟烂果实，散发着酒的香味。

In Hotan, I visited a fig tree. This kind of huge life form grew from a small plant to a deity in its own right. When entering its fragrant shade, I smell its breath, botanically delicate and yet something more – I feel like I am smelling the breath of a scholarly recluse or ancient sage, the breath of thought. The fruits that it has dropped on the ground give off the scent of liquor.

巴音布鲁克天鹅
Bayanbuluk's Swans

在巴音布鲁克草原，天鹅是离生活最近也最远的生灵。那些在湖中嬉戏的天鹅，无意向人们展示祥和与安宁，但人们分明领受到了一种和谐之美，一种启示。比照之下，人们心中安稳了许多，没有理由不很好地生活下去；而来自远方的讯息和寄予远方的希望，也都由随季节迁徙的这些精灵们不经意完成了。

On the Bayanbuluk Prairie, swans are the spirits farthest from and closest to life. The swans that play upon the water unwittingly represent peace and good fortune to humans, as we are moved by their harmonious beauty. Compared to humans, they live a relatively peaceful existence and have no reason not to continue doing so. This message from afar and the hope that we send afar are every year moved with the seasons, as the birds migrate with the weather.

鸟类的理想栖息地

A Nice Place for Birds

新疆地处亚欧板块的中心，远离海洋，高山环抱，沙漠浩瀚，草原辽阔，绿洲和湖泊湿地点布，鸟类资源丰富，约占中国鸟类种数的 34%。新疆是观鸟的天堂，相当一部分鸟类属于全国特有物种，一些还来自欧洲、中亚。近年来，新疆屡屡出现中国鸟类新纪录，如白尾麦鸡、白顶鹛、白兀鹫、高山雨燕等。

Xinjiang is located in the centre of Eurasia, away from the sea, surrounded by mountains, and covered by grasslands, deserts, oases, and some lakes. There are many avian species, accounting for almost 34% of China's biodiversity in this category. Xinjiang is a paradise for bird-watching, with some of China's endangered species being here, in addition to those from Europe and Central Asia. In recent years, numerous new species of birds have been discovered, such as the white-tailed lapwing, Emberiza stewarti, Neophron percnopterus, alpine swifts (nubifuga), and others.

胡杨

Poplars

粗糙的皮肤，丑怪的造型。这种沧桑，是记忆，也是未来的路标。这是一些第三纪的孑遗植物，距今已有 6500 万年以上的历史，是新疆最古老的珍奇树种之一，是唯一能在干旱沙漠环境中形成森林的乔木树种。

Rough skin and a grotesque form. These kinds of changes are memories, and markers on the road of the future. This is a relic of a plant from the Triassic era, approximately 65 million years old, and one of the most precious ancient trees in Xinjiang – the only kind that can form forests in the dry desert environment.

摄影：魏顺德

放大的猫和缩小的老虎
Enlarged Cats and Shrunken Tigers

雪豹是放大了的猫和缩小了的老虎。雪豹是边疆生活的一个图腾。它出没于高山峻岭，如游兵散勇，将自己放逐于偏远、孤寂和坚卓，其珍稀性更多地呈现出精神生态的象征意义，仿佛神明的作品横空出世——是的，它耀眼的环纹正是神明之手赋予的胎印。

A snow leopard is like an enlarged cat or shrunken tiger. The snow leopard is totemic of life in the border areas of Xinjiang. They appear high in the mountains, like a brave soldier, travelling far away, alone and resolute; its value is more apparent in the symbolism of its spiritual ecology, like a masterpiece that dazzles with its brilliant patterns.

伊犁马
Yili Horses

一个部落的目光最有分量的部分，都聚集在伊犁马腰臀。她的细腰凹陷，而肥臀却傲然凸起；她的双耳耸立，耳廓朝着迎风的地方摆动，仿佛耸峙的山峰，摩擦着宁静的天空；只有巨大的蹄子稳稳钉在大地上，在没有奔跑、没有形成风暴之前，如雕塑般的四肢，以树的笔直与沉默，构成速度爆发的前提。

What draws the eyes of the tribe most is a Yili horse's waist and rear – the waist is slim, and indented, whereas the rear is plump and protruding. Her ears stand erect, auricles pitched towards the wind, the shoulders stand like mountain peaks, almost scraping the sky. Only her huge hooves stand stably in the ground, and before she runs, before the dust is kicked into the air, her statuesque legs stand in the ground, straight as a pen, solid like trees – a herald of the speed to be unleashed.

摄影：双元

摄影：黄永中

鹰笛
Eagle Flutes

鹰笛也称"三孔骨笛"，管身多用鹫鹰的翅膀骨制作。那是不长的一截，只有手指粗细，鹰笛的下半部均匀地被凿出三个小孔，作为发声的孔道，其声没有竹木缠绵，也少了点儿金属的钢悍。它就像在肉体深处被激发的歌声，底蕴深厚而声波亮丽。这是骨头发出的声音啊！那些能够替代骨髓的东西，该是怎样的温暖而具有活力。

The "Eagle Flute", also known as the "Three-holed Bone Flute", has a body fashioned of the wing bone of an eagle. A short section only as wide as a human finger, this kind of flute is drilled with three holes at its lower part to make sound, not as lingering as that of bamboo, and without the metallic sound of a metal flute. The sound is a visceral one, a rich, deep and beautiful sound – this is the sound that bone makes. If you want to replace marrow with something else, it should be warm and lively.

草原雄鹰
Eagles on the Prairie

在巴音布鲁克草原上，有一只雄鹰突然向草地俯冲，那时我正坐在车上，它的速度让我颤抖，一只幼小的呱拉鸡立刻安静下来，这是鹰的搏击！我们也曾遇到同样一只鹰，受了伤的，有同伴想带走它，但最终把它留在了草原，因为它是属于草原的生命。

On the Bayanbuluk Prairie, a lanneret suddenly swept down as I was sitting in a car, shocking me with its speed. A small chicken immediately stopped its cries – this was the eagle's attack! We previously found another eagle, this one injured, that my partner wanted to take with us, but we ended up leaving it on the prairie, as its life belongs there.

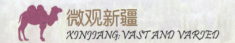

天地的信使：鹿石

Stone Deer

围着太阳神殿散布着的石柱，柱上刻着鹿等动物，是为鹿石。那鹿刻得很抽象，是鸟鹿合体的神兽，具有穿越天、地、人间三界的特殊神力，是天地之间的信使。

There are stone pillars around the temple of the sun, upon which there are animals like deer – these are called "stone deer". They are carved in an abstract manner, a merger of deer and birds, with the ability to operate in the realms of heaven, earth, and with human beings – they are the messengers between heaven and earth.

摄影：刘学堂

摄影：王民富

红柳舞轻沙
Dance of the
Sand

沙漠公路上，沙舞轻扬，天地昏暗。茫茫黄色之中，一抹生命的原色不时跳跃眼前，点缀着淡淡的红，散发着幽幽的香。就是弥漫黄尘中的这点儿红绿、些许幽香，美丽了沙漠戈壁，成就了红柳美誉。

Sand dances around on the desert road, darkening the sky. Amidst a yellow storm, the colours of life jump before the eyes, interspersed with a shallow red, giving off a faint smell. The points of green and red, pervasive in the cloud of yellow, lend a touch and colour to the Gobi Desert – these are the contributions of the red willows.

新疆珍稀濒危动物
Precious
Endangered
Animals

新疆深居内陆，地域辽阔，是中国一个独特的生态地理区，成为保护珍稀、濒危动物种质资源的天然基因库。新疆有野生动物近700余种，占全国的11%。有国家重点保护动物116种，约占全国的三分之一，其中包括蒙古野马、藏野驴、藏羚羊、雪豹、新疆北鲵等国际濒危野生动物。

Xinjiang is a vast area far inland, and is China's only designated eco-geographic area in which endangered animals are protected – a kind of natural genetic store-room. Xinjiang boasts almost 700 species of wild animals, accounting for 11% of the national total, 116 of which are endangered – a third of the national total. These include the Mongolian horse, Tibetan donkey, Tibetan antelope, Ranodon sibiricus, and other animals internationally designated as endangered.

187

沙海之神
God of the
Sea of Sand

从某种视觉效果上看，沙漠和大海差别不大——都一望无际，都波浪起伏。如此，在沙海上，那些密如进港船桅的，是它们；那些倾斜如将没船只的，也是它们。胡杨，胡杨，宇宙洪荒；胡杨，胡杨，千古流芳。它就住在"死亡之海"，却比谁都活得久长。它的生命刻度是这样：生而不死 1000 年，死而不倒 1000 年，倒而不朽 1000 年。

In a way of looking at them, there isn't much difference between a desert and an ocean – a vast plain covered by waves. In this way, on the sea of sand, they are the masts of the ships that come into the harbour; they are also the tilting masts of the sinking ships. Poplars, primitive and chaotic, stalwart and strong, are the long-lived residents of the "sea of death". This stalwart plant can live for a thousand years, strong and steady, without toppling.

大风起兮
Strong Winds

邻近乌鲁木齐，一片巨大的风车阵令人震惊！这就是拥有 200 多台风车、年发电量达 1800 万瓦的达坂城风电厂——亚洲最大的风力发电站。新疆有九大风区，风能资源占中国陆上风能资源总量的 37%，居全国第二位。大风起兮云飞扬，风车转兮发电忙，喜得能源兮供四方！

Near to Urumqi, there is a field of windmills that is quite a sight to see. There are more than 200 windmills, generating 18 MW of power – the largest windmill array in Asia. Xinjiang has nine major windy areas which generate 37% of China's wind power, second in the nation. Wind blows the leaves of the poplar trees and gives us electricity to use – quite a nice benefit.

摄影：王恺元

摄影：王晖

**地毯将陋室变
成了宫殿**
Nice Rugs

在今天的新疆，即使最简陋的农舍，最不起眼的黄泥小屋，通常
也都有地毯出现。地上的毡毯，墙上的壁毯，炕上的花毯，还有
坐垫、鞍褥等……地毯将陋室变成了宫殿。地毯有时是"大地"
的隐喻。它比大地柔软，它是微型的大地、挂在墙上的大地、呵
护梦的大地……

Today in Xinjiang, even the meanest farmhouses and normal-looking mud
huts have rugs. A rug on the floor, rugs on the wall, a decorative rug on
the hearth, as well as cushions, saddlecloth – these transform the simplest
residence into a palace. Rugs evoke the earth – they are softer and smaller, can
be hung on walls and protect the dreams of the earth.

能源富集之地
Rich in Energy
Resources

新疆多沙漠戈壁，但大自然有它的逻辑，储量可观的能源就是自
然的馈赠之一。以世界上最重要的三种化石燃料——石油、天然
气和煤炭而言，据预测，新疆石油资源总量约为 228 亿吨，天然
气资源总量约为 17.5 万亿立方米，均占中国陆上资源量的三分之
一以上；煤炭储量 2.19 万亿吨，占中国储量的 40%。新疆堪称中
国能源富集之地。

Xinjiang has many deserts, but nature is logical – the stored energy resources
are one of the gifts that nature gives to us. The three major fuels in the
world today are petroleum, natural gas and coal – Xinjiang has reserves of
approximately 22.8 billion tonnes of petroleum, 17,500 billion cubic metres
of natural gas, constituting more than a third of China's reserves, in addition
to 2,190 billion tonnes of coal – 40% of China's total. Xinjiang is truly a place
rich in resources.

189

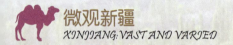
"小人参"：
恰玛古
"Little Ginseng"

说起新疆的蔬果特产，库尔勒的香梨、哈密瓜，吐鲁番的葡萄、雪莲花，无不声名远播。但柯坪县的恰玛古（维吾尔语"蔓菁"的音译），名头并不响亮。可就是这种生长于红色沙土中形似萝卜、有着落花生般"朴实"品格的"大头菜"，蕴藏着南疆维吾尔族人长寿的秘诀，近年来赢得了"小人参"的美誉。

Hami melons (a kind of cantaloupe), the fragrant pears of Korla, and the grapes and snowdrops of Turpan are all famous agricultural products of Xinjiang. Tubers of Keping County are not very well known, despite their excellence. Growing in the red earth, they are of specific cultivars that contain compounds that allow the local Uyghurs to live long, and have been compared to ginseng in recent years.

"风光"
无限好
A Limitless Scene

乌鲁木齐通往南山的景观大道上，有一道独特的"景观"，这便是矗立在路旁的新型节能路灯。新疆东部晴天多、日照强，是中国太阳能资源最丰富的地区之一，仅次于西藏。加之临近达坂城风区，风车加太阳能板的"二合一"节能灯就在这里派上了用场。"风光"无限好，科技引浪潮，路灯新景观，节能又环保。

On the road to Nanshan from Urumqi, there is a unique vista – new energy-saving lamps along the side of the road. Xinjiang has many clear days with strong sun, making it one of the best areas for solar power in the country, second only to Tibet. Additionally, when approaching the Dabancheng Windy Area, the "two-in-one" combo of solar and wind power comes into play. Advanced technology allows us to light the road in an energy-efficient manner – it's an amusing coincidence that the Chinese word for "scene" or "vista" is made up of the words "wind" and "light".

摄影：王怡元

舞姿奇异的花所根植的土壤
Fertile Soil

血统、宗教、地域、文化，几千年的力量微妙地传递下来，传递在移动的肢体上，体现了无形力量的控驭，这就是舞姿奇异的花所根植的土壤。那些跳刀郎舞的人们，那些农民，粗手大脚，裕祥里灌满了沙子，胡须里和头发里也灌满了沙子。他们的舞没有观众，他们把舞当成一种风俗习惯。

Bloodlines, religion, regions, cultures – the power of millennia passed down subtle via flexible, mobile bodies, carrying the shapeless power of control and conciliation – this is the soil in which the roots and flowers of dance grow. Those who dance the Dolan dances are farmers – thick hands and large legs, robes full of sand, as well as in their beards and hair. Their dances have no audience – they turn into a custom.

木卡姆
Muqam

木卡姆源于西域民族文化，又深受伊斯兰文化影响。木卡姆在维吾尔语中指"大型套曲"，包括文学、音乐、舞蹈、说唱、戏剧等多种艺术成分，被称为维吾尔族历史和社会生活的百科全书。其形式有"十二木卡姆""刀郎木卡姆""哈密木卡姆""吐鲁番木卡姆"等，2005 年获得"世界非物质文化遗产"称号。

Muqam originates from the cultures of the Western Region, and has been heavily influenced by Islam. Muqam is like the divertimento of the Uyghur language, combining literature, music, dance, spoken word, drama, and other artistic elements. It has been referred to as the encyclopaedia of Uyghur history and society, taking the forms such as "Twelve Muqam", "Dolan Muqam", "Hami Muqam", "Turpan Muqam", and the like. In 2005 it was awarded world intangible cultural heritage status.

贝伦舞
Belem

流传在察布查尔锡伯自治县等锡伯族聚居区的贝伦舞，不选时间，不择场地，只要点燃了舞意，乐手用东布尔弹起贝伦舞曲，人们便翩翩起舞。贝伦舞源于古代锡伯族的渔猎生活，锡伯族西迁之后，经过一代又一代民间艺人的再创作，贝伦舞成为在锡伯族民间非常流行、几乎人人会跳的一种民间舞蹈。

In the Qapqal Xibe Autonomous County and other areas in which Xibe people congregate, all it takes is a little bit of music to get the belem dance going – any time, any place, once the tunes start up, people start dancing. Belem dance originated from among the fishers and hunters who were the ancestors of the modern-day Xibe people, and once they had migrated west, it was changed and reinvented by folk artists generation after generation, making it a very popular dance among the Xibe people which almost all of them are capable of dancing.

十二木卡姆
The Twelve Muqams

蜿蜒的叶尔羌河，分出了12条支流，十二木卡姆是一只大魔法盒，它将歌、诗、乐、舞统统装进去。十二木卡姆是这个世界表示时间的另一种方式。

The zigzagging Yarkant River has twelve lesser streams. The Twelve Muqams are like a large magic box that combines song, poetry, music, and dance. The Twelve Muqams are another way of representing time in this world.

摄影：韩连赟

冬不拉的传说
The Tamboura

冬不拉只有两根弦，却能模仿大自然的各种声音。哈萨克族都喜欢弹奏，像阿肯弹唱、歌舞表演、诗歌朗诵等都离不开冬不拉伴奏。冬不拉就像激情，就像酒话，能让人忘记孤独和寂寞。真正的音乐不是一件乐器的外形能决定的，而是乐师的灵魂和乐器的灵魂神秘地合二为一，变成音乐的精灵。

The tamboura only has two strings, but can replicate all kinds of sounds from the natural world. The Kazakhs like to play it solo, such as in the Aken festival, where people sing, dance and perform songs and poems, the accompaniment of the tamboura. The tamboura is like passion, or drunken talk – it lets one forget one's loneliness or solitude. True music isn't something decided by the shape of the instrument, but rather by merger of the souls of the musician and the instrument, which makes it into the spirit of the music.

193

摄影：黄永中

刀郎木卡姆
Dolan Muqam

这样的歌唱，是胸腔里的牧歌，喉咙里的决口，是琴弦在流泪，嗓子在开花。一个火的歌喉，雄性的歌喉，是人声，也是天籁。荒漠里的长歌，旷野上的摇滚，在拯救大荒中不安的心灵。

This kind of singing is that of the nomads, where the pastoral songs emanate from within the chest and are realised by the throat. They are the tears of the instruments, and the blooming of the voice. When a man is giving it his all whist singing, one hears not just his voice but also the sound of nature. Long songs against a desolate backdrop, lilting ballads upon the prairie – these comfort the restless soul in its desolate setting.

阿曼尼莎与木卡姆套曲
Ammanisha and Muqam

相传叶尔羌汗国的第二代汗王拉失德，带随从去塔克拉玛干打猎。听到阿曼尼莎的异常绝妙的弹拨尔琴声，不禁产生了强烈的爱慕之情，于是把阿曼尼莎迎娶进宫。成为王妃的阿曼尼莎，系统收集、整理了民间流传的木卡姆套曲。

The second khan of the Kingdom of Yarkant, Abdurashid Khan, went with his entourage to Taklimakan to hunt. When he heard the enchanting melodies of the pi-pa played by Ammanisha, he was instantly overcome with adoration and took Ammanisha with him to the place to be his bride. As his consort, she systematically collected and arranged muqam, the ethnic melodies of the region.

塔吉克族的民间道具舞
Puppet Dance

民间道具舞使用马、牦牛、羊等道具表演，形式接近汉族人的《跑旱船》《跑驴》。演员的下半身是布帘扎成的马、牛的身体，前有首后有尾，以夸张的木偶模样边唱边舞。这是塔吉克族民间的传统娱乐方式。

Readily-available props for dancing include horses, yaks, and lambs, similar to some uses in the Han culture. The lower half of the performer's body may be a horse's or cow's body made out of a cloth drape, with a head and tail, to be used when singing and dancing an exaggerated, puppet-like dance. This is one of the traditional forms of entertainment among ethnic Tajiks.

麦西来甫
Maixilaipu

麦西来甫是绿洲居民一种公共的集歌、舞、乐为一体的民间娱乐大"派对"。麦西来甫在节日里举行，也在平日里随时举办。麦西来甫在室内也在室外，在村庄也在荒野，在婚礼上也在麻扎里……麦西来甫无处不在，人们乐在其中，忘却烦恼，如痴如醉，因为麦西来甫就是"集体的欢腾"，是绿洲上的狂欢节。

Maixilaipu is a kind of gathering among the residents of oases in which they sing, dance and entertain each other. These gatherings are held on festival days, as well as ad-hoc on ordinary days. They can be conducted both indoors and outdoors, both in the village and out in the fields, at weddings and mazars. Maixilaipu is everywhere, and people take delight in them, forgetting their worries and letting go – these are the group celebrations, and occasions for jubilation in the oasis.

摄影：韩连赟

刀郎歌舞
Dolan Dances

它来自于刀郎人早年的生活，只要音乐响起来（卡龙琴、热瓦甫、艾捷克、手鼓一齐奏响），无论是歌者还是舞者，那种忘情投入，在其他的文化形态中少有匹敌。这样的歌舞不局限于哪一天，也不局限于哪一个地方，而是随时随地，在田间地头，在农家小院……

Dolan dance originated from the early life of Dolan people. It just needs music (such as an assemblage of qanun, rawap, aijieke and hand drums) to make both the singers and dancers really get into it – this kind of cultural form appears rarely elsewhere. Such songs and dances aren't good for only a specific time or place, and instead can be enjoyed anywhere – in the fields, or at home…

摄影：麻军

音乐圣人
苏祗婆
Mother Suzhi

隋朝初年有位善弹胡琵琶而且精通音律的乐师，用西域音乐改革中原音乐，造就新的音乐体系，对宋词、元曲发展影响深远，这个乐师就是西域龟兹国少数民族音乐家苏祗婆。苏氏乐调体系对汉民族乐律的发展做出了卓越的贡献，琵琶也因此大盛，成为我国民族乐器家族的重要成员。

In the early years of the Sui dynasty there was a skilled musician who excelled at playing the pi-pa as well as musical theory. She used music of the Western Region to revolutionise the music of the Central Plains area, creating a new musical system, which deeply influenced Song poems and Yuan melodies – she was Mother Suzhi of the kingdom of Kocha. The work she did on her musical system represented a great contribution to Han ethnic music. She was also quite influential in the field of the pi-pa, and is one of the most important ethnic musicians in Chinese history.

和布克赛的牧仁
Mu Ren

和布克赛的牧仁，会拉马头琴，会弹托布秀尔，还会唱呼麦，还爱喝酒。每一次他来看我们，我们都会喝掉好几公斤奶酒。毡房整夜都会传出美妙的琴声和额吉辽远悠长的蒙古长调。

Mu Ren, from Hoboksar, can play the horse-head fiddle, sing hoomii songs, and likes to drink. Every time he comes to see us, we drink litres of milk liquor. Beautiful songs emanate from the yurt, mingling with the sounds of the instrument, far into the distance.

舞蹈，土地上的灵魂
The Soul of the Earth

狩猎、种植、放牧，山川、大地、河湖，百兽、草原、树木，传说、激情、梦想、欢乐、孤独、悲伤，宗教、祭祀、战场，丰收、爱情、婚丧，无一不在新疆的舞蹈中呈现。舞蹈，是这片土地上的灵魂。舞蹈是生命最直接、最本质、最强烈、最尖锐、最单纯而又最充分的表现。

Hunting, sowing, herding, landscapes, geographic features, lakes, animals, prairies, trees, legends, excitement, dreams, enjoyment, loneliness, tragedy, religion, ritual, battle, harvest, marriages, funerals – all of these happen accompanied with dance in Xinjiang. Dance is the soul of the local culture. In the expressions of life, dancing is the most direct, the most innate, the strongest, most genius, purest and fullest.

摄影：麻军

罗布人的"狮子舞"

The Lion Dance

罗布人的"狮子舞"与汉族的"狮子舞"完全不同，主要再现狮子生活中的抓、挠、扑、跳等幽默调皮的动作，把狮子的顽皮可爱表现得惟妙惟肖。"狮子舞"的鼓点，有锣鼓的意味。

The Lop Nur people's "lion dance" and that of the Han Chinese are completely different. With silly re-enactments of hunting, scratching, sneaking and jumping in the dance, the lion is recreated as a tricky and cute character. The percussion instruments that accompany the dance, however, are evocative of the traditional gong and drum.

长调

Long Songs

长调是蒙古族在草原上长久维持下来的自由歌谣，以游牧民族的生存景象为主要表现内容。蒙古语称其为"乌日听道"，意思是"悠长的歌曲"。在长调盛行的地方有一个说法："儿童会走路便会骑马，会说话便会唱歌。"长调是蒙古族的另一册历史，也是蒙古族牧民的精神诗歌。

Long songs are the ballads of the Mongolians on the grasslands preserved over the ages, contents mainly consisting of scenes of nomadic life. These songs are called Wuritingdao, meaning "long songs" in the Mongolian language. In areas where the long songs are popular, there is a saying: "Young children can walk and ride, speak and sing". Long songs are a photo album of ethnic Mongolian history, as well as the spiritual songs of the people.

摄影：双元

摄影：麻军

鹰舞
Eagle Dance

鹰舞是塔吉克族传统舞蹈，男舞者两臂前高后低，两肩微微上下抖动，步伐矫健灵活，盘旋俯仰，有如鹰起隼落，刚强有力，尽显宽广的情怀和豪迈的性格。女舞者双手高举在头上部，向里外旋转，柔和中藏蓄矫健。伴奏只有鹰笛和手鼓，舞者的双脚、腰肩、眼睛、眉毛、嘴唇都随着悠扬节奏形成了完整的舞蹈结构。

The eagle dance is a traditional dance among the Tajiks, in which the male dancer's shoulders are alternately positioned high and low as the arms are shaking – the movements are quick and flexible, whirling and rising like an eagle in flight, strong, powerful and heroic. Female dancers raise their hands over their heads and twirl outwards, strength and vigour hidden in their grace. The musical accompaniment consists solely of flutes and hand drums – the dancer's legs, waists, shoulders, eyes, eyebrows, and lips all respond to the rhythm of the music, becoming part of the dance.

用木头和羊肠制作的冬不拉
Making a Tamboura

古时候，有一只山羊，失足从山崖上摔了下来，恰巧腹部被崖壁的树枝划破，肠子被拉扯出来。后来，羊肠子慢慢干了。有一天，一位牧人从山崖下走过，听见了美妙的音乐声。他抬起头来，看见了树枝上挂着的干肠子，经过风的吹拂，发出悦耳动听的声音。牧人由此得到启发，用木头和羊肠制作了冬不拉。

In ancient times, there was a lamb that lost its footing and fell from a precipice. Unfortunately, its abdomen was ripped open by a branch on the cliff face, and its intestines spilled out. Later, they gradually dried. One day, a herder was walking down the cliff, and heard a beautiful sound. He raised his head to see the intestines hanging there, blowing in the wind, emitting a wonderful sound. From this, he was inspired to make the tamboura out of wood and lamb parts.

蒙古族舞蹈沙吾尔登
Shawurdon

沙吾尔登是蒙古族土尔扈特等部最具代表性的传统舞蹈，是土尔扈特人独创的民间舞蹈，在西域蒙古族中广为流传。沙吾尔登的特点是手臂动作丰富，下肢移位不大，有独舞、对舞和群舞。

Shawurdon is a dance most representative of the traditional dances of Torghut and other ethnic Mongolians. It is created by the Torghut themselves, and popular among the Mongolians of the Western Region. Shawurdon incorporates many movements of the shoulders, while the legs move little – it can be danced individually, in pairs, or in groups.

摄影：韩连赟

草原哈萨克族的天籁"斯布孜格"
The Heart Flute

"斯布孜格"被哈萨克族人称为"心笛"，实际上是一种竖笛，类似汉族的箫。"斯布孜格"最适于演奏老歌和慢歌。吹奏时把管口湿点水，放入口中用舌尖堵住管口，并留一小口吹气。吹奏时随吹奏艺人的吹吸气和手的动作发出不同的音色，并用喉头发低音，就形成了双音部。音色柔和、沉稳、悠扬，有如"天籁"。

The "sibuzige" is called the "heart flute" by the Kazakhs. It's actually a kind of clarinet, similar to the Han Chinese flute (xiao). The sibuzige is most suited to old or slow songs. When playing, the mouthpiece is wet, and the tongue is inserted with a bit of air held in the mouth. When playing, the instrumentalist's breath and hand movements make different sounds, in addition to the actions of the larynx which contribute bass tones – in such a way double notes are created.

段蔷与《新疆乐器图谱》

Dictionary of Xinjiang Musical Instruments

70 多岁的段蔷，一生坎坷，却酷爱音乐。21 年的牢狱生活，手指被打残，不能再演奏小提琴，于是他用几十年时间走遍新疆大地，用汉语、维吾尔语、哈萨克语、柯尔克孜语完成了自己的田野调查，最后成就了一套《新疆乐器图谱》，为世界留下了很多濒临失传的新疆乃至中亚地区的乐器资料。

Duan Qiang, in his seventies, has had a hard life, but loves music. During his 21 years in jail, his fingers were destroyed, and he can't play the violin any more. For this reason he spent more than a decade travelling across Xinjiang, speaking Chinese, Uyghur, Kazakh, and Kyrgyz to complete a field survey that he turned into his *Dictionary of Xinjiang Musical Instruments*, documenting the musical instruments of Xinjiang and the Central Asia that would otherwise be lost.

刀郎人的驼舞

The Camel Dance

乌鲁却勒镇位于塔克拉玛干沙漠的北部边缘的叶尔羌河边，是典型的刀郎人聚居地。骆驼舞主要反映了历史上丝绸之路上的驼客艰辛的商旅生活，经过长途跋涉来到古驿站，和大家欢乐地跳麦西来甫的情景。这一舞蹈至今完整地在乌鲁却勒保留了下来。

Wuluquele Township is situated on the northern fringe of the Taklimakan Desert, near the Yarkant River, and is the most typical example of a Dolan community. The "camel dance" mainly reflects the hardships of merchants travelling with camels on the historical Silk Road; after a long trek to an outpost on the route, everyone would celebrate and dance happily. This dance has been preserved to the present day in Wuluquele Township.

摄影：韩连赟

摄影：韩连赟

新疆的回族 "花儿"
Huar

"花儿"流传于中国甘肃、宁夏、青海、新疆等地，有独唱、对唱、联唱。"新疆花儿"是由西迁的回族带入新疆的，不同于内地"花儿"，它融入强烈的地域特色和回族音乐风格。

Huar ("flower") is popular in Gansu, Ningxia, Qinghai, Xinjiang, and other areas, and can be sung solo, as a duet, or in a chorus. "Xinjiang Huar" was brought by Hui people into Xinjiang, and is different from the huar in the eastern provinces of China – it incorporates strong regional characteristics and Hui musical principles.

城市中的音乐、人与酒
Music, People and Alcohol

20 世纪 90 年代的某个下午，西部歌王王洛宾和段蔷在街头相遇，老友相见，于是买酒，进了街边的餐馆。一个乞丐走到桌边，伸手要钱。王洛宾说，坐下一起吃吧。饭毕，王洛宾把剩下的半瓶酒塞给乞丐说："老哥，拿着吧，今晚还不知在哪儿过夜呢，可以挡挡寒气。"音乐、人与酒，在这个城市，相依为命。

On an afternoon in the 1990s, "King of Songs of the West" Wang Luobin met Duan Qiang on the street – the old friends bought liquor and entered a restaurant. A beggar approached the table and extended his hand. Wang Luobin invited him to have a seat. After they ate, Wang Luobin gave the half-full bottle of the liquor to the beggar, telling him to take it to stave off the cold at night. Music, people, and liquor all keep each other connected in this city.

人与音乐
People and
Music

音乐是乌鲁木齐向人叙说的另一种方式，是人内在的声音——人是可以通过"听"来认知的。对歌舞的热爱，已经不是某一个民族的特质，而是这个城市共同的语言。在牧场变为城市之后，那些歌舞一同进入了城市的大街小巷。从史诗到小曲，有创作者、传播者、变革者，还有守卫者。

Music is a tale told to people by Urumqi. It is the internal voice of people, and people perceive the world by listening. A love for music isn't a characteristic of a single, specific group, but rather the common language of a city. After pastures became cities, the same songs entered into their large streets and small lanes. From poetry to melodies, there are composers, disseminators, reformers and guardians.

新疆曲子
Melodies of
Xinjiang

流传于新疆的哈密、昌吉、乌鲁木齐、伊犁、塔城地区和南疆的库尔勒、焉耆等地的新疆曲子戏，是由新疆汉、回、锡伯等民族共创共享的地方戏剧剧种。它发源于陕西曲子、青海平弦、兰州鼓子、西北民歌等，并融入了新疆各民族音乐。

The quzi opera popular in Hami, Changji, Urumqi, Yili, Tacheng, Korla, Yanqi and other areas in Xinjiang are the result of joint creation between the Han, Hui, Xibe and other ethnic groups. They originated from the songs of Shaanxi, the pingxuan melodies of Qinghai, the drums of Lanzhou, the songs of the Northwest cultures, and integrated with the local ethnic music of various groups in Xinjiang.

摄影：韩连赟

勇敢者的游戏：
达瓦孜
Dawaz

它是体育，是杂技，是表演艺术，也是国家级非物质文化遗产。这就是"达瓦孜"——一项勇敢者的游戏。在高空绳索上行走、睡卧、倒立、舞蹈翻腾、弯腰采莲，你看得惊心动魄，大睁着眼，捏一把汗，恨不得气都不敢喘，表演者却似信步于庭前。

Combining sport, acrobatics, and performance art, "dawaz" is designated as a national intangible cultural relic in China. It is a game for the brave. One uses a tensed rope suspended in air to walk, lie, stand, dance, jump, and perform various other acrobatic feats upon. It's a captivating spectacle that will make you sweat and widen your eyes as you hold your breath, watching the performer's feats.

萨巴依
Sabay

萨巴依，维吾尔族和乌兹别克族的民间乐器，常用于歌舞伴奏。萨巴依有类似沙槌的声响，似乎从身体里出来一种战栗，通过身体、手臂传向萨巴依的木柄和铁环，不停地抖动。在坟园、荒地和尘土飞扬的路旁，你能听到一种有节奏的"沙沙"声。萨巴依歌唱者通常是乞丐、流浪汉、残疾人和苦修者。

The sabay is a traditional Uyghur and Uzbek instrument which is used for musical accompaniment to dances. It has a sound similar to a cabasa. The instrument carries the shivers of the body through the arm into the wooden handle and metal rings of the instrument which vibrate continuously. In cemeteries and wastelands, where the dust flies in the wind, you can hear the rhythmic sandy sound of the instrument. Frequent users of the sabay are beggars, vagabonds, disabled people, and ascetics.

摄影：党向华

摄影：党向华

阿希克
Asiks

在新疆的维吾尔族中，有一些抱着特殊生存态度、拥有特殊生活方式的人——"阿希克"。他们是游唱者、江湖艺人、宗教苦修者，或是一些游走的灵魂？在新疆南部喀什、和田等绿洲上的大小城镇，时常能够在街头巷尾见到手持萨巴依的行吟者阿希克。

Among the Uyghurs in Xinjiang, some maintain a special lifestyle – they are called the "asiks". Are they travelling singers, bards, ascetics, or wandering souls? In Kashgar, Hotan and other oasis cities in Xinjiang, large and small, one can frequently see them on the small streets, carrying sabays and chanting as they walk along.

贪婪的真实
Greed and Truth

"你要想嫁人不要嫁给别人，一定要嫁给我，带着你的嫁妆，领着你的妹妹，赶着那马车来。"不光要人家姑娘，还要人家的嫁妆和妹妹，多贪婪，多真实，也多直露！这首著名的新疆民歌一点不装模作样，不故弄玄虚，这才是一个人的真实的灵魂和感情。

"If you want to get married, don't marry anyone but me. Get ready your dowry, bring your sister, and hop on the cart to come to me." Not just wanting the girl, but also the dowry and her sister – how greedy, how true, and how direct! This famous song from Xinjiang puts on no pretences or airs – it is a revelation of true soul and feeling.

新疆歌舞
Xinjiang's Songs and Dances

古代的先人们为了获得诸神的善待，求得人畜平安与兴旺，祈祷并试图与神灵沟通，一种新的表达形式——音乐与舞蹈，在这一过程中一步步发展了起来。新疆的歌舞依然保留着远古的光影，并化为生活的一部分，充满烟火气，里面有绿洲、草原、牛羊、骏马，以及痛苦、快乐、爱情等人类生活的细节……

In order to curry favour with the gods, and ask for peace and prosperity for man and beast alike, to pray and attempt to communicate with spirits, people turned to the media of song and dance, which gradually evolved into what we see today. The songs and dances of Xinjiang still maintain traces of this legacy, which have become part of people's lives, filled with fire and smoke. Within are contained details such as the oases, prairies, cows, sheep, horses, pain, happiness, love, and other fixtures of human life.

一首叫《塔里木》的歌
A Song Called Tarim

在新疆民间，有一首叫《塔里木》的歌："哎，塔里木，茫茫戈壁大沙漠，我要进入你的怀抱，亲人哪亲人别难过……"这绝不是你经常听到的那首欢快的《塔里木河》。它更能道出大地的苍茫、辽远，以及人面对塔里木盆地时的百感交集。这首特悲凉、特感人的歌，曾经使好多人情不自禁流泪。

In Xinjiang, there is a song called "Tarim", the lyrics of which are as such: "Tarim, of the boundless and vast Gobi, I want to enter your embrace, my darling, my darling, don't be sad…" This is different from the happy song well-known in China, "Tarim River". This song is about the wild, the distant, the spectrum of emotions that people face when in the Tarim basin. The song is sad and moving, and has brought many people to tears over the years.

江格尔故乡
The Ancient Village

被誉为"江格尔故乡"的和布克赛尔蒙古自治县，是中国三大史诗之一《江格尔》的发源地。诗中唱到："他的人民长生不老，永葆二十五岁的青春。他的国家四季长青，到处洋溢着欢声笑语。他的家园没有冬天，始终散发着春天的气息……微风习习地吹拂，细雨绵绵地降落，圣主江格尔汗的家园，犹如仙境一般。"

Known as "The Village of Ancient Jangar", the Hoboksar Mongolian Autonomous County is the origin of the Jangar depicted in the epic poems. A poem describes it: "The residents do not grow old, always having a youthful appearance of 25 years of age. The country is green all year round, and smiles and laughter can be heard all about. Their homes have no winter, always smelling of spring. Soft wind blows gently, while light rain falls softly – the heavenly homes of Jangar are like a paradise."

江格尔奇传人

加·朱乃老人是新疆草原上最负盛名的江格尔奇，这位新疆西北部和布克赛尔蒙古自治县那仁和布克牧场的牧民，出生于江格尔奇世家，是第十三代江格尔奇传人。他是当地最为德高望重、演唱《江格尔》章部最多的江格尔奇。

Jia Zhunai is the most famous of the performers of the epic *Jangar*, set on the grasslands of Xinjiang. Living in the Hoboksar Mongolian Autonomous County in northwestern Xinjiang, he is the 13th generation of a line of performers of *Jangar*. He is highly respected, and the performer capable of singing the most parts of the epic.

加·朱乃 摄影：韩连赟

乐器村
Musical Instrument Village

地处阿克苏新和县的加依村，有350多年的历史，全村215户人家，105户人家都从事乐器制作，而且越来越多的年轻人开始学习乐器制作。乐器不仅使他们面目安详、目光清澈，还使他们发家致富。就算不做乐器的那些人家，也有不少在闲暇时光弹弹唱唱，好像生在"乐器村"就活在音乐中。

Jiayi Village, in Xinhe County, Aksu, has more than 350 years of history and 215 registered families, 105 of which are involved in the production of musical instruments, a trade which more and more young people are taking up. It is not only an activity which interests and captivates them, it also generates income for families. Many members of the families not involved in the industry still play instruments and sing in their free time – music is a big part of life in the "musical instrument village".

"当代荷马" 居素甫·玛玛依
Gusev Mamay

《玛纳斯》是柯尔克孜族的英雄史诗，中国三大英雄史诗之一。史诗讴歌了英雄玛纳斯及其七代子孙前仆后继，率领柯尔克孜人民与外来侵略者、各种邪恶势力进行斗争的事迹。居素甫·玛玛依，是世界上唯一一位能完整演唱8部、23万行史诗《玛纳斯》的大师，被誉为"当代荷马"。

Manas is a Kyrgyz epic poem of heroism, one of the three greatest of its kind in China. The poem celebrates in song the hero Manas and seven generations of his descendants, leading the Kyrgyz against foreign invaders and in all kinds of military campaigns against evil opponents. Gusev Mamay is the only person in the world capable of singing all eight parts, comprising 230,000 lines in total – he is known as the "Modern Homer" for this reason.

居素甫·玛玛依　摄影：韩连赟

摄影：李建民

乐器王
King of Instruments

艾依提·依明是新和县的民族乐器手工制作师，他是远近闻名的"乐器王"。之所以能被人以"王"敬称，是因为他做的乐器根本不用自己去卖，那些慕名者会像蜜蜂一样找到花道，敲开绿荫深处的家门。艾依提·依明对待造访者像王一样从容，好像每一位都是他多年的邻居。

Aiyiti Yiming, a maker of ethnic musical instruments in Xinhe County, is widely known as the "king of instruments". He is so called as he doesn't have to go out and sell any of the instruments he makes, because customers flock to his wares like bees to honey, always showing up knocking at his door. He is a kind king before his customers, treating them all as if they are neighbours of many years.

民间诗人祖拉
Poems of the People

祖拉是位年轻的牧民，还是个诗人。他放羊，放着放着就突然会写诗了。他的诗印成铅字，发表在乌鲁木齐的报刊杂志上。他说："诗是我另外的羊群。"

Zu La is a young herder, and also a poet. He suddenly comes up with poems while herding his sheep. His poems become type-printed in Urumqi newspapers and magazines. He says "poems are my other flock".

209

在音乐里融化

Immersed in Music

在南疆乡间，我突然听到了十二木卡姆里的"赛莱姆"，不知为什么，一股苍凉忧伤的情感攫住了我，我仿佛变成了一个赤足的维吾尔族女子，逆着一条奔涌的大河跑去，又仿佛站在高高的穹顶，茫然四顾，不知该往哪里去。在这个语言不通的村庄里，我第一次感到自己已成为他们中的一个，正在慢慢融化……

In a small village in southern Xinjiang, I happened to hear the salem of the twelve muqams. For some reason, I was gripped by a desolate sadness, as if I had become a young Uyghur girl myself, running barefoot against the current of a strong river, standing upon a dome, looking all around, not knowing where to go. In this village where I did not speak the language, I, for the first time, felt like one of them, slowly being assimilated.

赛骆驼

Camel Racing

骆驼，似乎总是一副慢吞吞的面孔，负重耐劳是它的强项，说起竞速，总觉得不大灵光。但如果在伊犁，目睹了蒙古族、哈萨克族的赛骆驼，你的认知会被彻底颠覆，"沙漠之舟"变身为"草上飞"，奔跑时速可达70—80公里，非一般骏马可及！骆驼左跃右蹬、左右摇摆的跑姿，也绝对是一种全新的视觉体验。

Camels have an almost irritatingly slow expression on their faces – they excel at working hard, rather than at feats of speed. However, in Yili, when you see the camel races of the Kazakhs and Mongolians, your understanding will be completely changed as you see the "barges of the desert" fly across the grass. They run at up to 70 – 80 kilometres per hour, faster than many horses. They run with a flailing gait, shaking back and forth in their running posture – a completely new kind of experience.

摄影：黄永中

摄影：黄永中

马上叼羊
Buzkashi

马和羊，是与新疆哈萨克、柯尔克孜、塔吉克等"马背民族"关系最密切的生灵。在一项运动中，马和主人一起成为"参赛者"，羊成为运动"器材"，这就是"马上叼羊"。叼羊运动形式多样，分组叼最具特色，两队对抗，冲群叼夺，追赶阻挡，前拉后推，左右护卫，突围达阵，激烈刺激的对抗，堪比橄榄球赛。

Horses and sheep are the animals most closely connected to the culture of ridership among ethnic Kazakh, Kyrgyz and Tajik people in Xinjiang. In a certain sport, the horse and rider become the contestants, and the sheep the equipment. This is "Buzkashi". There are many varieties to the sport, in which the team play variant is most distinctive – two teams face off each other, charging at each other and trying to block the opponent's advances as one protects the flanks as well as front and rear of one team's formation. When one punctures an opponent's formation, energetic competition ensues, much like in a rugby game.

传统民间游艺体育活动
Traditional Activities

新疆各民族传统的游艺体育多姿多彩。民间的传统游艺体育活动中，竞技有摔跤、拔河、秋千、达瓦孜、叼羊、赛马、赛骆驼等；游艺有叼戒指、姑娘追、打皇宫、瞎子摸象、打狼护羊等。

Xinjiang's various ethnic groups have all kinds of entertaining physical activities. These include wrestling, tug of war, swings, dawaz, Buzkashi, horse racing, camel racing, and others. "Ring taking", "being chased by girls", "attacking the palace", "pin the tail on the donkey", and "protecting the flock" are just a few of the games commonly played.

射箭
Archery

历史上，鸣镝骑射、戍边卫国的锡伯族人，擅长射箭。男婴呱呱坠地，家族长者便在结绳家谱"喜利妈妈"新绳上，挂一副用红丝绳和柳条扎成的小弓箭，寄托家族诞生神射手的期望。北京奥运会上，国家射箭队总教练郭梅珍和队员薛海峰就是从察布查尔走出来的锡伯族人，他们传承着"射箭民族"的血统和荣耀。

Historically, the Xibe people have been a key part of border defence as they are masters of the bow and arrow. When boys are still infants, the head of household fashions a miniature bow and arrow out of red silk cord and willow twigs, as part of the culture of archery that is instilled into the young child. At the Beijing 2008 Olympics, head of the national archery team Guo Haizhen and team member Xue Haifeng were both ethnic Xibe people from Qapqal, carrying on the bloodline and tradition of glorious archers.

摔跤
Wrestling

摔跤是维吾尔族人喜欢的竞技，维吾尔语叫"切里西"，场地要求简单，规则也不复杂，没有统一的服装要求和时间规定，大多在节日、巴扎日或聚会、郊游、农闲时举行。"切里西"植根于草根，不设门槛，体现力量、胆量和技艺。"切里西"是民间文化娱乐盛宴，正可谓摔有摔的乐儿，看有看的趣儿。

Wrestling is popular among Uyghurs, called "keris" by them. The requirements for a venue are quite simple, the rules are not complex, and there are no unified requirements for uniforms or time. Most of the meets occur during holidays, bazaars, parties, trips, and times of leisure. The sport is a grassroots one, with no barrier to entry – all one needs is strength, gall, and skill. "Keris" is a kind of cultural celebration, both fun to participate in and watch.

摄影：黄永中

摄影：黄永中

斗羊
Fighting Rams

斗羊，是维吾尔族人在聚会、节假日举行的喜闻乐见的传统民间游戏。高大、雄壮、力足、盘角粗壮的斗羊，一改平日里的温顺形象，在"力比多"的原始动力驱使下，成为野性十足的"斗士"。《史记》说"很（狠）如羊"，是很有道理的。莫道斗羊太残忍，这其实还是优胜劣汰、防止羊种退化的一种方式。

Sheep battles are an occurrence at Uyghur gatherings and holidays. Large, strong, powerful, and with big horns – the normally gentle sheep under the drive of their powerful libido become savage warriors. *The Shi Ji (Historical Records)* makes a reference to being "savage as a sheep", quite logically. Rather than being a savage sport, it's quite a practical application of survival of the fittest, ensuring the stock stays strong.

歌的生命
A Life of Songs

"西部曲兮流于民唇，承洛宾兮识而传真。驹无伯乐兮无以千里，曲无洛宾兮中外寡闻。民间瑰宝兮撷之于民，人间绝唱兮得之于心。传歌之志兮可嘉可钦，洛宾之功兮青史永存。"这是"西部歌王"王洛宾的墓志铭，他曾制定过一个 500 年艺术生命计划，努力写出能传唱 500 年的歌曲。我们相信，好歌的生命不止 500 年。

"The songs of the west originate from the mouths of the people, transmitted through Luobin. As Bo Le (a famous judge of talents) evaluated horses, so does Luobin disseminate songs. Treasures are picked from the common people, spread around through the work of Luobin so they may last." These are the words upon the tomb of Wang Luobin, "King of Songs of the West". He once wrote a 500-year artistic life plan, and songs to be sung and transmitted for 500 years to go with it. We believe that good songs may last longer than that.

213

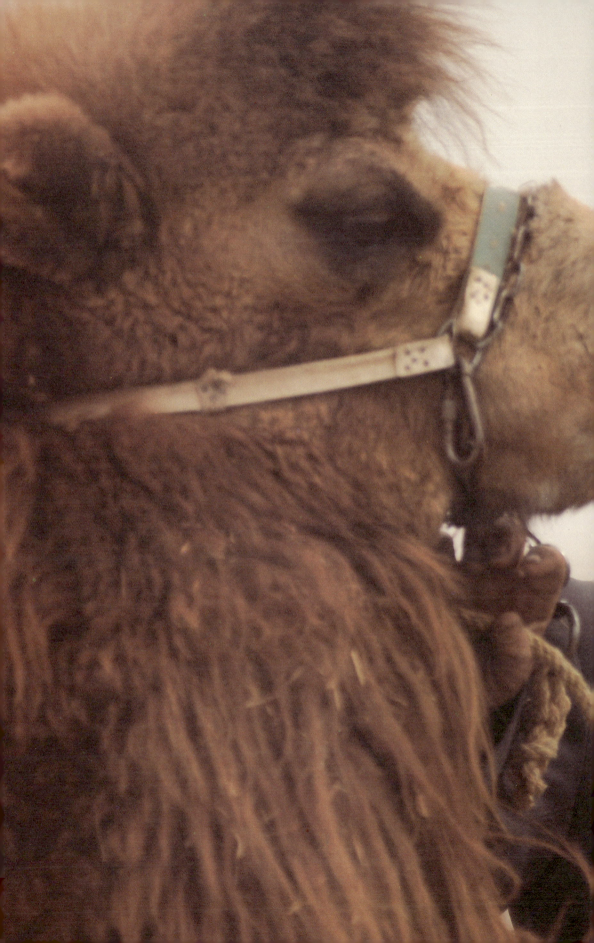

语言·杂话
Languages and Stories

"疆"字的解读 Interpretation of the Character "jiang"	"疆"字仿佛专为说明新疆而设。这个字左右结构，左边是张弓守土，右边分别是"三横两田"。"三横"由上至下排列，分别代表三条山脉：阿尔泰山脉、天山山脉和昆仑山脉。上"田"为北，是准噶尔盆地；下"田"为南，是塔里木盆地。这是新疆人的一种意会，无关字理。 The character for "jiang" in Xinjiang can be said to have been made specifically for the region. It is composed of a bow protecting soil on the right, and the right shows three horizontals amongst two fields. The three lines horizontals, from top to bottom, can be seen as three mountain ranges: Altay, Tianshan, and Kunlun. The upper "field" is the north of the Junggar Basin, and the lower "field" is the southern Tarmin Basin. This is, of course, a folk etymology.
酒 Liquor	维吾尔族人说：酒嘛，睡在瓶子里老实得很，跑到人的肚子里就调皮得很。 Uyghurs say: alcohol is well-behaved in the bottle, and a troublemaker in the stomach.
卡瓦一样的脑袋 A Brain Like a Kawa	南疆人说某个人不聪明，脑子有问题，不会说脑子进水了，而是说"卡瓦一样的脑袋"。"卡瓦"是维吾尔族人对葫芦或南瓜的称谓，与汉语中的"傻瓜"有异曲同工之妙，不过更形象生动。 When the people of southern Xinjiang describe someone as being stupid or crazy, they say, rather than the "brain is leaking", but that the person's head is "like a kawa". A "kawa" is a word in southern Xinjiang for a gourd or pumpkin – this curiously mirrors the Chinese language in which "dummy" is called a "stupid melon".
父亲的歌 Father's Song	在新疆，我听到一位蒙古族老人这样唱："十五的月亮和十五岁的女儿一样，它是爸爸妈妈心上的灯笼。二十五的月亮和二十五岁的女儿一样，它是爸爸妈妈四人心上的灯笼。"这是结了婚的月亮。显然除了自己的父母，她还在公公和婆婆的心里。 In Xinjiang, I heard an old Mongolian singing: "the moon of the 15th day is like a 15-year-old girl – the lantern in her father and mother's hearts. The moon of the 25th day is like a 25-year-old daughter – the lantern in the hearts of her four parents…" This is a married moon. Of course, aside from being in her parents' heart, the lantern also shines in that of her in-laws.

这马儿调皮得很

An Unruly Horse

裕民县山花节，遇一哈族老汉，单人匹马踽踽独行山草间。友人想秀一把骑术，老汉眼睛俏皮地一挤，嘴巴轻快地一"嗒"，用最艺术的方式婉拒："这马儿调皮得很！"不说你骑术堪忧，不说我不情愿，却说那马儿，婉曲而不失风度，幽默却不油滑，令人不禁心生敬意，折服于这最修辞化的表达。

At the Mountain Flower Festival of Yumin County, an old Kazakh man was walking along with his horse in the grass. A friend wished to show off his riding talent, but the old man simply made a clicking sound with his mouth, refusing the offer in the most graceful of ways – the horse is unruly! Rather than doubting the rider's skill, or being unwilling himself, the horse was simply unfit for the task. The man's manner of refusal was graceful, humorous, and geniuine, inspiring one to respect him.

摄影：王晖

217

春天
Spring

那些说来就来的雪，说化就化了，新疆人说雪站不住了，这个"站"字用得多么传神，仿佛挺立了一冬的雪，是得了什么病而忽然骨酥筋麻，软软地躺倒了。

People say let it snow, and let the snow melt when the time comes – in Xinjiang people say the snow can't stand its ground – after standing all winter, it becomes weary and has no choice but to simply give in and lie down.

喀纳斯的狗
Dogs in Kanas

前些年，游人不多的时候，喀纳斯的狗比较厉害，但有一种人它不咬，就是走路摇晃的人，它觉得这才是本地人。那些年在喀纳斯，好多男人早晨起来一般还醉着呢。

In the times when travellers were sparse, the dogs of Kanas were more aggressive, but they wouldn't bite those who swayed as they walked, for they believed them to be locals. In those years in Kanas, many men woke up in the morning still drunk.

二转子
Second Rotation

新疆历来是多民族聚集之地，民族间的通婚混血自古有之，比如在塔城，一个家庭可能会是几个民族组成的。一个民族与另一个民族混血的结晶俗称"二转子"，二转子如果再与一个不同民族混血，产生的后代就被称为"三转子"。

Xinjiang has historically been a place in which many ethnic groups came together, with marriages between groups occurring since ancient times. In Tacheng, a family may be composed of a few different groups. When people of two ethnic groups marry, this is commonly termed the "second rotation". If the product of such a union marries a member of yet another ethnic group, it would be a "third rotation".

鸡蛋妈妈的丈夫
Husband of the Egg's Mother

鸡蛋妈妈的丈夫，这不用猜，就是指"公鸡"，这是新疆刚学汉语的少数民族朋友对公鸡的表述。

The husband of the egg's mother is of course the cock – "husband chicken" in Chinese. This is a kind of expression used by ethnic group members in Xinjiang who are learning Chinese as a second language.

牙好的时候多吃肉
Eat More While You Have Good Teeth

新疆有句维吾尔谚语：牙好的时候多吃肉，腿好的时候多走路。

There is a saying amongst the Uyghurs of Xinjiang: "When your teeth are in good shape, eat more meat. When your legs are in good shape, walk more."

草原上没有公厕

No Public Toilets

牧民说，草原上狗多，狗改不了吃屎。所以，草原干净得很，不需要建公厕。

Herders say that with so many dogs on the prairie, given their love of eating excrement, there's no need to build public toilets as they will always keep the landscape clean.

一层一层的年纪

Layers of Age

秋天，和一位维吾尔族老人坐在树下聊天时，看见树叶飘落下来。老人说："树叶黄了叶子会落，人的岁数嘛也是一层压着一层，落叶归根，人也一样的。"

In autumn, when sitting down chatting with an old Uyghur, I saw the leaves fall. He remarked: "As the leaves turn yellow they will fall, just like age piles upon humans – leaves return to the roots, and so will we."

把脸也洗一下

Wash Your Face

维吾尔族老人说："水是最圣洁的，请你在洗手的同时，把脸也洗一下。"意思是说如果别人好心帮助了你，你也顺便把其他需要帮助的人帮一下！

An old Uyghur said: "Water is the most sacred. When washing your hands, also wash your face." This means that when someone does the favour of helping you, you should also help those around you!

摄影：刘力

多语新疆

Multilingual
Xinjiang

即便是偏远如喀什，这种集国家通用语言文字（汉语）、民族语言文字（维语或哈语、蒙语、柯语、锡语）、外国语言文字（英语、俄语、日语等）于一身的路牌也并不鲜见。"语言文字生态"诠释一种生活，也映射一种心态。随处可见的多语和谐并用现象，是新疆开放包容、多元异彩文化特质最直接的注脚。

Even in far-off Kashgar, the common language of the country (Standard Chinese), ethnic scripts (Uyghur, Kazakh, Mongol, Kyrgyz, Xibe) and foreign languages (English, Russian, Japanese and others) are commonly seen on road signs together. The linguistic ecosystem reflects the state of the region itself. Multilingualism is common, as Xinjiang is open and inclusive to all the varied cultures.

摄影：王晖

绰号不是人人都能得到
Nicknames Aren't Free

一个维吾尔族老汉说："我叫依明・阔西卡尔。依明是我的名字，阔西卡尔是我的绰号，公羊的意思。你可别笑，绰号在我们这里可不是人人都能得到的，只有那些有特点、有一定影响力的人才能获得。公羊就是领头羊。"

An old Uyghur said: "My name is Yiming Kuoxikar. Yiming is my name, Kuoxikar is my nickname, meaning "ram". Don't laugh. Not all of us have nicknames here – only the special do. Only those with enough influence are granted one. The ram is the leader of the sheep."

杂语交融的地方
A Place of Many Languages

新疆是个杂语交融的地方。历史上，民族交往频繁，中外商贾云集，东西文明交汇，使这里语言纷繁复杂。30 余种的古文字，让语言文字学家费尽心机、穷毕生精力仍难解真谛。

Xinjiang is a place where many languages mix – historically as ethnic tribes had a high degree of contact with each other, merchants passed through, and interactions took place between east and west, the languages of the region became more complicated. With more than 30 kinds of ancient scripts, this region has attracted much scholarship among linguists, some who have spent their entire lives studying them.

给力的神"马"
Like a Horse

自古至今，新疆人对马充满深情和钟爱，这些都烙在语言当中了，比如"骏马是男人的翅膀"（哈萨克族谚语），"好马只需一鞭"（维吾尔族谚语），"你给别人一只山羊，别人给你一匹骏马"（柯尔克孜族谚语）。在新疆你可以听到笑成马了、累成马了、能成马了、倔成马了。给力的神"马"，让语言都"活"啦！

From ancient times, the people of Xinjiang have had strong feelings for horses that are reflected in the language itself. A Kazakh proverb holds "a good horse is a man's wings". A Mongolian proverb states "a good horse only needs one lash". A Kyrgyz proverb says "give someone a goat, and they give you a horse." In Xinjiang, you hear phrases like "laughing like a horse", "tired as a horse", "capable as a horse", "stubborn as a horse" – this amazing animal really brings the languages to life.

没有结婚的羊
Unmarried Sheep

在乌鲁木齐，当你从在烤肉摊或烤全羊摊前走过，让你馋涎欲滴的不光是色香味，还有这句："没有结婚的羊"。

In Urumqi, when you pass by a skewer stand or a stand that sells roast lamb, you are filled with desire for the flavor – what people refer to as "unmarried sheep".

孔雀河
Konqi River

孔雀河流经库尔勒，维吾尔语称为"昆其达里雅"，意为皮匠河，因当地皮革业发达。据研究，"昆其"是汉语"髡者"的音译，髡者本指理发匠，维吾尔语转指皮匠（给牛羊"理发"的人）。新中国成立后，根据维吾尔语读音，把"昆其"雅化，译为"孔雀"。孔雀河是民族文化交融汇流的"语源学"证明。

The Konqi River passes through Korla, and is called "kunqidaliya" by the Uyghurs, meaning "cobbler's river", as the industry is well-developed there. According to research, "kunqi" is a Uyghur pronunciation of the old Chinese word "kunzhe" – a shaver of heads, which came to mean "cobbler" in Uyghur as these people "styled the hair" of sheep and lambs. After the establishment of the People's Republic, "kunqi" was changed to the better sounding "kongque", meaning "peacock" in Mandarin. Thus the Chinese name for the river, Kongque He, is a testament to the linguistic interaction in the area.

秦尼巴克
China Garden

秦尼巴克意为"中国花园"，是一个中西合璧的词。秦尼是英文"中国"的译音，巴克则是维吾尔语"花园"的意思。秦尼巴克也是一座中西合璧的花园，是维吾尔园林的浪漫情调与英式庭院的典雅风格的一次有机结合。作为曾经的英国驻喀什总领事馆所在地，秦尼巴克见证了半个多世纪中亚史的跌宕起伏和新疆大地上的风云变幻。

Meaning "China Garden", Qinnibake is a word that incorporates east and west – in Chinese "qin ni" is the approximation of the English word "China", and "ba ke" is Uyghur for "garden". Qinnibake is an Eastern and Western style garden – a Uyghur garden that incorporates elements of English architecture. As the former site of the English consulate in Kashgar, Qinnibake is a testament to more than half a century of happenings in Central Asia and ups and downs in the Xinjiang region.

坎土曼的传说
Legend of the Kantuman

坎土曼被维吾尔族视为万能农具，锄地、挖土、间苗、开渠都离不开它。维吾尔族有句谚语："坎土曼的苦头手知道，粮食的甜头嘴知道。"坎土曼烙下劳苦的印记，但也创造收获的幸福。当父亲把坎土曼传递给儿子时，劳动和收获的真谛，儿子一定会体悟得相当真切。

The kantuman is seen by the Uyghurs as an all-purpose agricultural tool, used for tilling, digging, sowing, and trenching. There is a Uyghur saying: "The hands know the bitter taste of the kantuman, and the mouth knows the sweet taste of the grain". The kantuman bears the marks of hard work but also reaps benefits. When a father gives his son his kantuman, the son will understand the true essence of labour and benefit.

儿子娃娃
Baby Boy

可别急，也别恼，新疆人这么说你时，绝对是赞！儿子娃娃是新疆人对男性的夸赞之词，涵盖勇敢、豪爽、说到做到、讲情义等诸多褒扬之意，换个说法，那就是纯爷们儿、真汉子！

Don't hurry or worry – when people in Xinjiang say this to you, it's a good thing. "Baby boy" is a common appellation for young males that implies the values of being bold, forthright, brave, capable, and so on – that is to say, it's a term for a real guy.

古丽
Guli

风情的花帽头巾，弯弯的画眉，精巧的小辫，是新疆维吾尔女孩——古丽们的群体肖像。在维吾尔语中，古丽是"花儿""花朵"的意思，常泛指年轻女孩，也是维吾尔女性取名字喜欢用的字眼儿，像克孜力古丽（玫瑰花）、阿娜尔古丽（石榴花）、阿依古丽（月亮花），或者干脆叫美丽古丽，听着就可爱漂亮！

The flowered hat and headscarf, painted eyebrows, and small braids – these are the characteristics of the girls of Xinjiang. In Uyghur, the common name "Guli" means "flower", and is frequently used to describe young girls. Names such as Kizliguli (rose), Anarguli (pomegranate flower), Ayguli (moon flower) and the like are all common.

摄影：黄永中

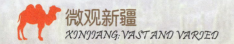
眼睛装不下的美
Unfakeable

这是为新疆阿勒泰旅游区创作的广告词：眼睛装不下的美。其实，这也适合整个新疆。

An ad for the Altay Tourist Area in Xinjiang described it as "beauty that can only be real". This could be said of all of Xinjiang.

巴郎子
Little Balang

巴郎，是维吾尔语"小伙子"的汉语音译词。小男孩，可以叫"小巴郎子"，现在也广泛使用在新疆人对男孩子的昵称上。

Balang means "little guy" in Uyghur. Little boys can be called "little balang", and the word can be used to refer to boys in general in Xinjiang.

摄影：王晖

学习维语 "三板斧"
Three Phrases

语言是沟通感情最便当的媒介，来新疆学几句维语，会瞬间拉近与维吾尔族群众的距离：亚克西是"好""棒"（再多三个音节，亚克西姆斯兹是"你好"），热合买提是"谢谢"，霍希是"再见"，也是"干杯"（记不住就说"和谐"）。学会这三句，你就像拥有了程咬金三把斧，可以微笑着、比画着畅游新疆啦！

Language is the most convenient medium for communicating emotions – when you learn a few Uyghur phrases in Xinjiang, the distance between you and the people will be shortened – "yaksi" is "good", and "yaksi musz" is "how do you do". Rehemai is "thank you", "hosh" is "goodbye" as well as "bottoms up". With these three phrases, you have the keys that you need to head out in Xinjiang.

你好吗
How Are You?

由于工作的关系，我认识了一位叫伊布拉音的维吾尔族朋友。每次他来电话，第一句必定是：你好，我是伊大哥。然后就殷勤地问候：你好吗，我的朋友？孩子好吗？宏志兄弟好吗？华莎妹妹好吗？周总好吗？恨不能把我们的朋友交集挨个儿问候一遍。每当这时，我总是忙不迭地说：好好好，都很好！谢谢伊大哥惦记！

Through my work I met a Uyghur friend named Ibrahim. Every time he called, the first sentence would be "Hello, it's me, Ibrahim". Then, he would ask: "How are you, my friend? How are your children? How are your brothers? How is your mother, and your boss?" If only he could come up for a collective term for all of them. Every time, I would say "fine, fine, fine, everyone's fine! Thanks for your concern, Ibrahim!"

新疆杂话
Xinjiang Stories

"有一回，他醉倒在马路边，吃的东西吐了一大摊。一条老狗走过来，吃完还围着老张转，看他嘴上还沾了点，伸出舌头又去舔。"这是新疆杂话《张翻翻》的一个片段，一个醉汉形象跳脱眼前，令人忍俊不禁。新疆杂话植根于本土方言，合辙押韵、通俗风趣，堪称新疆的地域名片，已列入国家级非物质文化遗产。

"One time, he collapsed, drunken, at the side of the road, blowing chunks all over. An old dog walked over, and after eating his vomit, saw there was still some on his mouth, and licked it off his face." These are lines from the Xinjiang story Zhang Fanfan – people can't help laughing as a drunk man appears. These Xinjiang stories originate in local dialects, and with their rhymes, puns, and common themes, are almost name cards for Xinjiang – they have been listed as a national intangible cultural heritage in China.

布尔津：三岁的公骆驼
Burqin: A Three-Year-Old Camel

布尔津河是额尔齐斯河最大的支流，因古时候有一位名不见经传的老人在这里放牧骆驼为生而得名。如此尊重平民的地名让人立即亲近了这条河！布尔，卫拉特蒙古语，意思是三岁的公骆驼。津，放牧之意。

The Burqin River is the largest tributary of the Ertix River. It takes its name from a relatively unknown camel herder in ancient times – it's remarkable how the river is named after someone so ordinary! Bur, in Oirat Mongolian, means "three-year-old camel". Qin means "herding".

新疆河南话
Henan Dialect in Xinjiang

新疆的东疆、北疆和兵团一些团场，流行河南话，甚至有"河南方言岛"现象，据说和 20 世纪五六十年代河南人大规模支边移民有关。至今仍流传着这样的笑话——上课时老师领读、学生跟诵：杏，横姿哩横！麦，美姿哩美！白，倍舔哩倍！家，甲听哩甲！当然，随着全国各地人来到新疆，普通话正逐渐流行。

In eastern and northern Xinjiang, at some farms of the Xinjiang Production and Construction Corps, Henan Dialect is widely spoken to the extent that these places are almost dialect enclaves – this is due to the large number of people from Henan who took part in the large-scale migration to the border areas in the 1950's and 1960's. Even now there are various jokes about the prevalence of the dialect in Xinjiang, but as more people from various parts of the country arrived in Xinjiang, standard Mandarin has become more and more common instead.

新疆话的风采
Interesting Language

新疆人说话喜欢"出格"，用"牙长的一截截"形容路途近，把风骚女子叫"骚孔雀"，生气说成"肚子胀"；新疆人还喜欢用形容词生动形式，比如甜兮兮、柔乃乃、湿浃浃、胖曩曩，冰叽哇嗒（冰凉）、疙瘩哇匙（凹凸不平）、黑嘛窟蠹（漆黑）。稀松平常的话，这么历历如绘地一用，真是风采尽显，情态顿出！

The people of Xinjiang like "breaking the pattern", using phrases like "a tooth coming in crooked" to describe a route being short, calling a coquettish girl a "coquettish peahen", saying one's "stomach is bloating" to describe someone as angry. They also like using expressive adjectival phrases, such as "sweet as sugar", "soft as silk", "wet as water", "fat as a pig", "cold as ice", "bumpy as a pre-teen's pizza face", "black as coal", and so on. This kind of jocular language used in such a vibrant manner allows them to really make their language come alive.

喧荒
Xuanhuang

照片上是喀什街头"喧荒"的维吾尔族老人。"喧荒"是新疆汉语方言，相当于聊天、拉呱儿、侃大山、扯闲篇，其造词之意，颇能彰显新疆地广人稀、性格豪迈的神韵，你可以可着劲儿地、漫无边际地东拉西扯——从奶茶馕饼、玉石玛瑙，到巴郎古丽、巴扎淘宝，从天山昆仑、大漠戈壁，到丝路西域、罗布泊、阿凡提。

The picture is of two "xuanhuang" old men on the streets of Kashgar. "Xuanhuang" is Xinjiang Mandarin Dialect for chatting idly – the word describes a specific type of behaviour among the people of Xinjiang – bold and generous, romantic and charming; you can go on and on, dragging in all sorts of irrelevant matters – from milk tea, bread, agate, jade, to girls, to shopping, to the Kunlun mountains and Gobi desert, to the Silk Road, Lop Nur, and Avanti.

摄影：双元

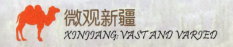

沟里的秘密
Secrets in the Gully

地名是探秘地理人文的一把钥匙。在新疆有一个地方，辖区地名多带"沟"字，有水西沟、水磨沟、板房沟、白杨沟、碾子沟、鱼儿沟、榆树沟、芦草沟、甘沟、东沟、后沟，这个地方叫乌鲁木齐。乌鲁木齐名字来源于蒙古语，意为"优美的牧场"，这么多"沟"汇聚，是为这座中亚第二大城市"释名"的最好注解。

Place names are words that geographers use as keys. In Xinjiang, there is a place in which many of the sub-jurisdictions have names with "gou" ("gully"or "valley"). Suixigou, Shuimogou, Banfanggou, Baiyanggou, Nianzigou, Yu'ergou, Yushugou, Lucaogou, Gangou, Donggou, Hougou – these are all place names in Urumqi. The name "Urumqi" originates from the Mongolian language, meaning "excellent pasture". All these names containing "gou" are used to keep track of various places in Central Asia's second largest city.

在那……遥远的地方
A Place Far Away

在新疆，如果你问路，恰巧碰到一位哈萨克族朋友，他说在那边，一般不会太远；他说在那…边，就会有一定距离；他若说在那……边，你得有受点儿累的准备；如果说在那…………边，那可能表示不知要翻几座山了。不用词汇手段，省却语法手段，就靠语音的长短，距离的远近就表达得淋漓尽致！

In Xinjiang, when asking directions, should you meet a Kazakh, when he says "over there", he means nearby. "Over… there" means there's a bit of distance involved, and "over… … there" means you should be prepared for a bit of a journey. If he says "over… … … …there" may mean you might have to cross a mountain range, or something on that order of magnitude. Using fewer words, and eschewing linguistic encumbrance, simply the length of words or pauses can be used to convey distance in this way.

爱"子"的新疆人
Different Suffixes

新疆人粗犷爽直，在语言上也有反映，比方说新疆方言喜欢用"子"缀。别处说凉皮儿、揪片儿，新疆人说凉皮子、揪片子，听着就有劲道；羊肝儿、毛驴儿，到新疆人嘴里就说成羊肝子、毛驴子，听着就大气。其他还有酸奶子、皮芽子，以及更好玩儿的虫虫子、眼眼子、一堆堆子、一筐筐子，极具韵致，很有味道。

People in Xinjiang are rough and straightforward, which is reflected in their language – they like to use the simple suffix "-zi" where other speakers use the more eloquent "-er". Common words such as liangpi and jiupian, two kinds of noodles, become liangpizi and jiupianzi rather than liangpir and jiupianr. Words for foods and animals can seem to have more of an effect to other Chinese speakers. There are a number of words like this which people find quite amusing.

"马上"在新疆
On the Horse

2014 年流行"马上"体，但是不少人吐槽，新疆人说的"马上"，谁知道有多久！请不要埋怨新疆人不守时，如果到过新疆，你就会了解，那辽阔的大地，就是跨上了马，也是要跑上一阵子的，咱们不也有一句话叫"远看山近跑死马"？语言交流讲究社会语境，所以在新疆听到"马上"，你千万别猴急猴急的。

The topic of "ma shang" (meaning "on horseback" and also "immediately") became popular in 2014, but who can only guess how long the concept has been popular in Xinjiang! Don't fault those in Xinjiang for not being punctual –in such a broad landscape, distances are vast. Language communication requires for a social context. Thus, you needn't rush or hurry when you hear someone say "mashang" in Xinjiang.

台子
Taizi

台子作为地名，常与古烽火台相关，如头台子、双台子。乌鲁木齐周边"台子"也不少，多属山梁阔地。南台子，取其方位；高台子，因其海拔；平草台子、菊花台子、苜蓿台子，名以植被；月亮台子，不知名之所由，听着挺神秘。这些台子，初夏以后花草丰茂，林木葱郁，牛马徜徉，鹰鸟轻翔，是休闲避暑的胜地。

"Taizi" is a place name that is a common component of the names of ancient beacon towers, scuh as Toutaizi and Shuangtaizi. There are a number of places in Urumqi with names of this type, mostly located on the ridges of mountains. Nantaizi (nan: "south") is so named for its position, Gaotaizi (gao: "high") is so named for its elevation, and Pingcaotaizi (pingcao: "grass plain") and Juhuataizi (juhua: "chrysanthemum") are named for their vegetative cover. Yueliangtaizi (yueliang: "moon") is a name of unclear origin, so it sounds mysterious. These "taizi" are covered in lush vegetation in summertime each year, and grazing horses and cattle, along with birds flying overhead, make them nice places to relax and avoid the heat.

摄影：王晖

攒劲得很
Really Great

新疆人食重味，衣重彩，说话重情态。"……得很"，是"很……"的加强版，比后者更利于表达状态和程度，它因此得到了新疆人的青睐，比如威（厉害）得很、尖（聪明）得很、能干得很、拐杖（坏）得很、蛋屁话（废话）多得很。套用一句新疆话，那就是：这种结构攒劲（给力）得很！

People in Xinjiang eat thick food, wear thick clothing, and talk in a thick spirit – in Mandarin Chinese even the placement of adjectival modifiers for words such as "very" is changed for extra emphasis in a number of phrases, for example, wei (powerful) de hen "quite formidable", jian (sharp) de hen "quite clever", nenggan de hen "quite capable", guaizhang (cane) de hen "quite wicked", danpihua (nonsense) duo de hen "quite ludicrous", and so on. In terms of the local dialect in Xinjiang, one can say that its structure is zanjin de hen (really great)!

侃大山
Talking about Mountains

几位朋友聚会，夸起家乡名山，几位内地朋友三山五岳、四大名山一通狂侃，自豪之情溢于言表。发现新疆朋友一直笑而不语，劝道："你也说一下嘛。""咱新疆嘛，就三座山还算说得出口，一座叫昆仑山，万山之祖；一座用'天'命名，叫天山，口气有点大；还有一座阿尔泰山，也不懂得低调，小名叫金山。"

At a gathering with friends, people were talking about their hometown mountains. A number of people from the inland provinces of China were talking about the famous "five mountains" (Taishan, Huashan, Hengshan, Songshan and Hengshan) and other geographical features quite proudly. I found one of my friends from Xinjiang chuckling. He said: "Talking about mountains, in Xinjiang a few mountains here and there don't mean much. We have the Kunlun Range, with its myriad peaks, the famous Tianshan Mountains, and of course the Altay Range, which we nickname 'golden mountain', which is admittedly a bit much."

地名二合一
Two-in-One

新疆托克逊县，有个李毛坎儿孜村。李毛，是维吾尔族人对卷发李姓人的戏称，坎儿孜即坎儿井，"李毛坎儿孜"是汉语、维吾尔语地名合词。在新和县也有类似的地名，叫"裁缝铁热克村"，原先有汉族裁缝居住在此，"铁热克"维语意为"白杨树"。汉族和维吾尔族互相离不开，这二合一的地名，就是一种印记。

In Xinjiang's Toksun County, there is a village called Limao Kanerz – Limao is a name the Uyghurs gave to a curly-haired man surnamed Li, and kanerz is the Uyghur word for a qanat – the name of the village is thus half-Chinese, half-Uyghur. In Xinhe County, there are many similar place names – Caifeng Terek is a similar one, caifeng meaning "tailor" in Chinese and Terek being Uyghur for "white poplar". These place names are a reminder of how inextricably linked the Han and Uyghur peoples are.

过分、放肆
Overdoing It

过分和放肆是典型的贬义词，塔城人偏偏这样用：咱塔城，天蓝得有些过分，花开得有些放肆！听听，人家自我"批评"做得多么有豪情。塔城环境没说的，塔城人也真没说的，把"贬词褒用"修辞方法运用得真是妙。

"Overdone" and "unbridled" are two terms with negative connotations, which the people of Tacheng use thus: The blue sky in Tacheng is a bit overdone, and the flowers bloom unbridled! It seems a bit lofty to "criticise" oneself in such a way. Tacheng and its people are really great, using words with negative connotations in such a way.

奠基之石
Marking Stones

西白杨沟小学是乌鲁木齐南郊的一所农牧区双语学校，学校操场上原本寻常的石头，在师生们的巧思下，竟孕育出新的"生命"：一个字、一个拼音、一幅画，国家通用语言文字就这样生动地"图解"到石头上，走入同学们眼里、心里。语言文字是文化的基石，也是民族沟通、和睦、团结的奠基之石。

Xibaiyanggou Elementary School is a bilingual school in a semi-farming and semi-herding area in the southern suburbs of Urumqi. A stone on the athletic ground of the school has been given a new life by the students and teachers through their ingenuity – a Chinese character, pinyin, and a picture have been carved upon the stone depicting various concepts in Mandarin so that the students may remember them. Language is the foundation of culture, and is also the foundation upon which various ethnic groups communicate, make friends, and stick together.

摄影：王晖

三大名海
The Three Big Seas

中国三大名海你知道吗？新疆朋友的答案是这样的："第一名海嘛，大家都知道，在北京，叫中南海；第二名海嘛，大家也熟悉，叫上海；第三名海嘛，人家不张扬，记住啦，在新疆，叫福海（乌伦古湖）！"

Do you know the three famous "seas" of China? A friend in Xinjiang explained this way: "The first sea (hai) is of course in Beijing – Zhongnanhai. The second is of course "Shanghai" which we are all familiar with, and the third, less widely known is in Xinjiang – Fuhai! (Fuhai is another name for Ulungur Lake.)

渐行渐远的味道
A Fading Flavour

莫合烟是俄语"玛合勒嘎"的音译兼意译，据说劲大，口感粗犷似雄浑大漠。莫合烟流行的另一原因是它的 DIY，自卷自抽，还可以递一片报纸，撮一撮烟丝给朋友，便宜简约，又不失面子。在产业政策的调控下，莫合烟在本世纪初逐渐退出销售市场，这种曾经的新疆味道已渐行渐远，化为一个时代的集体记忆了。

Mohe Tobacco, or mahorka in Russian, is a strong tobacco with a rough flavor. It's popular for those who roll their own cigarettes (DIY cigarettes), and friends frequently send each other packages wrapped in newspaper. It's cheap and simple, but still a nice gift. With changes in policy, it's fallen out of use in this century, and what was once a hallmark of the local culture is quickly becoming only a memory.

石榴
Pomegranate

石榴在维吾尔语中叫"阿娜尔"。许多姑娘取名为"阿娜尔汗"（石榴姑娘）或"阿娜尔古丽"（石榴花），读起来有一种音乐和色彩的美感。当花朵和果实为人名所借用，就足以说明这种植物的深入人心以及在这个民族日常生活中的重要性了。

Pomegranates are called "anar" in Xinjiang, and many girls are named Anarhan ("pomegranate girl") or Anarguli ("pomegranate flower") – reading these words invokes a colourful, musical feeling. When we take the names of fruits and flowers as personal names, it shows that we are closely connected to them, and underscores their importance to a certain group of people.

吃得豪爽
Eating Style

我喜欢看新疆人进食的样子，比如说吃拉面，几个人闷头于比自己的脸盘儿大许多的大号搪瓷盘上，呼啦啦地吃出一片声响，谁也不会顾忌什么。哪怕是一位女士，也会加入到这一片激越的交响中，大汗淋漓、痛哉快哉！

I like the way people in Xinjiang eat – for instance, when eating noodles, you may see a group of people hunched over large enamelled bowls, emitting a chorus of noises as they slurp them down – there's nothing wrong with this. Sometimes, you may even see a girl tucking in and participating in the symphony, really giving it her all.

大拌筋
Dabanjin

新疆人称为拉条子的面食，还有一个别名叫大拌筋。想起来就让人流口水。如果一个人在疆外漂泊了一个月，一踏进新疆的街市就忙死颠颠地到处找拌面馆，他准是个地地道道的新疆人。

The noodles that people in Xinjiang call latiaozi are also known by the name dabanjin. Just thinking about them makes the mouth water. If after a month travelling outside of Xinjiang, the first thing you do upon returning is fervently look for a noodle house, then you are a real Xinjiang guy.

拉条子
Latiaozi

什么是新疆？从面食上说，"拉条子"就是新疆。

What is Xinjiang? In terms of noodles, it would be latiaozi – Xinjiang-style mixed noodles.

摄影：韩连赟

摄影：刘力、韩连赟

馕
Nang

馕，是全中国只有新疆才有的食品，它没有经过铁器的接触，不会有丝毫铁的腥锈味儿，只有来自泥土的厚重的香味。从馕坑里取出的馕，黄灿灿的，四射着豪光，如日月般的馕饼，辉映了多少晦暗的日子。

The nang is a kind of bread that is unique to Xinjiang. As it doesn't come into contact with iron implements, it lacks the metallic tinge that some kinds of bread have; instead, it tastes only of rich earth. When it emerges from the oven, it glows with its yellow light – like the sun and the moon, illuminating many gloomy days.

抓饭的吃法
Eating with One's Hands

手抓饭的吃法，不能依字面的理解满把去抓，而只动用拇指、食指和中指即可。面对一盘抓饭，还要保持一颗感恩的心，然后用食指和中指将盘中餐的一部分拨拢到盘边，再用拇指配合，压实，形成油汪汪的一撮，送入口中。你会觉得无数次吃手抓饭，只有用手抓的那一次最够滋味也最正宗。

Xinjiang-style rice pilaf, or shouzhuafan, meaning "rice eaten with the hand", is eaten with the thumb, index and middle fingers. When you're faced with a plate of it, you should have a grateful heart – when only a bit of rice remains, you use your index and middle finger to push it to the side of the plate, and then use your thumb to compress it into a coherent unit that you pop into your mouth. No matter how many times you've tried shouzhuafan, you've not experienced it at its most authentic until you've eaten it with your hand.

摄影：刘力

吃面识厨师
Noodle Experts

看做新疆拌面，是非常有意思的一件事。如果扯面的是条汉子，你会看出一种气势；如果抻面的是个女子，你会看出一种韵味。据说有经验的吃客根本不用到后堂去看，端上来的面只要一入口，便知道做拌面的师傅是汉子还是女子。

The process through which Xinjiang mixed noodles are made is quite interesting. If the noodle maker is a guy, you will feel his vigour in the noodles; if the noodle maker is a girl, you will feel her lasting charm. It's said that experienced noodle consumers can tell whether the noodles they are eating have been made by a guy or a girl without even seeing into the kitchen – all they need is to taste one bite.

熏马肠
Smoked Horse Intestine

熏马肠是草原哈萨克族人的重要美食。在每年过冬之前膘肥马壮的深秋季节，哈萨克族人都要进行"冬宰"（索古姆）。他们把肋巴肉条子装入1米长短洗净的马肠里（也有把马肉、马油搓上调料和盐装入马肠的），两头扎紧，挂在凉房里晾干，用牛粪或用爬地松点烟慢慢熏熟，以便随时蒸熟待客享用。

Smoked horse intestine is an important delicacy among the Kazakhs of the prairie. Every year before winter, when the horses are fat in late fall, the Kazakhs conduct their "winter slaughter" (sogum). They put strips of fatty meat into a cleaned horse intestine along with lean meat, fat, seasonings and salt, twist the ends tight, and hang the intestine in a cold room to dry, and smoke it with manure or wood, so that it can be cooked up for guests whenever they arrive.

烤馕包烤肉
Chinese Tacos

新疆街头最常见的一景就是，几个人站在烤肉摊前，手里都拎着一个大圆馕，二三十串烤好的羊肉被一起退下铁扦子，裹在馕饼里。这便是和美国人的热狗一样的快捷午餐，经济实惠，味美营养，站着吞咽，很有气势也很有野趣。

A common sight on the streets of Xinjiang is to see a few people standing around a skewer stand with a large round nang bread in hand, sliding the meat of twenty or thirty skewers off into the nang. This is like the fast food hot dogs eaten by Americans – economically practical, delicious, nourishing, edible while standing, well-constructed and fun.

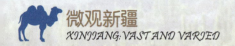
手抓肉
Cooking Meats

哈萨克族的老妈妈会像守着婴儿摇篮一样守着那锅肉，在水刚烧开、水花翻滚的时候，她会用大铁勺轻轻地将沸水逼出的血水泡沫撇去，以保持汤水的洁净，这个过程需要相当一段时间。老妈妈的沉静与耐心，完全进入到了这锅肉里，那种慈爱的投入，真的会让手抓肉与众不同！

An old Kazakh woman watches over the pot of meat as if it were a cradle with a baby in it – as soon as the water starts to boil, she uses a large spoon to gently scoop off the foam, thus keeping the water clean. This is a process that takes some time. The woman is quiet and patient, completely immersed in the task of tending to the pot – her emotional investment makes this the best meat for rice pilaf.

盐碱地里的牛羊
Salty Earth

我的蒙古族朋友郎图告诉我：盐碱地里跑着长大的牛羊的肉最好吃，肉质细嫩，味道鲜美且毫无膻味。所以，千万不要狭隘地以为贫瘠的土地没有价值。

My Mongolian friend, Langtu, told me: the meat of cows and sheep who walk in saline soil is the best – tender and fine, with a great flavour that has no trace of a goaty odour. Thus, it's quite narrow-minded to think that barren earth is not valuable.

味蕾的念想
Missing Home

去往新疆以外的任何地方，都要上千公里。这种空间上的距离，更容易让一个游子产生怀乡之情，他们常常会用想老婆、想孩子来强调对那片塞外之地的思念，其实严格意义上说，是胃和味蕾对那片土地的念想。

When travelling anywhere out of Xinjiang, a journey of more than a thousand kilometres is involved – this kind of spatial distance makes travellers even more prone to longing for home. They frequently refer to missing their wives and children to emphasize their feelings of separation from their homes. Actually, in a strict sense, it's the stomach and taste buds missing the land back there.

游玩的最高形式是请你吃肉
Having Fun Eating

在新疆最常见的一种情形是，有人请你去山野、草原游玩，风景固然怡人，固然重要，但最终的目的却归结在吃羊上。看着绿茸茸的草原上撒满洁白的羊群，每一个人都会发出类似"太美了"的赞叹。而把这美的一部分，变成盘中更美的一部分，其过程却是被普遍接受的。游玩的最高形式是请你吃肉。

A common occurrence in Xinjiang is to be invited to go to the mountains or grasslands for fun – the scenery and people are of course great, but the ultimate goal is to eat mutton. Everyone admires the beauty of seeing the beautiful white sheep on the luxuriant green fields. Turning this beauty into a dish on a plate is a universally accepted process. The best part of travelling in these regions is eating meat.

发现之旅
Journey of Discovery

八月到九月，是水果成熟的季节，曾经被造物主隐藏的各种色彩，开始趋于丰富、饱和。这样的时间，是享受的时间；这样的旅行，是发现之旅——美景与美食，是上天赐给人类的礼物，是形而上与形而下的完美统一。在新疆，以乌鲁木齐为原点，走向天山南北，去享受这样的发现之旅。

August and September are the season for fruits ripening, where the colours of nature previously hidden all come out – everything becomes plentiful and full. A time like this is a time for enjoyment. A trip like this is a trip of discovery – beautiful scenery and great food are the gifts from nature to us – the union of metaphysics and physics. In Xinjiang, starting from Urumqi, whether one goes north or south of the Tianshan Mountains, there is a journey of discovery lying in wait.

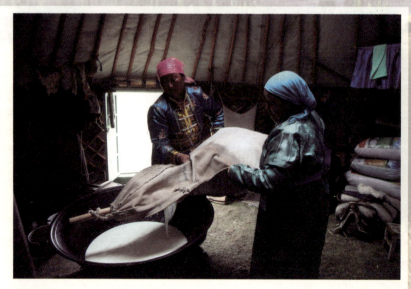

摄影：韩连赟

蒙古族的白食和红食
White and Red Food

蒙古语"查干伊得"指以奶为原料制成的食品，意为圣洁、纯净的食品，即"白食"，包括酸奶干、奶豆腐、奶皮子、奶油等。家里来了小客人，主人会蘸一点奶皮子或奶油涂抹在小孩儿的额头，表示祝福。以肉类为原料制成的食品，称"乌兰伊得"，意为"红食"。为了便于保存，牧民还常把牛羊肉制成风干肉。

The term "chagan yide" in Mongolian refers to food made from milk – the word means "clean" or "pure" – "white food". This includes yoghurt jerky, milk tofu, vrum (milk-skin), cream, and other dairy products. When young guests come to visit, the host dabs a bit of vrum or cream on his forehead as a form of blessing. Foods derived from meat are known as "ulan yide", or "red food". In order to better store them, the herders frequently make jerky out of beef and mutton.

关于新疆美食的一个段子
A Story about Foods

揪片子和拉条子结婚，烤包子很不愿意，就找来黄面和烤肉进行阻拦，大盘鸡一声令下，酒席上的丸子汤撒了一地，烤全羊被溅得黄了脸，嘴里说道："大家都是吃货，何必为个炮仗子丢了美食的名誉？"

When the two pulled noodles want to get married, the baked buns object, and turn to the yellow noodles and barbeque meat to stop them – the big plate chicken cries out and the meatball soup at the banquet is spilled all over. The cooked whole lamb is enraged at being splashed all over, and says: "You guys are all gluttons – why must you fight and harm our reputation as foods?"

哈密瓜之美
Beauty of the Hami Melon

看一看哈密瓜吧，她的色泽斑斓而凝重，黄的灿烂耀目，绿的沉静内敛，青的生机盎然；而那些花纹，仿佛是大师的精心设计，被用心雕镂镌刻上去的。细的如蚁和蚓之爬痕，极尽柔美，粗的如行草之笔触，极尽豪放。

When looking at a Hami melon, its gorgeous colour and lustre, glowing yellow on the outside and green within, we see it is full of life. The patterns on the outside look as if they were designed by a great master, carved on the surface of the melon. The thin, lacelike lines are soft and beautiful, with the thicker ones looking like the bold strokes of an ink brush.

摄影：徐纯

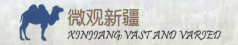
羊的肩胛骨肉
Shoulder Meat

在新疆的蒙古族人家做客，主人会端上一盘香喷喷的羊肉，其中有一块叫作达楞玛合的肉，这是一块羊的肩胛骨肉。宴请客人时，主人会当着客人的面削下上面的肉，专门送给男人吃。据说，这块肉蓄藏着 70 个勇士的力量，可以供 70 个男人享用。

When you visit a family of Mongolians in Xinjiang, the host will serve a plate of fragrant mutton, with a piece of meat called the dalengmaha in the middle – this is the meat on the shoulder bone. When holding a banquet, the host will carve off meat in front of the guests, specially for the males to eat. It's said that this meat has the power of seventy men, and can feed seventy men.

苦尽甘来的瓜果
Bitter and Sweet

凡苦涩盐碱太盛之地，瓜果必奇甜无比。新疆就是这么一个能化腐朽为神奇、化苦涩为甘甜的地方。因此新疆的瓜果就不应该是一般意义上的水果，它包含了太多内容，那些跨越时间、洞穿历史的藤蔓和根须，吮吸了太多的苦难和酸楚。当它以果实的面目出现的时候，我们才理解了何为苦尽甘来。

In a landscape full of bitterness, astringency, and salinity, the fruits and melons are wonderfully sweet. Xinjiang turns the rotten into the wonderful, the bitter into the sweet. For this reason, the fruits and melons of Xinjiang are no normal fruit in the ordinary sense of the word – it contains too much content – the tendrils and vines that have extended through time and penetrated history have absorbed too much bitterness and grief. However, when they appear as fruits, we truly understand the phrase "after the bitter comes the sweet".

摄影：徐纯

242

新疆鹰嘴豆
Chickpeas

鹰嘴豆在新疆俗称诺胡提，又称羊角状鹰嘴豆。因其面形奇特，尖如鹰嘴，故称此名。鹰嘴豆是糖尿病、高血压和肾虚体弱者理想的健康食品。新疆木垒县是鹰嘴豆的主产区，鹰嘴豆具有平衡膳食的独特功用，素有"长寿豆"的美誉。

Chickpeas are commonly known as nuohuti in Xinjiang, or "ram's horn chickpeas". Because of their unique shape, like the beak of an eagle, they are known as "eagle beak peas" in Chinese. They are healthy food for diabetics, those with high blood pressure, and those with kidney deficiencies. The Mori Kazakh Autonomous County in Xinjiang is the major producer of chickpeas. They are a good part of a balanced diet, and have been called "long-life peas".

趾高气扬的皮芽子
Piyazi

在新疆，洋葱又叫皮芽子。"皮芽子在蔬菜中趾高气扬，胡萝卜在茄子面前炫耀自己的堂皇。"（则勒力：《萨克诗简》）皮芽子在新疆饮食中占有重要位置，炒肉、拌凉菜都离不开它。当你饥肠辘辘走在街上时，街边的大锅抓饭馋得你直咽口水，皮芽子会拦截住你，因为它的香味在抓饭里。

Onions are called piyazi in Xinjiang. "Piyazi can hold their head up high in an audience of vegetables, and the carrots show off their grandeur in front of the aubergine". (These are words from a book of poems.) Piyazi have an important place in the food culture of Xinjiang, as they are necessary for both stir-fried and cold vegetable dishes. When you are walking hungrily along the road, the big woks of rice pilaf will tempt you, and the onions will drag you in, as their scent is in the rice.

新疆女人的三大最爱
My Three Loves

新疆女人的三大最爱，不是美容、高跟鞋，而是国内舶来品——凉皮、米粉、麻辣烫。它们不是新疆土产，却因新疆女人的独特嗜好而将她们与其他地方的女人分割开来。如果一个女人说"这三样是我的最爱"，没错，她肯定是新疆女人。

The three things that Xinjiang girls love the most are not beauty salons or high heels, but rather products from elsewhere in China: steamed cold noodles, rice noodles, and malatang (tingling spicy hot pot). These products are not from Xinjiang, but as they are so popular among girls there, they have become something that distinguishes Xinjiang girls from girls of other places. If a girl says "these three things are my favourites", she is definitely a girl from Xinjiang.

奶乡奶香
Milk Products

仿佛是上苍的特别恩惠，新疆成为全国著名的奶乡。这里奶种丰富，不仅有常见的牛奶、羊奶，还有马奶、驴奶、骆驼奶等珍稀奶品；这里奶制品花样繁多，鲜奶、酸奶、奶茶、奶酒、奶酪、奶皮子、奶疙瘩、奶豆腐各领风骚。朋友，如果你尝过天山南北好客的牧民制作的奶制品，你一定想醉在奶香飘溢的新疆。

Almost like a gift from above, Xinjiang is the most famous place in China for milk. The milk in Xinjiang is plentiful – not just the common cow and goat milk, but also horse, donkey, camel and other kinds of precious milk sources. The milk here is processed into all kinds of products – fresh milk, yoghurt, milk tea, milk liquor, cheese, milk skin, dried milk, milk tofu, and other delights. If you've tried the milk products either north of south of the Tianshan Mountains, you will find your memory of them in Xinjiang simply unforgettable.

深入人心的酒
Getting in to Liquor

还有什么能像酒那样深入人心？一顿酒到另一顿酒的距离，代表着理想的一次次飞升。每顿酒的形式都大同小异，从开启第一瓶的庄重到最后一瓶的癫狂，从啜饮第一口的审慎到最后的大碗不拒，从平静到晕眩，从客客气气到咄咄逼人，从细声低语到高歌猛进，可以看到酒奔突于新疆人的血液中所踢踏起的阵阵烟尘。

What else can enter into people's hearts like liquor? The distance between one round and another round of drinking represents a logical flight between them. Each is the same in essentials while differing in minor points – from the solemnity of the first bottle to the craziness of the last, from the first cautious sip to the last big bowl of liquor, from calm to wild, from polite to bombastic, from a small, low voice to roaring fury, we can see how liquor runs madly in the blood of the people of Xinjiang, stirring up a furious storm.

俄罗斯老太太格瓦斯
Real Kvass

格瓦斯，最早产于中世纪基辅公国的东斯拉夫，是俄罗斯民族非常酷爱的一种酵饮。谷物、啤酒花、蜂蜜和水的完美结合带给了人美妙的口感。如今，布尔津夜市上吉娜售出的格瓦斯瓶子上一律贴着白胶布，写上"俄罗斯老太太"。据她讲，这个手艺是妈妈在世时教给自己的，她的格瓦斯绝对正宗。

Kvass was first produced in the eastern Slavic Kiev Kingdom in the Middle Ages. It is a fermented drink well-loved by many groups in Russia. It is made of grain, hops, honey and water, and has a great flavour and mouth feel. Even now, the bottles of kvass sold at the night market by a woman named Jin in Burqin have white stickers on them that say "Russian Mother". She explains that when her mother was still alive, she taught her how to make the drink, and for this reason her product is very authentic.

牛羊肉与海鲜的区别

Meat and Seafood

新疆人总结牛羊肉与海鲜的最大区别，前者是肉包着骨头，后者则是骨头包着肉。

The people of Xinjiang describe the difference between beef, mutton, and seafood as being that the former two are meat on bones, and the latter is meat in bones.

香约玫瑰

Rose Products

每年5月，和田县阿勒热乡的人们就忙碌起来，采摘加工盛期玫瑰。这里的玫瑰干花、玫瑰精油、玫瑰蜜、玫瑰酱享誉四方。据说成就香妃芳名的是"清而不浊，和而不猛"的玫瑰酱，初尝便使人唇齿留芳，经常食用，连毛孔里沁出的都是香气。

Every year in May, the people in Alage Township of Hotan County have a lot of work to do, picking and processing roses – the dried roses, rose oil, rose honey and rose paste are all famous products of the area. It's said that this rose paste, famous for being "clear and not murky, nice and not savage", is what the Fragrant Concubine frequently used. When using it for the first time it leaves a fragrance on one's lips; when eaten regularly all one's pores will emit a pleasant fragrance.

摄影：王晖

245

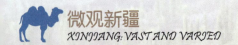
新疆是什么味儿
Flavour of Xinjiang

新疆是什么味儿？难道仅仅是牛羊的膻腥？其实，我们的思维、行动、说话方式、面部表情，甚至呼吸的节奏，这些综合因素在人的外部显露出来的东西，属于那个特定区域中每一位个体无意中形成的共性，也就是吃新疆饭、喝新疆水长大的人必须发散出的气息。这气息是不能被装扮出来的。

What is the flavour of Xinjiang? Is it just the goaty taste of mutton? Actually, our thoughts, actions, manner of speaking, facial expressions, even the pace at which we breathe – the amalgamation of these things that we display to others are the common characteristics that we all unconsciously share with each other. Our breath comes out of our bodies that grew up eating Xinjiang food and drinking Xinjiang water – these things can't be faked.

自然的味道
A Natural Flavour

鼻子把我们带向一个个美丽的去处。在新疆，烤肉烤包子的羊肉香味，奶茶馕饼子的草原气息，大盘鸡大盘鱼的豪放之气，都有一种西部的、草原的、自然的味道，由此开启的是另一段色香之旅。

Our noses take us to a beautiful place. In Xinjiang, the fragrance of mutton in barbecue and baked buns, the scents of milk tea and nang bread evocative of the prairie, the great scent of big plate chicken and big plate fish – all these have a natural scent characteristic of the Western Region, of the prairie – they take us on a journey of scents.

摄影：唐朝晖

穆萨莱斯
Musalaisi

穆萨莱斯，是南疆阿瓦提县维吾尔民间的土酿葡萄酒，又被人戏称为"没事来事"。有人说它是葡萄酒的历史标本，有诗人称其为"葡萄血"。酿造时，在发酵的葡萄中掺入鸽子血或鸽子肉、羊腰子、肉苁蓉等大补之物，酒劲绵柔中暗含不可思议的力量。有人说它是酒，又有人说，它是一种灵魂。

Musalaisi is a type of local grape wine made in Avati County in Southern Xinjiang, which has been jocularly called "meishilaishi" ("find trouble if there is none afoot") in Mandarin. Some people have said that it is a historical reference point for wine, with others calling it the "blood of grapes". When brewed, pigeon blood or pigeon meat, lamb kidneys, and Herba cistanches are added to the mixture, giving the wine an amazing power. Some people say it is a kind of liquor, and others say it is a kind of "spirit".

闻香识味
Knowing Scents

曾经，在古丝路上，印度和阿拉伯地区的香料源源不断地被商人们运了过来，那种神秘悠远的香如西域的天空和历史，又像某段老城墙下的斑驳光影和驼铃声声，绵延千年之后，以更为丰富多彩的新疆以及世界各地品牌的面目出现在这座城市的大街小巷。乌鲁木齐最为阴柔的部分，是那些缭绕千年的氤氲香气。

In the past, on the old Silk Road, perfumes from India and the Middle East were continuously brought here by merchants; the mysterious, distant sky and fragrance of the Western Region were like the motley crew of shapes mingling with the sound of camel bells under a section of an old city wall. After a millennium, the many brands of Xinjiang and places elsewhere in the world appear in the streets and alleys of the city. The most tender parts of Urumqi are coiled up in the fragrances of the millennium past.

从一而终
All Along

一个人的教养，也不时从餐饮的品位中折射出。味蕾的高贵或卑琐，靠后天的培养是能够完成的，但它也有不以人的意志为转移的情况，其主要原因是面对纷繁的味源，一时的迷失在所难免。而迷失一定是暂时性的，不确定的，最终它还是会回到原初被培养的基点上，对新疆饭从一而终。

A person's upbringing is frequently represented in their taste in food and drink. Both refined and base tastes are acquired rather than innate, but sometimes there are purposeful shifts, a main reason for this being that when faced with various flavours, it is easy to become temporarily disoriented. This disorientation is of course temporary and uncertain – after a certain time one will invariably return to the foundation one was raised with – Xinjiang food will never let its adherents go.

牛羊对人的异化

Animal Character

餐饮以牛羊肉主打的新疆人，牛气与羊势皆已潜入体内。他们走路的姿势、说话的腔调，甚至手势都大异于其他地方的人。他们既有牛的倔强和坚韧，又有羊的温柔与顺从，眼神中有羊的纯净和牛的强悍。

In a culture where people eat large amounts of beef and mutton, the character of the animals enters into the body – the way in which people walk, talk, and even their gesticulation differs from people of other places. They have the stubborn tenacity of cattle, and the soft docility of sheep – even their eyes have the purity of sheep and the valiant character of bulls.

艾德莱斯绸

Aidelaisi Silk

艾德莱斯绸是一种扎染丝花绸，别称"玉波甫纳卡娜提古丽"，意思是布谷鸟翅膀花，隐喻这种花绸能像布谷鸟一样给大地带来春天的气息。民间用土法织绸，用草根、核桃皮、石榴皮和吐曼花浸泡的植物颜料染色。图案简洁、抽象，有一种荒凉中的绚烂。世界总是这样，最艳丽的色彩往往藏在最荒凉的地方。

Aidelaisi is a kind of dyed silk, which is also called "Yubo Funa Kanatiguli", meaning "flowers of the wings of the cuckoo", a metaphor for the silk being able to bring tidings of spring, like the cuckoo. It is locally produced with traditional methods, leveraging grass roots, walnut peels, pomegranate peels, Tuman flowers, and other plants for dye bases. The patterns are simple, abstract, and have a feeling of something splendid against a desolate backdrop. This is how the world always is – the most beautiful of colours are hidden within the most bleak places.

摄影：韩连赟

摄影：王晖

九碗三行子
Nine Bowls

"九碗三行（hàng）子"，不是一道菜，而是新疆回族正宗的宴席，九碗菜摆成每边三碗的正方形，横竖左右看，都成三行，故名"九碗三行"。如果取掉中间的汤菜，便是一个回族的"回"字，九在回族人心目中，是个大吉的数目，当九碗三行的"菜阵"摆列开来时，主人的祝福也随着菜肴浓浓的香气上桌啦！

"The three lines of the nine bowls" is not a kind of food, but rather the authentic banquet style of the Hui people in Xinjiang – nine bowls of food are placed in a 3x3 grid, thus giving the banquet its name. If the middle bowl of soup is removed, it becomes the Chinese character for "Hui". The number nine is also a lucky number in Hui culture, and when the bowls are arranged in the pattern, the good wishes of the host will also permeate the table like the smell of the food.

新疆餐饮格局
Big Food

生活在新疆这么一个山大水阔的地方，就一定会有与之相对应的饮食习惯。新疆的餐饮格局一言以蔽之便是一个"大"，以大盘鸡为标志的新疆大盘系列菜，粗猛豪迈，纵横捭阖，带有明显的西域性格特征。

Living in a place with natural scenes as vast as Xinjiang, there will of course be corresponding dietary customs to the place. The food of Xinjiang is characterised by an important aspect – it is "big". "Big plate chicken" is one of the more representative Xinjiang dishes, rough and bold, large in dimension, with clear characteristics of the Western Region.

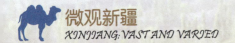

柯尔克孜族的服饰
Kyrgyz
Costumes

"阿合卡巴克"白毡帽，下沿镶黑，向上翻卷，据说源于传统宗教中对白山黑水有灵的崇拜，被称为柯尔克孜族的"圣帽"。柯尔克孜男子喜穿白色衬衣，领口、袖口绣有图案，外穿夹衣长袍。女子大都喜欢红色服饰，在大草原上尤为耀眼，多配有脖饰、发饰、手饰、耳环、手镯等。

The white felt hats, or "ahekabak", are lined with black at the bottom, and rolled at the top – this is said to be a reflection of traditional religions worshipping the white-capped black mountains as having souls, and for this reason the Kyrgyz call these hats "saintly hats". The shirts that Kyrgyz men like to wear are white with patterns upon the collar and cuffs, and are worn under a long garment. Girls like red clothing and accessories, which look great out on the plains – common accessories are neck ornaments, hair accessories, hand ornaments, earrings, bracelets, and the like.

摄影：韩连赟

三个朋友
Three Friends

在新疆的朋友并不考虑移民，他说，哪里去吃地道的烤羊肉、喝正宗的格瓦斯？定居北京的新疆女孩挂在嘴边的一句话是"我还想回新疆去"；而移民澳大利亚六年的女孩则显得更加慌乱："我没给我的故乡新疆留下些什么，它却让我魂牵梦萦。"

My friend in Xinjiang has never considered emigration, saying no matter where he goes, there wouldn't be good mutton barbecue or authentic kvass. A girl from Xinjiang resident in Beijing always talks of her desire to return to Xinjiang. A girl who emigrated from Xinjiang to Australia six years ago says: "I didn't leave anything for my homeland of Xinjiang, but it still makes me miss it very much."

沙子烤羊肉
Sandy Barbecue

新疆人把羊肉的烹调做到了极致，阿克苏附近沙湖的沙子·烤羊肉你可能闻所未闻。所谓"沙子·烤羊肉"，就是先是在沙漠上点起炭火，燃烧三四个小时，把沙子烤得滚烫，然后把羊羔肉放进羊肚里，加入秘制的佐料，最后用铁丝扎紧肚口，埋在被烧得滚烫的沙子里。两个小时以后，用刀割开羊肚，一股浓香扑鼻而来。

In Xinjiang, there is some of the best cooked mutton anywhere. You may have never heard of the "sandy barbecued mutton" of Shahu Lake, near Aksu. Making this so-called "sandy barbecue" involves first lighting a fire on the desert, and letting it burn for three or four hours; once the sand is very hot, mutton is stuffed into a sheep's stomach along with seasonings. The stomach is then bound with iron wire, and buried in the burnt sand. Two hours later, when you extract the stomach and cut it open, your nose will be positively assaulted with enchanting flavour.

汤饭
Xinjiang Dinner

初到新疆听说汤饭，还以为是汤泡饭的简称呢，端上桌才知道，人家和米饭根本不搭界。这是一种带汤汁的面食，面剂子任意捏、揪、拉、搓成各种形状，关键是汤料，各种蔬菜任意混搭，西红柿必不可少，再配上羊肉，口味酸辣，夏天吃消暑清口，冬季吃暖胃驱寒。汤饭是许多人家的晚饭，故有"新疆晚饭"之称。

When I first heard the term tangfan ("soup-rice") in Xinjiang, I thought it was a term for some kind of rice immersed in soup – only after it arrived on the table did I realise what it was – something with no relation to white rice. It's a kind of noodle in soup, where the noodles are randomly pulled, peeled or ripped off a block of dough into all kinds of shapes. The key is the soup, into which all kinds of vegetables are put, especially tomato, in addition to mutton. It's sour and spicy, and tastes great in the summer where it cleans your palette, and also in winter when it warms your stomach and drives off cold. Tangfan is a common dinner for many people, and has even been called "Xinjiang dinner".

蒙古族的刺绣

Mongolian Embroidery

刺绣，蒙古语叫"嗒塔戈玛拉"。自古以来，草原蒙古族姑娘从小跟母亲学习刺绣艺术，并伴其一生。蒙古族刺绣纹样粗犷、线条明快、色彩强烈，具有典型的北方游牧民族风格。蒙古族服饰在长袍、裤子、坎肩、靴、帽等服饰上均有刺绣装饰，花毡、枕套、门帘、马具等日常生活用品上也可见刺绣工艺。

Embroidery is called "tatagmala" in Mongolian. From ancient times to the present, the girls of the Mongolian grasslands have learned embroidery from their mothers at a young age and continued with the activity. The patterns used in Mongolian embroidery are bold and unconstrained with lively lines and bright colours – they display the classical character of the nomads of the north. Mongolians decorate their robes, trousers, waistcoats, boots, hats and other clothing with embroidery, as well as quilts, pillows, curtains, saddles, and other everyday objects.

摄影：韩连赟

感官的盛宴
A Feast for
the Senses

从来没有哪个地方能像新疆这样，同时让你的视觉、听觉、味觉、嗅觉和触觉得到满足。你会看到无法用语言描绘的色彩，你会听到仿若天籁的乐音，你会品尝到让人垂涎的美食，你会闻到令人窒息的芬芳，你会触摸到远古和现代。这是调动所有感官的一次盛宴，是一种全方位的精神大餐。

There has never been another place like Xinjiang which satisfies your senses of sight, sound, taste and smell. You will see colours that you struggle to describe in words, hear sounds that are almost heavenly, taste food that will make you drool, smell intoxicating fragrance, and touch both the past and present. It's a banquet for all your senses – a full range of spiritual feast.

**和时间抗衡的
干果**
Dried Fruits

美食和人一样，都是时间面前的失败者，只有很少的一些可以和时间抗衡——比如干果。它们存储了足够的西域的阳光与雪水，以不同的色彩向人展示时光之美。葡萄、大枣、巴旦木、核桃、无花果……无不是时光的化身，为男人把根留住，为女人把美留住。

Food is like people – both collapse when faced with the eventual ravages of time. Only a few can compete with it – such as dried fruits. They store the sunlight and snowmelt of the Western Region, showing off their various colours. Grapes, jujubes, Xinjiang apricots, walnuts, figs – all of these are fossilisations of time. They sustain men's root, and women's beauty.

食在新疆
Eating in
Xinjiang

新疆是一个多民族的地区，各地的美食美不胜收，譬如在和田总忘不掉烤鹅蛋、烤鸭蛋、烤包子、馕坑肉、架子肉；在阿克苏一定要吃当地鸽子肉拌面；在奇台总想吃那里的过油肉拌面、凉皮、大蒸饼；在布尔津一定要去俄罗斯餐店，尝尝俄罗斯列巴，喝一喝比瓦。

Xinjiang is a multi-ethnic area in which many cuisines compete with each other: Hotan has the baked goose egg, baked duck egg, baked bun, nang with meat, and large skewer. Aksu has the not-to-be-missed pigeon meat noodles. Qitai always tempts people with its meat noodles, cold steamed noodles, and big steamed cakes. In Burqin, there are excellent Russian restaurants and the excellent "huge bread", the size of a football, as well as beer to be drunk.

摄影：刘力

哈萨克族的 "斯尔玛克"
Sirmak

"斯尔玛克"绣品是哈萨克族最重要的生活物品之一。"斯尔玛克"花毡，做工精细，用料讲究，喜用丝线和金线，多用对比色，图案多选材于草原、山水、云朵、树木和花卉，古朴、大方、艳丽，反映出哈萨克族人独特的审美情趣，具有浓郁的牧区生活气息。

"Sirmak" embroidery is one of the most important objects in the lives of ethnic Kazakhs. "Sirmak" felt is finely fashioned with skill, employing silk and gold threads, many contrasting colours, and designs representing prairies, landscapes, clouds, trees, and flowers in a style that is simple, unsophisticated, generous, beautiful, and reflects the unique aesthetic values of the Kazakh people, filled with the spirit of pastoral life.

摄影：韩连赟

古代西域服饰
Ancient Clothing of the Western Region

考古发现，早在 3000 多年前的先秦时期，西域的毛纺织业就已经发展起来。生活在那里的人们擅长纺织毛布，并用彩色颜料在上面绘染各种美丽的图案。他们的衣装样式粗犷，装饰古朴，喜用鸟禽羽毛作为配饰，形成了暖裘烂漫、毛布绚丽的服饰风格。

Archaeologists have discovered that in the pre-Qin era, more than 3,000 years ago, the Western Region already had a developed weaving industry. The people who lived there excelled at weaving and using dyes to create all kinds of beautiful patterns on the cloth produced. Their styles of decoration, rough and simple, incorporated bird feathers on brightly coloured garments, making them distinctive and beautiful.

塔吉克族服饰
Tajik Costumes

塔吉克族男子爱穿无领对襟的黑色长外套，内搭白衬衣，头戴圆形高筒帽。妇女一年四季都喜欢穿连衣裙，尤其喜欢红色的。无论男女，在帽沿、领口、袖口、衣襟处都绣有美丽的花纹。妇女的圆形花帽上装饰着金银片和色彩鲜丽的珠子，裙边上花纹灿烂，走起路来随风摇曳，犹如仙女从云端飘落人间。

Tajik men wear a long black coat that is tailored without lapels, a white shirt underneath and a round hat on the head. Women wear dresses all year round, especially favouring the colour red. Both men's and women's costumes feature beautiful embroidery around the edges of the hat, collar, sleeves and lapels. The edges of the women's round hats are decorated with small plates of gold and silver, with brilliant patterns at the edges, and their dresses flutter in the wind like fairies descending to earth.

摄影：黄永中

花帽
Flower Caps

花帽，维吾尔语称为"朵帕"。维吾尔族花帽品种繁多，造型古朴，花色或华贵艳丽或庄重素雅，深受人们喜爱。图案多以新疆常见花卉、果实等为素材，如常见的男式花帽巴旦木花帽，其花纹是巴旦木的变形和修饰，多为黑底白花，庄重大方。女式花帽则多用金银线、各色小珠子绣成鲜花图案，五彩缤纷，精致可爱。

Flower caps, called "dopa" in the Uyghur language, come in many varieties, ranging from simple to very fancy – they are quite popular. Common patterns include local flowers, fruits and the like. The commonly seen Baddam Flowered Hat worn by men is decorated with Baddam patterns, a black base with white flowers for an impressive visual effect. Hats for women usually include gold and silver thread with coloured beads and a rainbow of decorations that make them both elegant and cute.

2500 年前的时尚
Fashions from 2500 Years Ago

新疆维吾尔自治区博物馆收藏的一件可爱的圆领、套头式女童连衣裙。裙子用红、浅黄、褐、蓝等多种颜色撞色设计，以几何图形巧妙拼接，下摆两侧各加一块三角形布，形成宽松的 A 字型下摆，显得非常活泼俏丽。该裙装保存比较完整，虽历经 2500 年，色彩依旧鲜艳，时尚气息扑面而来。

In the Xinjiang Uyghur Autonomous Region Museum, there is a cute pullover girl's dress with a round collar. The dress is composed of components in red, light yellow, brown, blue and other colours, the pieces of which are geometrically arranged. The lower hem has attached at either side a triangular piece of cloth, making up a wide and loose lower hem in the shape of the letter "A", and producing a very nice visual effect. The dress is well-preserved, and even after 2,500 years the colours are bright and the garment is fashionable.

新疆大盘鸡
Big Plate
Chicken

没有一个新疆人不认识它，只有盲人，但盲人一旦动了筷子，也就认识它了。

Everyone in Xinjiang knows it, except maybe the blind, but even they get clued in after taking a bite.

袷袢
Qiapan

维吾尔族男子的传统装扮是头戴花帽，身着"袷袢"，腰系长带，下穿长裤、长靴。"袷袢"里配套头式白衬衣，衬衣领口、袖口处绣有精致的花边。袷袢是一种齐膝长袍，多用竖条纹彩色绸布做成。新疆维吾尔自治区博物馆藏的这件毛织袷袢质地柔软，花纹精美，色彩艳丽，是清代维吾尔族服装的代表样式。

A traditional costume for Uyghur men consists of a flower cap and a Qiapan, with a belt, long trousers, and long boots. A pullover white shirt is worn inside, and the collar and sleeves of the shirt are embroidered with floral patterns. The Qiapan is a knee-length garment made of vertical bands of cloth in various colours. The Xinjiang Uyghur Autonomous Region Museum has displayed a Qiapan with a soft character, beautiful floral patterns and vibrant colours – it is a representative piece of clothing for Uyghurs from the Qing Dynasty.

索引 | Index |

A

阿尔金山	Altun	47
阿尔泰山	The Altay Mountains	7
阿曼尼莎与木卡姆套曲	Ammanisha and Muqam	194
阿斯塔那古墓群	The Astana Tombs	54
阿希克	Asiks	205
艾德莱斯绸	Aidelaisi Silk	248
艾青在兵团	Ai Qing and the Corps	158
爱"子"的新疆人	Different Suffixes	228
爱喝酒的猫	Drunk Kitty	175
安集海	Anjihai	137
敖包特庙	Ovoot Temple	134
奥尔德克	Ordik: A Normal Man	165

B

八卦城	City of Eight Trigrams	119
八千湘女上天山	Calling for Reinforcements	151
八窍头骨	Orifices and Bones	55
巴郎子	Little Balang	224
巴斯拜捐飞机	I'm Gonna Buy You a Plane	74
巴音布鲁克天鹅	Bayanbuluk's Swans	182
巴扎	Bazaar	76
巴扎天的毛驴车	Bazaar Day	104
把脸也洗一下	Wash Your Face	219
把你的儿子借我用一下	Loan Me Your Son	174
把新疆带回家	Take Xinjiang Home	19
白哈巴	Baihaba	50
白桦林的眼泪	Tears of a Birch Forest	19
白桦林里许个愿	Make a Wish to a Birch	39
白杨、红柳、雪松都知道兵团	The Military Corps Is Known by All	155
百岁老人村	A Village of Centenarians	173
拜火教	Zoroastrianism	99

贝伦舞	Belem	192
边防的魅力	The Allure of the Border	151
边境线	The Border	150
冰山之父：慕士塔格峰	Muztag Peak	36
冰雪中的温暖	Warmth in the Snow	79
兵团的维吾尔人	Uyghurs as Corps Members	156
兵团生活	Military Life	150
兵团中的特殊群体	Special Groups in the Corps	158
波马古墓之谜	Riddle of the Poma Tomb	55
博格达峰	Bogda Peak	22
不黏腻的新疆	Feeling Good	24
不想伤害，也不想掩埋	Respectful Distance	97
不一样的买卖	A Different Form of Commerce	105
布尔津：三岁的公骆驼	Burqin: A Three-Year-Old Camel	226

C

彩陶之路	The Road of Coloured Pottery	52
彩云归处是家乡	A Sense of Home	112
苍茫尽处是繁华	A Bustling, Vast Space	17
草原	Grasslands	29
草原哈萨克族的天籁 "斯布孜格"	The Heart Flute	200
草原花	Grassland Flowers	48
草原上的美容	Beauty on the Prairie	99
草原上的女人	Women on the Grassland	101
草原上的游牧民族	Nomads on the Grassland	31
草原上没有公厕	No Public Toilets	219
草原石人	Stone People	63
草原守护神	Protector of the Grassland	169
草原雄鹰	Eagles on the Prairie	185
草原与小马驹	Animals on the Prairie	21
长发是这样养成的	Haircare	104
长调	Long Songs	198
"楚呼楚" 泉的传说	Legend of a Spring	174
绰号不是人人都能得到	Nicknames Aren't Free	221
城市中的音乐、人与酒	Music, People and Alcohol	202
吃得豪爽	Eating Style	234
吃面识厨师	Noodle Experts	237

吃羊的湖怪	Monster in the Lake	171
冲出塔克拉玛干	Out of Taklimakan	34
传统的交通工具	Traditional Transit	43
传统民间游艺体育活动	Traditional Activities	211
春天	Spring	218
从马背上下来的城市	From Horseback to City	108
从一而终	All Along	247

D

达里雅布依：塔克拉玛干沙漠的肚脐	Daliyabuyi	70
打掌人	Making Shoes for Animals	130
大巴扎的色彩	Colours of the Bazaar	123
大拌筋	Dabanjin	234
大地的工业艺术	Karamay	135
大地的乳房	The Earth's Bosom	175
大地的颂词	Geographic Eulogy	22
大风起兮	Strong Winds	188
大海子	The Great Sea	41
大河向北流	Flow to the North	41
大漠"老兵村"	A Village of Old Soldiers	158
大西洋的最后一滴眼泪：赛里木湖	Sayram Lake	42
大与野的新疆	Big and Wild Xinjiang	3
单车少年	A Lad Riding a Bike	143
"当代荷马"居素甫·玛玛依	Gusev Mamay	208
刀郎歌舞	Dolan Dances	196
刀郎木卡姆	Dolan Muqam	194
刀郎人	Dolan	87
刀郎人的驼舞	The Camel Dance	201
刀郎人狩猎遗俗	Dolan Hunters	93
刀郎乡的孩子	Children in Dolan	125
地名二合一	Two-in-One	230
地毯将陋室变成了宫殿	Nice Rugs	189
地窝子	Ground Nest	153
奠基之石	Marking Stones	231
冬不拉的传说	The Tamboura	193
冬季出生的孩子	Winter Children	99
冬天的和布克赛尔	Hoboksar in Winter	133

冬天里的塔里木	Tarim in Winter	49
冬窝子	Winter Nest	126
动物崇拜	Animal Worship	102
斗羊	Fighting Rams	213
都瓦祈福	Duwa Prayers	106
独特的起名方式	Naming Names	96
段蕾与《新疆乐器图谱》	Dictionary of Xinjiang Musical Instruments	201
断裂的文明	Interrupted Civilization	167
蹲在鱼身上钓鱼	Fishing on a Fish	171
多变的云	Capricious Clouds	25
多浪河	Duolang River	138
多语新疆	Multilingual Xinjiang	220

E

俄罗斯式风情	Russian Flavour	142
俄罗斯老太太格瓦斯	Real Kvass	244
儿子娃娃	Baby Boy	223
二道桥	Erdao Bridge	108
二转子	Second Rotation	218

F

发现之旅	Journey of Discovery	239
反差综合体	Great Contrasts	37
反扣西瓜皮	Useful Leftovers	175
放大的猫和缩小的老虎	Enlarged Cats and Shrunken Tigers	184
丰富奇特的地貌景观	Rich and Varied Scenery	9
丰饶的塔尔巴哈台	Plenty in Tarbagatay	133
"风光"无限好	A Limitless Scene	190
冯夫人定西域	Madam Feng	168
佛教圣地：苏巴什故城	Subas Old City	58
《福乐智慧》	Fortune, Happiness and Wisdom	62
伏羲女娲图	Fuxi and Nüwa	53
父亲的歌	Father's Song	216

G

| 甘英西使 | The Emissary | 165 |

感官的盛宴	A Feast for the Senses	253
戈壁上长出的城市	Out of the Gobi	140
歌的生命	A Life of Songs	213
歌舞刀郎乡	The Songs of Dolan	124
各民族通婚最多的地方	A Remarkable Place of Inter-ethnic Marriage	134
给黄牛立的墓碑	Stele for an Ox	160
给力的神"马"	Like a Horse	221
给洗手水	Hand-washing Water	83
给自己接生的接生婆	Doing it Yourself	99
公主堡	A Home for a Princess	166
公主私情	Princess Tactics	168
供奉宗喀巴和成吉思汗的蒙古族	Tsongkhapa and Genghis Khan	102
沟里的秘密	Secrets in the Gully	228
狗鱼和鹰	A Pike and an Eagle	34
孤独的毡房，我的家	Lonely Yurt	116
古代西域服饰	Ancient Clothing of the Western Region	255
古尔班通古特沙漠	The Gurbantunggut Desert	13
古尔图	Gurt	49
古丽	Guli	223
骨头游戏	The Bone Game	98
怪石沟	Guaishigou	48
怪异胡须墓	Odd Graves	61
关于新疆美食的一个段子	A Story about Foods	240
观蹄印识羊	Resilience	97
硅化木园	Petrified Forest	24
过分、放肆	Overdoing It	231

H

哈密瓜	Hami Melon	34
哈密瓜之美	Beauty of the Hami Melon	241
哈萨克族的"斯尔玛克"	Sirmak	254
哈萨克族摇床礼	Cradle Ceremony	91
孩子出生的习俗	New Children	102
旱獭	Marmots	135
豪气的大床	A Big Bed	105
禾木印象	Impressions of Hemu	139
和布克赛的牧仁	Mu Ren	197

和时间抗衡的干果	Dried Fruits	253
和田的尘土	Dust in Hotan	132
和田的浮尘	Hotan's Dust	112
和云说话的人	Speaking to the Clouds	162
红柳舞轻沙	Dance of the Sand	187
红其拉甫	Khonjirap	159
红山	Hongshan	143
胡杨	Poplars	183
胡杨木	Poplars	170
花儿沟	Hua'ergou	123
花开如礼炮	A Floral Salute	24
花开震四野	Say "Bloom"	23
花帽	Flower Caps	256
花树之城	City of Trees	145
会报警的树木	Alarmed Wood	166
活着的历史	Living History	116

J

鸡蛋妈妈的丈夫	Husband of the Egg's Mother	218
"吉卜赛人" 村落	The Gypsy Village	70
家家是哨所	Watchhouses Everywhere	150
驾着 "驴的" 赶巴扎	Donkey Taxies	145
坚硬的树瘤	Burrs on Trees	97
兼容并包的乌鲁木齐	Compatible Urumqi	108
渐行渐远的味道	A Fading Flavour	232
江布拉克	Jiangburak	27
江格尔故乡	The Ancient Village	206
江格尔奇传人	A Performer of Jangar	207
"疆" 字的解读	Interpretation of the Character "jiang"	216
街道是草原的坐标	Markers of Grasslands	136
节省布料的军装	Saving Cloth	156
洁身自好的白桦	Trees with True Integrity	39
截然不同的美	Different Beauty	35
解忧公主	Princess Jieyou	61
金山银水之地	Rivers of Silver	179
进城的靴子	Boots and Customs	84
精灵之城布尔津	Exquisite Burqin	135

精神的雕刻	Jade Carvings	179
鸠摩罗什	Kumarajiva	95
九龙壁	A Nine-Dragon Wall	54
九碗三行子	Nine Bowls	249
酒	Liquor	216
镌刻誓言	Carving Promises	28
军垦第一犁	The First Ploughs for Reclamation	152
军垦第一哨	The First Sentry	157

K

喀拉峻草原	Kalajun Grassland	119
喀纳斯的春天	Spring in Kanas	122
喀纳斯的狗	Dogs in Kanas	218
喀纳斯的野花	Wild Flowers in Kanas	120
喀纳斯的雨	Rain over Kanas	38
喀纳斯湖怪	The Monster of Kanas Lake	170
喀纳斯迷人的雾岚	Mist over Kanas	37
喀什的高台民居	Old Residences	121
喀什的遥远	Distant Kashgar	113
喀什噶尔的古老街区	Kashgar's Old Streets	114
喀什噶尔的夜晚	Night in Kashgar	41
喀什小巷	Kashgar's Alleys	111
卡瓦一样的脑袋	A Brain Like a Kawa	216
开国大典的国旗手李冠英	Standard-Bearer Li Guanying	152
坎儿井	Qanat	118
坎土曼的传说	Legend of the Kantuman	222
侃大山	Talking about Mountains	230
烤馕包烤肉	Chinese Tacos	237
柯尔克孜族的服饰	Kyrgyz Costumes	250
可可托海	The Koktokay Sea	44
孔雀河	Konqi River	222
恐龙沟	Dinosaur Gulley	59
苦尽甘来的瓜果	Bitter and Sweet	242
库车王府	Kuqa Palace	129
快乐的巴扎古丽	Having a Good Time	144
奎屯	Kuytun	146
昆仑的大逻辑	Kunlun Logic	178

L

拉条子	Latiaozi	234
来者不拒的新疆	Welcoming Xinjiang	43
狼背羊	The Wolf	169
狼哺乌孙王	Raised by a Wolf	171
狼图腾的民族	Wolf Totem	172
狼用尿解围	Fight or Flee	164
老铁匠	An Old Master	67
老温的弟弟	Mr. Wen's Brother	165
2500 年前的时尚	Fashions from 2500 Years Ago	256
两种光芒照耀新疆大地	Two Kinds of Light	178
流星是懒汉变的	Shooting Stars Are Lazy Guys	172
笼屉匠人	Fine Craftsmanship	72
楼兰姑娘	Loulan Girl	72
露天博物馆：吐鲁番	Turpan: An Open-Air Museum	52
轮台城	Luntai City	55
罗布人	Lop Nur	131
罗布人村寨	Lop Nur Villages	68
罗布人的"狮子舞"	The Lion Dance	198
骆驼石	The Camel Rock	60
旅行的困惑	The Confusion of Travel	2
绿色宝库	A Treasure-Trove of Green	18
绿色原野：可克达拉	Kekedala	160
绿洲的夏天	Summer Oasis	17
绿洲	Oasis	20

M

麻扎	Mazar	77
马上叼羊	Buzkashi	211
"马上"在新疆	On the Horse	229
马与草	Horses and Grass	110
马与蒙古族人	Mongolians and Horses	89
麦西来甫	Maixilaipu	195
卖恰玛古的老奶奶	Selling Herbs	141
没有结婚的羊	Unmarried Sheep	221
没有小偷儿的县	A Place without Thieves	114

美少女和漂亮驹	A Girl and a Colt	137
美玉拒绝庸俗	The Natural Beauty of Jade	178
蒙古族的白食和红食	White and Red Food	240
蒙古族的刺绣	Mongolian Embroidery	252
蒙古族人不吃马肉	No Horse Meat for Mongolians	98
蒙古族舞蹈沙吾尔登	Mongolian Dances	200
蒙王府热气泉	The Hot Springs	47
梦幻神仙湾	A Dreamy Bay	45
民间诗人祖拉	Poems of the People	209
魔鬼城	Ghost City	44
魔鬼城雅丹地貌	Yardang Landform	31
木卡姆	Muqam	192
牧归	Herder's Duties	140
牧人	Herders	113
穆萨莱斯	Musalaisi	247

N

那花，那马，那少年	Back Then	138
那拉提草原	Nalati	144
奶乡奶香	Milk Products	244
男人的喉结	A Man's Throat	174
南疆	Southern Xinjiang	119
难懂的喀什	Enchanting Kashgar	115
难以概括的新疆	Describing Xinjiang	2
馕	Nang	235
馕高于一切	Nang above All	93
能源富集之地	Rich in Energy Resources	189
尼雅城	Niya Ancient City	68
你好吗	How Are You?	225
年轻的城	A Young City	157
鸟类的理想栖息地	A Nice Place for Birds	183
牛羊对人的异化	Animal Character	248
牛羊肉与海鲜的区别	Meat and Seafood	245
农工	Farmers or Workers?	154
女儿的第一次化妆	First Make-up	104
女性化的玉	Feminised Jade	179

P

帕米尔高原上的塔吉克人	Tajik on the Pamir Plateau	27
拍打无花果	Beating the Fig	87
漂泊的克里雅人	The Kerians	90
飘香的城市与女人	Scents of the City	112
葡萄王	Grape King	181
蒲昌古城	Puchang	74
朴素的乡村婚礼	Village Weddings	126

Q

"七"之谜	The Mystery of "Seven"	167
骑手醉伏在马背上	Sleep it off on the Horseback	81
袷袢	Qiapan	257
亲近沙漠的城市	A City Next to the Desert	129
秦尼巴克	China Garden	222
清晨的劳作	Rising Early	139
龟兹	Kuqa	132
秋日的胡杨	Autumn Poplars	128

R

| 让你一次吃个够 | Eating your Fill | 100 |
| 人与音乐 | People and Music | 203 |

S

萨巴依	Sabay	204
萨满教	Shamanism	96
萨满乐舞	Shaman Dances	83
赛骆驼	Camel Racing	210
三大名海	The Three Big Seas	232
三道海子巨石堆	A Pile of Giant Stones	57
三个朋友	Three Friends	251
三只虱子	Three Fleas	173
桑皮纸	Good Paper	103
沙海之神	God of the Sea of Desert	188
沙漠绿岛：阿拉尔	Alar: A Green Island	159

沙枣花	Oleaster Flowers	110
沙枣花香的女人	A Perfumed Lady	162
沙子烤羊肉	Sandy Barbecue	251
山的表情	Mountains and Expressions	90
射箭	Archery	212
深埋在沙石下面的冰块	Ice Blocks Buried in the Desert Sand	88
深入人心的酒	Getting in to Liquor	244
神秘米兰城	Mysterious Milan	69
神木园	The Mysterious Garden	8
神奇新疆	Mysterious Xinjiang	130
生殖崇拜：康定石门子岩画	An Old Rock Painting	60
圣佑庙	The Temple of Divine Protection	82
盛开的花朵：新疆女子	Girls in Xinjiang	80
十二木卡姆	The Twelve Muqams	193
石榴	Pomegranate	232
石中美者为玉	Jade: The Best Stones	180
时光的挽留	The Strings of Time	109
时间是一笔糊涂账	Through Time	83
食在新疆	Eating in Xinjiang	253
世界上最大的村子	World's Largest Village	112
世界上最早的毛皮滑雪板	The Earliest Skis	59
收获的季节	Harvest Seasons	28
手抓肉	Cooking Meats	238
守墓的老兵	Keeping Watch over Fallen Comrades	156
摔跤	Wrestling	212
丝绸之路	The Silk Road	5
丝路商人	Merchants on the Silk Road	64
丝路要冲	On the Silk Road	3
丝路遗韵	The Sound of Silk	35
"酸奶"泉	Yoghurt Spring	168

T

塔城	Tacheng	127
塔城的家庭餐馆	Home Cooking	135
塔城上空的明媚	Oasis of Light	120
塔河边的月亮湾	Crescent Bay	16
塔吉克墓葬	Tajik Tombs	86

塔吉克族人的播种节	Sowing Seeds	95
塔吉克族的崇拜	Tajik Beliefs	102
塔吉克族的春节	Tajik Spring Festival	101
塔吉克族的民间道具舞	Puppet Dance	195
塔吉克族服饰	Tajik Costumes	255
塔克拉玛干沙漠之谜	The Mystery of the Taklimakan Desert	13
塔兰奇	Taranchi	68
塔里木河	The Tarim River	12
塔里木盆地	The Tarim Basin	5
台特玛湖	Lake Taitema	49
台子	Taizi	229
贪婪的真实	Greed and Truth	205
汤饭	Xinjiang Dinner	251
唐王城	Tangwang City	70
陶器上的巫觋	Wizards on a Far	63
剃头匠	A Fancy Shave?	73
天地的信使：鹿石	Stone Deer	186
天然饮品白桦树液	Natural Drinks	98
天山	The Tianshan Mountains	9
天山的传说	Legend of Tianshan	172
天山深处的英雄路：独库公路	A Road Through Tianshan	153
天山是金雕	A Golden Eagle	36
天山天池	Tianshan Tianchi	29
天山雪莲	The Snow Lotus	181
铜匠世家	Copper Work	69
童话边城布尔津	Fairy-tale Burqin	120
童子笑	Laughing Children	147
图木舒克	Tumushuke	159
土尔扈特部东归	The Torghut Return	66
土尔扈特蒙古族人的见面礼	Saying Hi	95
吐峪沟	Tuyugou	81
托包克游戏	Tobuk: A Traditional Game	88
脱离庸常之美	Unusual Beauty	18

W

| 完美废墟：交河故城 | Perfect Remains: The Ancient Jiaohe City | 57 |
| 万山之祖：昆仑山 | The Kunlun Range | 12 |

王国	The Kingdom	61
"微型水库"云杉	Spruce: A "Mini Reservoir"	164
维吾尔族巴扎上的"毕德克"	Bidek: A Middleman	92
维吾尔族的见面礼	Pleasantries	97
维吾尔族民居	Nice Homes	94
维吾尔族女性见面礼	Meetings and Greetings	106
味蕾的念想	Missing Home	239
温宿大峡谷	Grand Wensu Canyon	23
文明的交汇地	Cultural Nexus	20
闻香识味	Knowing Scents	247
我是一个兵	I Am a Soldier	154
卧牛石	Rocks and Ox	46
五百岁无花果王	A Kingly Tree	182
五星出东方利中国	China Will Rise	53
舞蹈，土地上的灵魂	The Soul of the Earth	197
舞姿奇异的花所根植的土壤	Fertile Soil	192

X

西迁节	Migration to the West	78
锡伯族人的供奉与崇拜	Xibe Beliefs	101
锡伯族人的婚礼	Xibe Weddings	92
锡伯族西迁	The Xibe Migration	64
夏尔希里	Xia'erxili	42
夏塔古道	The Xiata Passage	62
香料之城	City of Perfume	109
香约玫瑰	Rose Products	245
镶着雪山边儿的草原	Grasslands in the Snow	14
肖尔布拉克	Schorburak	154
小白杨哨所	Xiaobaiyang Watchhouse	151
小草与大草	Grasses	15
小河墓地	The Xiaohe Tomb Site	56
小木匠	A Young Carpenter	71
小女孩的愿望	A Girl's Wish	128
"小人参"：恰玛古	"Little Ginseng"	190
卸落在地的马鞍	Saddle on the Ground	91
新疆餐饮格局	Big Food	249
新疆曾是一片汪洋	Xinjiang Was a Sea	59

新疆大盘鸡	Big Plate Chicken	257
新疆大视野	A Vast Space	6
新疆的包容美	The Beauty of Xinjiang	4
新疆的河	Xinjiang's Rivers	14
新疆的回族 "花儿"	Huar	202
新疆的落差	Extremes in Xinjiang	7
新疆的图瓦人	The Tuva	168
新疆扉页：吐鲁番	Turpan: The Title Page in the Book of Xinjiang	50
新疆歌舞	Xinjiang's Songs and Dances	206
新疆姑娘的小辫子	Take it Seriously	85
新疆河南话	Henan Dialect in Xinjiang	226
新疆话的风采	Interesting Language	226
新疆金秋	Golden Autumn in Xinjiang	33
新疆客新疆人	Guests and Locals	155
新疆女人	Xinjiang's Ladies	84
新疆女人的三大最爱	My Three Loves	243
新疆曲子	Melodies of Xinjiang	203
新疆是什么味儿	Flavour of Xinjiang	246
新疆夏天的绿	Summer Green in Xinjiang	32
新疆鹰嘴豆	Chickpeas	243
新疆杂话	Xinjiang Stories	225
新疆珍稀濒危动物	Endangered Species	187
新疆之 "新"	"New" in Xinjiang	4
星星峡	Xingxingxia	47
喧荒	Xuanhuang	227
学习维语 "三板斧"	Three Phrases	225
雪山的力量	The Power of Snow-capped Mountains	88
熏马肠	Smoked Horse Intestine	237
薰衣草蜂蜜	Valley of Lavender	180
薰衣草神秘之旅	An Enchanting Journey	16

y

牙好的时候多吃肉	Eat More While You Have Good Teeth	218
亚军事风俗	Semi-military Customs	150
沿着一条河流的方向	Along the River	38
盐碱地里的牛羊	Salty Earth	238
眼睛装不下的美	Unfakeable	224

羊的冬天	Winter Sheep	136
羊的肩胛骨肉	Shoulder Meat	242
羊是长不大的婴儿	Young Sheep	111
阳光的味道	The Flavour of Sunlight	33
"野兔子"之地	Wild Rabbits	45
叶尔羌河流过的地方	The Flow of the Yarkant River	125
一炮成功	Easy Work	65
一层一层的年纪	Layers of Age	219
一方水土一方人	You Are What You Eat	76
一首叫《塔里木》的歌	A Song Called Tarim	206
一只野鸭创造了大地	A Creation Myth	174
一种滋味：从舌尖到心田	Life's Sweet	146
一株野蛮的葡萄树	A Wild Grapevine	120
伊犁河	Yili River	119
伊犁马	Yili Horses	184
伊宁	Yining	141
伊宁汉人街	Hanren Street	116
驿站与巴扎	Post Station and Bazaar	62
音乐圣人苏祇婆	Mother Suzhi	196
鹰笛	Eagle Flutes	185
鹰舞	Eagle Dance	199
永不谢幕的民族博览会	Never-ending Meetings	84
勇敢者的游戏：达瓦孜	Dawaz	204
用木头和羊肠制作的冬不拉	Making a Tamboura	199
悠然见南山	A View of Nanshan	110
游牧挽歌	An Elegy for Nomadism	82
游玩的最高形式是请你吃肉	Having Fun Eating	239
有天马的地方	Heavenly Horses	65
鱼湖	Fish Lake	31
与边境有关	It's about the Border	160
玉石的时光之路	Jade Path	182
乐活人生	A Melodic Life	142
乐器村	Musical Instrument Village	208
乐器王	King of Instruments	209

Z

| 杂语交融的地方 | A Place of Many Languages | 221 |

宰牲	Sacrifice	86
在白哈巴的一个小店里	A Store in Baihaba	122
在麦盖提喝早茶	Morning Tea	127
在那……遥远的地方	A Place Far Away	228
在音乐里融化	Immersed in Music	210
攒劲得很	Really Great	230
张仲瀚的"吃喝玩乐"	Zhang Zhonghan	157
昭苏，一个连回忆都奢侈的地方	Zhaosu, a Wonderful Place	115
昭苏边境的格登碑	The Gurden Stele	153
昭苏草原之春	Spring in Zhaosu	27
昭苏盆地	Zhaosu Basin	32
这马儿调皮得很	An Unruly Horse	217
趾高气扬的皮芽子	Piyazi	243
中国最早的佛窟	Buddhist Caves	56
抓饭的吃法	Eating with One's Hands	236
转场	Livestock Transfer	78
准噶尔盆地	The Junggar Basin	8
自嘲	A Self-deprecating Joke	154
自然的味道	A Natural Flavour	246
自然生长的羊羔	Let Them Be	100
最封闭的村庄：牙通古斯	Most Isolated Village	163
醉爱	Intoxicated Love	49
左公柳	General Tso	65

图书在版编目(CIP)数据

微观新疆:汉英对照/左锋主编.—北京:商务印书馆,
2015
ISBN 978-7-100-11088-4

Ⅰ.①微⋯ Ⅱ.①左⋯ Ⅲ.①新疆—概况—摄影集
Ⅳ.①K924.5-64

中国版本图书馆 CIP 数据核字(2015)第 033305 号

微 观 新 疆
(汉英版)

XINJIANG：VAST AND VARIED

左 锋 主编

商 务 印 书 馆 出 版
(北京王府井大街 36 号 邮政编码 100710)
商 务 印 书 馆 发 行
北京中科印刷有限公司印刷
ISBN 978-7-100-11088-4

2015 年 2 月第 1 版　　　开本 787×1092　1/16
2015 年 2 月北京第 1 次印刷　　印张 18
定价:68.00 元